Rome, Parthia, India

Rome, Parthia, India

The Violent Emergence of a New World Order 150–140 BC

John D. Grainger

PRAETORIAN PRESS

First published in Great Britain in 2013 by
The Praetorian Press
an imprint of
Pen & Sword Books Ltd
47 Church Street
Barnsley
South Yorkshire
S70 2AS

Copyright © John D. Grainger 2013

ISBN 978 1 84884 825 2

Typeset in Ehrhardt by
Mac Style, Driffield, East Yorkshire
Printed and bound in the UK by CPI Group (UK) Ltd, Croydon,
CRO 4YY

Pen & Sword Books Ltd incorporates the Imprints of Pen & Sword
Aviation, Pen & Sword Maritime, Pen & Sword Military, Wharncliffe
Local History, Pen and Sword Select, Pen & Sword Military Classics,
Leo Cooper, The Praetorian Press, Remember When, Seaforth
Publishing and Frontline Publishing.

For a complete list of Pen & Sword titles please contact
PEN & SWORD BOOKS LIMITED
47 Church Street, Barnsley, South Yorkshire, S70 2AS, England
E-mail: enquiries@pen-and-sword.co.uk
Website: www.pen-and-sword.co.uk

Contents

Maps

Table

Maps

Introduction

In 1989 the President George Bush I proclaimed the emergence of a New World Order, which had resulted from the 'collapse of the Soviet Union' – this being the term which is the current phrase in Russia for these events. There is certainly a New World system emerging, though there seems for the moment little order in it, and it is nowhere near what Bush expected. But if he had been better versed in history the president would have known that this was scarcely the first of these sudden changes. They are usually in preparation for a generation or two, and when the change occurs it takes only a few years to happen. The result is a visible change in affairs, above all in international political alignments. So relatively lengthy periods of little change are followed by brief periods when the tensions developed in that time of peace are released and a new problem confirmed. The word 'earthquake' seems appropriate.

This pattern of relative placidity for a relatively lengthy period followed by a paroxysm of change, which is then followed by another period of relative placidity, is the result of a political system in which several, or many, states co-exist and compete. Europe for the past millennium is one such time and place. The periods of relative calm – 'placidity' is perhaps not the most accurate description – are not necessarily untroubled, but any troubles which occur are only local, or are confined to a particular part of the system. In terms of Europe since the eighteenth century, there was a 'placid' period between 1748 and 1792, and it was the French Revolution and the violent career of Napoleon Bonaparte, between 1792 and 1815, which was the paroxysm of change. This was followed by a period of calm until the 1860s, when Prussia's three victorious wars shook much of the old system. In the calm period of 1815–1864, there were certainly difficulties and changes – in the Netherlands, in Greece, in Spain, revolutions in France, the unification of Italy in awkward stages, the great revolutionary upheaval of 1848, rebellions against the Russians in Poland, the Crimean War – but the system as it was in 1864 was recognizably very similar to that in 1815; indeed the German wars between 1864 and 1871 may also be seen as another relatively minor and local difficulty, and the system as it was in 1914 could be seen in that of 1815.

But the Great War was clearly a paroxysm of change just as was that of 1792–1815, and this was repeated in 1938–1945. One must conclude that the long periods of relative calm allowed tensions to develop which could only be relieved by a paroxysm of warfare. The smaller changes in European affairs between 1815 and 1914 had not been enough to relieve that pressure.

The ancient Mediterranean and Middle Eastern world exhibits the same alternation of lengthy calm and sudden change. Things moved more slowly than in modern Europe, and such changes were less frequent, but the pattern is there. Taking in the whole civilized world from India to Spain, as this book does, the first of these paroxysms was probably the destruction of the Assyrian Empire in the late seventh century BC. A period of international tension between a set of great powers followed from about 600 BC, then the rapid creation of the Persian Empire between 546 and 522 is the next paroxysm of change. The Akhaimenid Empire was a long period of imperial peace which contained within it, like nineteenth century Europe, a series of local problems and disturbances which did not essentially disturb the whole: repeated rebellions in Egypt, the Greek wars, campaigns in Central Asia, rebellions by Persian aristocrats, *coups d'état* at the centre. But in 340 BC the situation was much as it had been in, say, 520 BC. And yet strains were clearly developing around the edges of the imperial system, in Macedon, in Greece, in Egypt, further afield in Italy – 342–340 is the crucial moment in the emergence of the Roman system – and in India with the expansion of the Magadha state as well.

Alexander's campaign and the Macedonian civil wars which followed (334–301) is another of the periods of sudden change, which was followed by the relative calm and minor changes of the Hellenistic period – again the 'calm' clearly does not exclude wars and changes, but they tended to be local. This book considers a fourth of these ancient world seismic periods, between 150 and 140 BC. This was when the Roman Republic suddenly emerged, after six decades of refusal to expand, as an empire controlling the Mediterranean world from the Aegean to Spain and Africa; simultaneously in the lands from Babylonia to India the small Parthian state swiftly grew into an empire stretching from the Euphrates to Central Asia; in India the tentative revival of the Maurya empire failed, but in Central Asia the Greek Baktrian state collapsed.

The significance of this period of change is that these developments laid the outline for the political world order for the next seven-and-a-half centuries, in which the central confrontation, around which everything else revolved, was that between the several Roman Empires – Republic, Principate, Dominate, Byzantium – and the successive Iranian empires of Parthia and the Sassanids.

Beside this constant conflict the inclusion of the West in the Roman state and the events in Central Asia and India were of only secondary importance. India was involved in western affairs because of Alexander, but became shut out once the Parthians interposed themselves between Syria and India; the western Mediterranean regions were included in Rome's empire, but affairs west and north of Italy were scarcely of the same importance as those which took place between Antioch and Babylon. Beside the confrontation in Mesopotamia, the loss of Spain and Gaul, even of Italy, was secondary.

Of course the situation of affairs as it was in 140 BC was as yet only a broad sketch of that which became fully formed by 50 BC. Yet the outline was clear: by 140 Rome and Parthia were the two great powers, and from 140 to 50 the only real question was where the line of division between them would finally be drawn.

The central event in this brief set of changes is the collapse of the Seleukid kingdom. It is this which opened the way for the expansion of the Parthian state, and its reduction to weakness also weakened the whole international political system, in Egypt, Asia Minor, Central Asia, and the western Mediterranean. The rise of Rome and Parthia to their dominating Great Power positions, which they clearly occupied from 140 onwards, was largely the result of the Seleukid collapse.

The world-shaking change, of course, happened in sections and in stages, involving apparently disconnected crises from eastern India to Spain, but the fact that they all took place in a brief period of a little over a decade is more than a mere coincidence. By 150 the world was ready, after half a century of placidity, to change.

This attempt to take a ten-year transect through the ancient world means that the chapters leap about from Italy to India to Greece to Africa. This is not random, since it is one of the claims being advanced here that all these areas affected one or other, even India and Italy; it is also a claim that the crucial area is not Italy or India, but the Fertile Crescent, the old civilized lands from the Nile to the Euphrates, but in particular Syria. Therefore it is in this area that the story must both begin and end. It was the collapse of the authority of the Seleukid kings in that central region around 150 BC which began the great crisis, and it was the definitive division of the Fertile Crescent, and the accompanying destruction of the Seleukid kingdom, which opened the way for the big confrontation between East and West, Rome and Iran, for the next seven centuries and more.

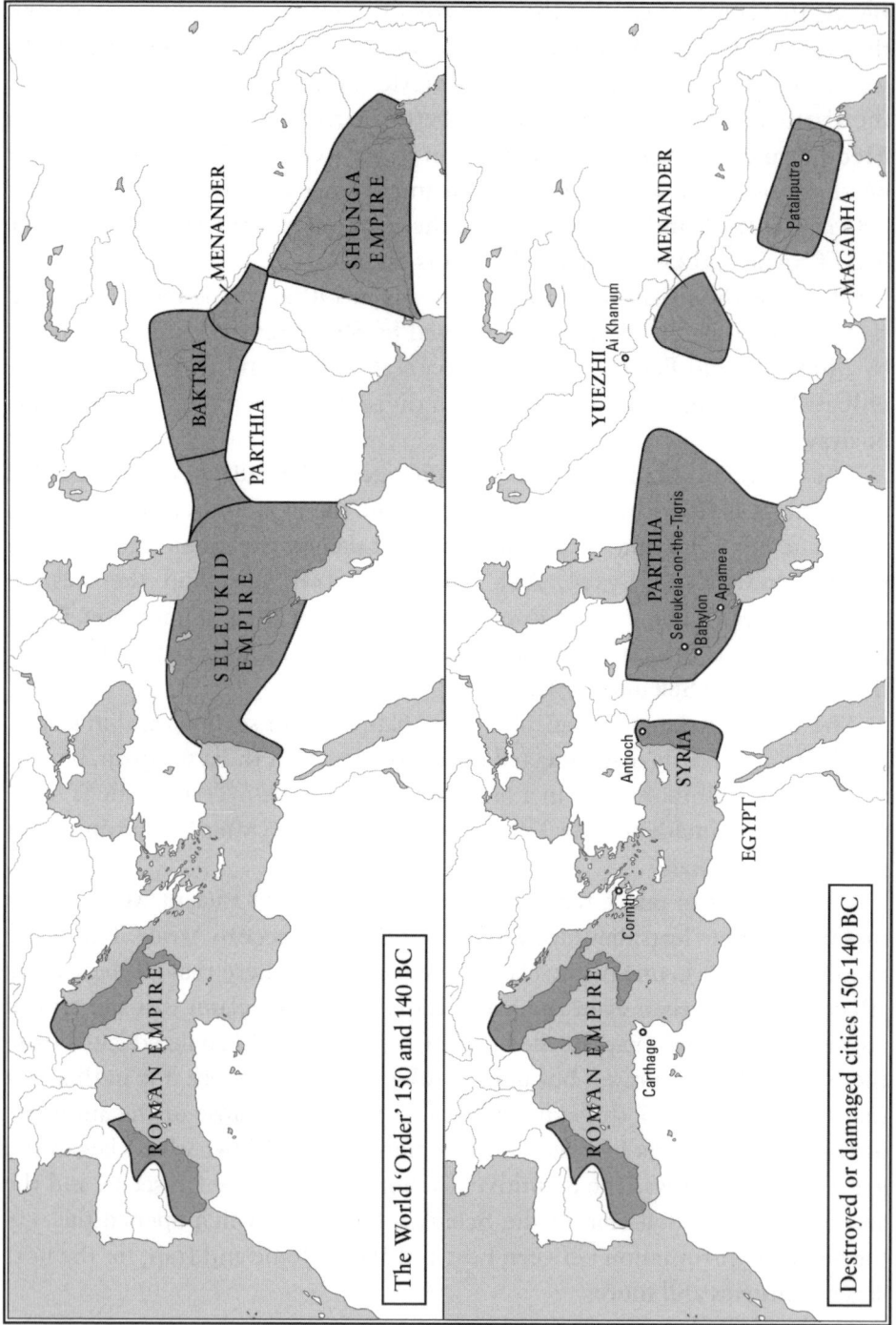

The World 'Order' 150 and 140 BC

Destroyed or damaged cities 150-140 BC

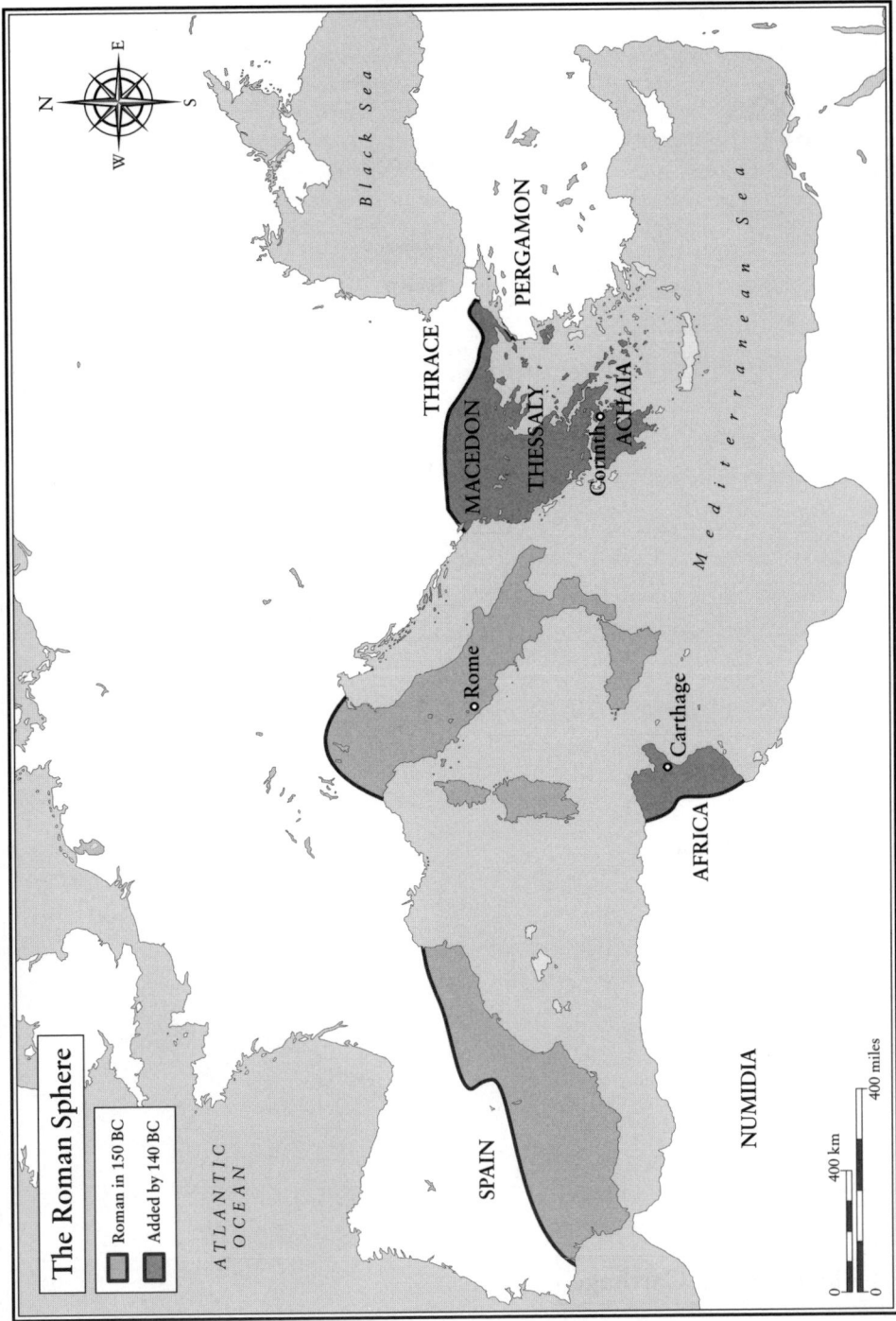

The Roman Sphere

Roman in 150 BC
Added by 140 BC

ATLANTIC
OCEAN

Black Sea

THRACE
PERGAMON
MACEDON
THESSALY
ACHAIA
Corinth
Mediterranean Sea

SPAIN

Rome

Carthage

AFRICA

NUMIDIA

400 km
400 miles

N

W   E

S

Utica ○

Carthage ○

Tunis ○

Aspis ○

Neapolis ○

AFRICA

Hadrumetum ○

Lepcis Minor ○

Thapsus ○

NUMIDIA

Acholla ○

The Lands of Carthage

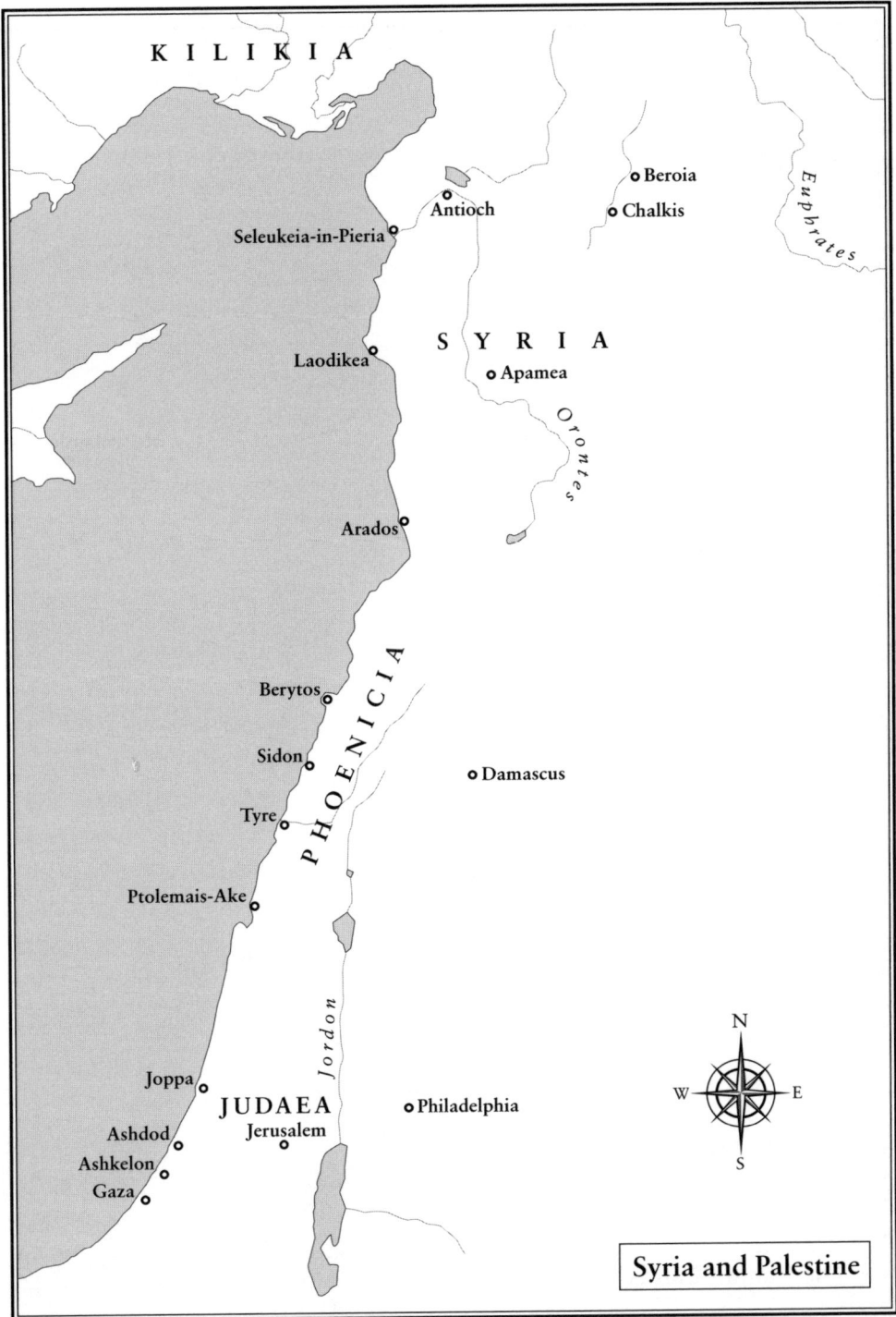

KILIKIA

Beroia

Antioch

Seleukeia-in-Pieria

Chalkis

SYRIA

Laodikea

Apamea

Orontes

Euphrates

Arados

Berytos

PHOENICIA

Sidon

Damascus

Tyre

Ptolemais-Ake

Jordon

N

W E

S

Joppa

JUDAEA

Philadelphia

Ashdod

Jerusalem

Ashkelon

Gaza

Syria and Palestine

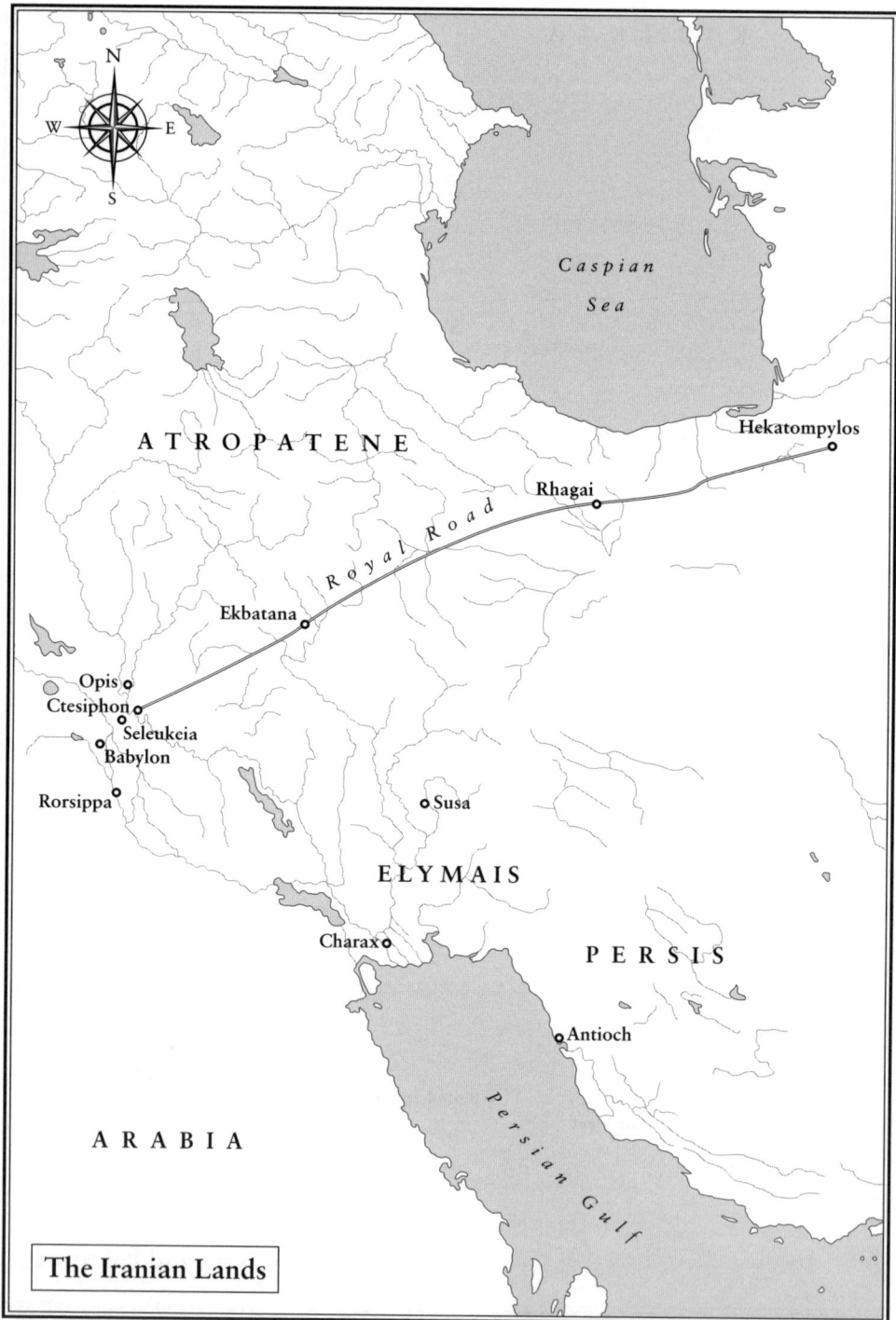

The Iranian Lands

Chapter 1

The World in 150 BC

To an educated and civilized man of the Mediterranean world in 150 BC or so, the known world stretched for about six thousand kilometres from Spain in the west to India in the east, though from north to south it was much narrower, sandwiched between the Sahara Desert and the Indian Ocean on the south, and the European forest and the Central Asian steppe on the north – a strip only a couple of thousand kilometres or so wide at the most. It was surrounded, even hemmed in, by those unknown regions, the lands of the barbarians, and it was penetrated by seas and divided by great mountain ranges. The edges of the civilized world were fuzzy, for the lands of the cities – the civilized regions – shaded off into the barbarian lands in all directions, and even enclosed some areas of barbarism. These lands were all divided among cities, states, and empires; the barbarians were divided into clans and tribes.

The political and cultural centre of this strip of civilized land was a relatively small area around the eastern part of the Mediterranean Sea. In that area the great cities of Athens, Rhodes, Pergamon, Antioch, and Alexandria dominated the culture and economy of all the rest. To the west the only comparable cities were Rome, Syracuse, and Carthage; they were smaller in size and not in the same league culturally as Antioch and Alexandria; to the east there were rather more notable centres: Babylon and Seleukeia-on-the-Tigris in Babylonia, others in Iran and Baktria; there were still more in India, particularly in the northern area, in the lowlands of the Indus and Ganges Valleys. The dependence of these eastern lands on the core region is quaintly illustrated by a quotation from the philosopher Klearchos of Soli which was carved at the Greek city of Ai Khanum in Baktria. Similarly in Rome in 155 there was great excitement when a trio of Athenian philosophers turned up as envoys – a taste of the cultural mainstream was clearly most unusual in that city. It was only along the shores of Greece, Anatolia, Syria, and Egypt, however, that there were the great economic, political, and cultural powers which radiated over all the rest. This was the centre of the world.

This was a world which was essentially Greek in language, religion, and culture. Klearchos' Delphian maxims and the philosopher Karneardes in

Rome were Greek and spoke Greek – the rest had to learn the language. There were other languages in use, of course, and other religions, but if a man knew Greek he could converse with people from Spain to India, and in no other language could he do that, even if the use of Greek did fade away at the fringes. The greatest states in this world used Greek as their language of administration and communication, both with their citizens and with other powers, though they all had other tongues in use as well. So in Egypt, where the great city of Alexandria was a vibrant Greek cultural centre, the majority of the population spoke Egyptian in their everyday lives, but they also needed Greek to communicate with their rulers. These administrators rarely bothered to learn Egyptian, and they kept their detailed records in Greek. In Syria, the local language was Aramaic, and this was intelligible in the lands to the east, as well, from Babylonia to the borders of India, where it had spread under the old Akhaimenid Empire, though it was being superseded by Greek.

In Italy Latin was slowly spreading to smother the many local dialects and languages of the peninsula – but even the Romans, particularly proud of themselves, used Greek in diplomacy and even at home; Greek held its own against Latin in the south of Italy for the next fifteen centuries. Iranians spoke a version of the Old Persian language, and this was used eastwards into Baktria, where there were Greek cities, though the people spoke other local languages as well; here Aramaic was also spoken, or at least written, and there were several others in use. Even in India Greek was one of the languages of some of the rulers. Most of the population spoke their local tongues, but a king in the Punjab, or a Yavana (that is, a Greek, or at least western) mercenary in the Ganges Valley or in the Deccan, could have conversed with a Baktrian horseman or a Syrian merchant or a Carthaginian-Spanish landowner or a Roman consul without an interpreter. In 150 BC it was a Greek-speaking world, and the great cities around the eastern Mediterranean were the founts and originators of that culture.

On the other hand, it was not always ethnic Greeks who were in control in those lands, and by no means was the worldwide cultural unity of Greeks and Greek replicated in international affairs. A string of major powers divided up much of the civilized world between them, and there were hundreds of minor powers around and between and beside them. It was a highly complex political world, and in this it contrasted sharply with its partial linguistic and cultural unity; in other words the political division mimicked, in a way, the underlying linguistic diversity rather than the superficial cultural unity.

The largest state in this political system was the kingdom ruled by kings of the Seleukid family. They were descended from Seleukos I Nikator, a companion, contemporary, and successor of Alexander the Great, and their kingdom stretched from Syria to eastern Iran, almost half of the civilized world, as defined above. It included the rich lands of Syria and Babylonia as well as the deserts of Iran. It was, therefore, if one reached back to the time even before Alexander, the heir of much of the defunct Persian Empire, though it was smaller. It was a century and a half old by 150 BC, but it was creaking at the joints by then. It had already shed large areas of the original kingdom into independence at its western and eastern extremes, and several of its regions were ambitious for their own separations. It also faced avid enemies on several of its frontiers. Nevertheless, in 150 it was still the same size as it had been for the last forty years.

To the east of the Seleukid state were Parthia and Baktria, both of them lands which had broken away from Seleukid rule. Parthia had become a separate state by the invasion by the nomad Parni, who conquered the province of Parthia – another instance of the cultural and political supremacy of the Greeks. It was ruled by kings who claimed, at least on their coins, to be philhellenes; its origin made it a complex society in which Greeks, Persians, and nomads interacted. Baktria had broken away from the Seleukid Kingdom by seceding, and was ruled by self-confidently Greek kings, though the majority population was Iranian. Baktria was now separated from its Seleukid parent both politically, by its independent local kings, and physically, by the interposition of Parthia. Politically Baktria's original unity at its secession into independence almost a century earlier had ended, and at least two families of kings, maybe more, now contended with one another.

One Baktrian king had seized the chance of Indian political divisions to emulate Alexander the Great and Seleukos I, to invade India; parts of the Punjab were thus under Greek rule, while areas beyond it had felt the sharp points of Greek spears in raids. Few Greeks had penetrated beyond the Indus Valley, though several, hoping to outdo Alexander, had held ambitions to conquer further afield. For much of the time since Alexander, however, this had been out of the question, for most of India had been under the rule of the Maurya family of emperors. These were now gone, though replaced by the Shunga dynasty. The Greco-Baktrian invaders had taken advantage of the empire's decline, and the rich Ganges Valley was thus open for enemies to attack.

The Parthian kingdom, between the quarrelling Baktrians and their Seleukid parent, was only a minor state. It was Iranian in language and religious practice, and looked back to the Akhaimenid Empire for inspiration. This no doubt appealed to the obstinately Iranian population of the Iranian plateau. After some vicissitudes, it was a well-established local power, with ambitions for expansion, and in this it was encouraged or helped by the loosening hold of the Seleukids in Iran. They held the great road along the north of the desert firmly, but southern Iran was semi-independent under local rulers. Persis, the original homeland of the old Persian empire's rulers, had its own kings and held to old traditions.

The southern neighbour of the Seleukid kingdom was the kingdom of the Ptolemies of Egypt, founded by another of Alexander's contemporaries. These two royal families were constant enemies, having fought each other in six major wars over the last century and a half. The bone of contention had been Palestine and Phoenicia, at least on the surface, though the deeper problem had been the perception of who was the greater power, and who had been the more faithful to the memory and legacy of Alexander. Ptolemy I had seized control of the body of Alexander in one of the earliest major acts of defiance of those hoping to hold Alexander's conquests together. He had interred the preserved corpse at Alexandria, Alexander's city, where it was revered and venerated; the priesthood of Alexander was the most prestigious in the kingdom.

Possession of Alexander's body was one way of legitimizing the power and kingship of Ptolemy and his descendents. The Seleukids, by contrast, had as part of their titles 'the Macedonian', just as the Persian Great Kings had proudly announced that each king was 'the Akhaimenid'. Seleukos I had come nearest of all Alexander's successors to taking control of the whole of the empire, only to be murdered − by a renegade Ptolemy − as he was about to gain control of Macedon as well. He and his family ruled all Alexander's lands − except for Macedon and Egypt. This, and their claim to be Macedonian, was part of their legitimization.

Asia Minor had been lost by the Seleukids forty years earlier, and was now occupied by a series of secondary powers. The Attalid kings ruled a considerable kingdom in the west of the peninsula, and the rest was divided among various kings and many cities. All of these were at enmity with each other, and all they still feared the power of the Seleukids. The treaty of Apamea of 188 which ended the Roman War of Antiochos III had included a prohibition to stop the Seleukids intruding into Asia Minor again, but this no longer applied once Antiochos was dead.

Greece was also, as ever, much divided. The city states of the Peloponnese were largely gathered into the Achaian League, though some of its members, above all Sparta, were reluctant. Other leagues, in Aitolia and Boeotia, were even weaker, even moribund. The one powerful state in the area had been Macedon, but it had suffered a destructive defeat by Rome two decades earlier. This was the third Romano–Macedonian war, and this time Rome had impatiently broken the kingdom up into four supposedly independent republics. The Macedonians were unhappy about this, and the weakness of the four unstable republics made them vulnerable to raids by Balkan peoples from the north. The Roman idea had been precisely what had resulted – to weaken the Macedonian kingdom so that it ceased to be a threat to Rome and her client states in Greece. But the weakness also left the republics vulnerable to nostalgia for the royal past, when the kingdom had been great and wealthy.

The West contained two major powers, Rome and Carthage, who confronted each other across the western half of the Mediterranean, as they had for more than a century. Two great wars, lasting in total almost forty years, had reduced Carthage from the dominant power in the western Mediterranean to its North African core, which had also been steadily reduced in the last fifty years by pressure from its neighbour King Massinissa of Numidia. Even so, the city remained one of the major urban centres of the world, rich, vigorous, and still relatively powerful; Massinissa could only chip away at Carthage's territory because Rome consistently favoured him; given the opportunity Carthage could have destroyed him, or at least could have stopped his raids.

Rome was the winner of the two wars which the two cities had fought. It had expanded during these wars from controlling peninsular Italy to securing an empire which made it the second largest state in the Western world, and its most formidable military power. It now ruled all Italy as far as the Alps, the great islands of Sicily, Sardinia, and Corsica, a considerable area of southern and eastern Spain, and the eastern coast of the Adriatic. Wars with Macedon had led her to dominate, but not actually control, the Greek cities and leagues in a curious type of imperialism by which Rome dominated from a distance and exercised a remote control by use of unscrupulous diplomacy and veiled threats. This method of control had taken time for the clients to understand, and it was a system which was disliked and resisted by those cities and kingdoms whose ideology was one of independence, that is, everyone in Greece.

This may be called Rome's 'informal' empire. There is no doubt that Rome considered these states to be under its power. They played up to this by referring their problems, internal and external, to the Senate, which might or might not respond. But power over the states did not always equate to control, and Rome's clients and allies were therefore a restless bunch. Rome's empire was thus a complex polity: it consisted of Italy, which was divided in a complicated way between Roman and allied territory; colonial conquests in Cisalpine Gaul, the islands, and Spain; and the 'informal' empire lay to the east. This complicated system existed to make it the more amenable to Roman control – divide and rule – but it also meant that it was thoroughly unstable. It was kept in some sort of order only by Rome's manifest military power, and by the skill with which its diplomats and senators alternately solved and stirred up problems.

Instability was not just a condition of the Roman Empire. Cities, independent or not, were liable to insurrection and revolution; kingdoms were likely to break up, and were liable to collapse into civil war, particularly over the question of the succession. Wars on a relatively small scale were endemic – in 150 there were wars in Asia Minor, on the borders of Macedon, in North Africa, Spain, Syria, and probably in Baktria. Greater wars could extinguish kingdoms and ruin cities. And all round the long narrow strip of civilized country which stretched from Gades in Spain to Pataliputra in India; barbarian tribes eyed its riches and threatened to invade. The wealth of the civilized lands was a constant lure, with the result that the frontiers of civilization were marked by even more constant warfare than were the borders of the civilized states.

Rome, for example, had been fighting in Spain almost continually since conquering the Carthaginian Spanish lands fifty years earlier, and had had to fight repeatedly in northern Italy to retain its grip on the rich Po Valley (Cisalpine Gaul). The Balkan peoples were a constant threat to Macedon and Greece, and the break-up of Macedon into the four republics had only encouraged more raids. Two Celtic kingdoms in particular, the Scordisci in the Belgrade area and the Tylis kingdom in Thrace, were constant menaces. In Anatolia another Celtic group, the Galatians, had been bludgeoned into some sort of submission, at least temporarily, by defeats and division, but were never quiet for long. Their main enemies, the Seleukid kings, were no longer interested in fighting them, and the task now lay with the kings of the Anatolian states. The Seleukids in Syria and the Ptolemies in Egypt were threatened by desert dwellers from Arabia and Libya, and Arabs were beginning to encroach into the old civilized and cultivated lands of Babylonia and Syria for the first time for several centuries. Iran had a mixture of tribes under little outside control; the cities and roads were strongly garrisoned by the Seleukids; there were near-independent kingdoms along the south, and the mountains held hostile tribes. The Parthians, who by now were one of those well-established kingdoms, were nevertheless regarded as barbarians because of their desert origin and Iranian ideology.

The barbarian frontier in Central Asia was the most active and dangerous of them all. The divisions between Baktrians and Parthians, the divisions among the Baktrians, and the siphoning off of Baktrian strength and attention into India rendered the whole region vulnerable to both raids and large-scale invasions. The frontier nomads themselves were under pressure from other nomads to the north and east, for a major tribe, the Yuezhi, had been migrating westwards from the frontiers of China for the past generation. By 150 they were pressing on the steppe frontier which was guarded by the Baktrians.

In India it was the Greek invaders who were the barbarians, foreigners following in the steps and perhaps using the methods of Alexander, whose campaign along the Indus had been particularly brutal. The disintegration of the Maurya Empire loosed conflicts over the remains among its fragments and invaders. For two generations a semblance of the old empire continued under a new dynasty founded by a military man, Pushyamitra Shunga. He was a vigorous ruler, and revived the empire with some success, though a Greek kingdom was successfully established in the Punjab, and the lands of the Deccan broke away. Pushyamitra, having ruled for perhaps thirty years, died not long before 150 BC, and was followed by much weaker rulers. The barbarians, Greeks and others, were thus once more a major threat.

If we move from east to west it is apparent that the forms of government in the civilized world shifted gradually. The Shungas ran their state as an autocratic empire, in which religion was one of the major instruments of royal power. The Mauryas, at least some of them, had been Buddhists of a sort, but their supplanter Pushyamitra was a Brahmin and a confident and assertive Hindu. One reason for his *coup* against the last of the Mauryas was that he aimed to 'restore' the practices of Hinduism, an early example of 'restoration' as an excuse for a revolution. Monarchy of a less comprehensive and determined sort was usual amongst the Greeks of Baktria, where the always incipient possibility of hostility between Iranians and Greeks was present, though the constant disputes and dynastic wars also limited both royal effectiveness and the personal freedoms of the subjects — but at least the people were not subjected to any religious dictation, Buddhist or Hindu, however ineffective.

From the borders of India west to the Aegean the normal political mode was monarchy, but modified by a deliberate delegation of authority to the local level, in particular to cities. The Seleukids had developed their kingdom into a state large enough to be an empire by deliberately founding many cities where they did not exist; they also accepted the existing cities, as in Babylonia and Phoenicia, as part of their system. These cities were often populated by Greek immigrants and their descendants, and since they had the surrounding lands assigned to them, this put the cities on the side of the kings; just to be sure, each city was garrisoned by a royal military force in its acropolis. In some areas, notably Syria, the whole land was effectively divided amongst the cities, and the kings were still active city founders. These cities all had an autonomous internal government, and they and the kings had an effective institutional link, a royally-appointed official called an *epistates*, who was a native of, or at least lived in, the city he was assigned to. This ensured a flexible and responsive administration. The system was effective in maintaining royal control, and there were few internal disputes – though the governors of provinces, who had command of the garrisons, and of regions where cities were absent, or frontier areas, could be obstreperous.

There was also a comprehensive royal administration, largely devoted to collecting taxes and spending the revenue on the war-making capacity of the kingdom. This required a fairly substantial bureaucracy, and was a government system which was imitated in Baktria and the Asia Minor kingdoms, and probably in Parthia. It was, of course, a major source of employment for the Greek-speaking population, though this did not exclude non-Greeks. All they had to do was to become Greek.

Ptolemaic Egypt was more of an autocratic monarchy, for the first Ptolemy happily adopted the native tradition of religious monarchy, but to hold on to this control the kings were necessarily active in conciliating the Egyptian population, even though they had to do so in Greek, and usually through the priests of the great temples. The Seleukid practice of founding cities had never been favoured by the Ptolemies, who relied for their control on an all-pervasive bureaucracy. This was much more intensive and unpleasant than in any other state, but it had produced enormous wealth for the kings. This and the fact that Greek was the administrative language of the state only emphasized the continuing foreignness of the ruling dynasty and its administrators. This foreignness and oppressiveness became a major source of weakness and several serious native Egyptian rebellions had taken place in the previous half-century. The great temples' priests had much influence over the people and so with the king; and the people, taxed to the limit and sometimes beyond, had successfully developed a species of strike, withdrawing their labour by fleeing into the desert when the taxation became too onerous. By 150 the kingdom was a Greco-Egyptian aristocracy of bureaucrats, military men, and native priests ruling over the toiling, hostile and disgruntled Egyptian peasantry. It took an exceptionally able king, vigorous and active, to control this unwieldy system. In 150 just about the last such king of the dynasty, Ptolemy VI, was ruling, and he had had to spend ten years reducing the country to order and peace.

The Parthian kingdom, established in a barren area and with few cities, had also evolved into a dualistic state, but here the contest was between the king and his barons, in which the king was merely the most powerful baron. The lords around him commanded their own armies, and were obligated to answer the call when the king went to war, a call they were quite capable of ignoring if it so suited them. The king controlled the largest of the forces, and had the resources to recruit mercenaries, which he could bring in from the desert lands to the north. It was a species of feudalism, but without the binding legal framework needed to make such a system work. The royal family, however, had devised ways to emphasize and elevate itself – by operating a calendrical era whose Year 1 was the invasion of Parthia from the steppes, and by each king taking the throne name of Arsakes, the personal name of the first king. In 150 the kingdom was still small, not much larger than the original Parthian province, and none of the political players, king or lords, had much power, but the kings had taken up the old Persian religion centred on the sacred fire, as a supplementary means of unifying their people.

Each of these kingdoms was thus different from its neighbours, in size, government, administration, population. In Asia Minor this variety continued. Some of the kingdoms there were virtually national states, with native rulers – Pontos and Bithynia along the north coast, for example, or Kappadokia in the centre, all of which had to keep careful watch on the turbulent Galatians who occupied the centre of the great peninsula. The Galatians were divided into three major tribes, not necessarily peacefully, and had a long tradition of raiding their neighbours, and their men of enlisting as mercenaries.

The main kingdom in Asia Minor was the Attalid, a collection of territories and cities only just held together by a dynasty of Greek kings notably adept at conciliation. The royal centre and capital was Pergamon, a city deliberately developed as a royal base and headquarters, but the kingdom also contained many Greek cities largely founded originally by other lords, or by the Seleukids who had ruled the interior intermittently from 281 to 190. These cities had inherited the autonomy of their origins, and could be awkward subjects – hence the royal need to be conciliatory. In addition the kingdom was the neighbour to a long sequence of cities, many of them very ancient by now, along the Aegean and Mediterranean coasts. All these places had long histories of independence, or at least of autonomy under a distant king. This pattern was being replicated in their way by the Attalid kings; the relations between the kingdom and the cities were thus inevitably unstable; all the cities would be much more content to be free of any royal supervision, and so could hardly be thought automatically loyal to the dynasty.

The major concern of any king was in what we now call foreign affairs. They were war-leaders and diplomats, and internally their main function was as judges, and tax collectors and spenders. They usually had a council of Friends (*philoi*) whom they could consult, and who could be used as military commanders and as envoys. The origin of the main kingdoms in the entourage of Alexander was reflected in the diplomatic practice of treaty making, by which a treaty between two kings lasted until one of them died. It could then be renewed by his successor if the other party agreed. More often, however, a royal death was the signal for a new bout of warfare. This practice, of course, did not apply to republican states, whose treaties with each other were thus much less durable.

At the Aegean, in moving from East to West, monarchies gave way to republics. Not entirely, for there were still kingdoms to the west, in highland Greece and in North Africa – but generally the mode of government from the Aegean westwards tended to be non-monarchical. The system was usually aristocratic or oligarchic, in that power in any particular city generally lay with the rich, whose wealth was mainly acquired by inheritance or by the ownership of land. Some cities had a wider franchise than others, some were dictatorships, many paid lip service to the practices and shibboleths of democracy, but in all cases the identifiable rulers constituted a relatively small group of wealthy men.

These non-monarchies extended from the coast of Asia Minor to southern Spain. The greatest of them, of course, was Rome, which had an intermittent anti-royal prejudice originating from its own experience of a dictatorial king; this had not prevented it from acting in a dictatorial way towards its non-Roman subjects. There were a few minor monarchies in Greece still, though three – Macedon, Epeiros, Sparta – had only recently been extinguished. Rome had destroyed the Sicilian monarchy. There were still kingly rulers among the Spanish tribes, but the only ruling kings of any power left within Roman reach were in North Africa, where the Numidian Massinissa had ruled as a Roman ally for half a century.

There was little to choose in political behaviour between monarchies and great republics. The constitutions of the monarchies usually consisted of the king attempting to control the rich aristocracy and/or a variety of cities – Greco-Egyptian, Greco-Iranian, Parthian barons, cities in Syria and Asia Minor. This was not all that different from the republics who were dominated by their own aristocracies or oligarchies. Republics tended to have a more open political life, where monarchies' politics were concentrated within the royal courts where the courtiers – the Friends – competed for royal favour. Whether under or on the surface, all the states were oligarchical.

The western, republican, region was also where slavery was a prime economic device. The kingdoms of the east used slaves, of course, but the presence of a numerous free peasantry meant that slaves were not particularly useful; they tended to be the domestic variety, except in mines and quarries. The countryside was generally inhabited by a well-rooted peasantry, tax-paying and hard-working, if non-Greek speaking, and the kings had no wish to change that situation. In the freedom-loving republics of the west, however, where liberty was often a catchphrase in politics, slave numbers were rising quickly, and the conditions of slavery were deteriorating. Rome was at the heart of the slave system. Large estates run by slaves had multiplied in southern Italy and Sicily in the last half-century since Hannibal's War, in part because the devastated lands in these areas had been left depopulated. The slaves were either captured in Rome's numerous wars, or were acquired by purchase from slave dealers, who in turn acquired their merchandise by buying prisoners captured in other wars, or merely by kidnapping free men and women. The slaves themselves were therefore generally non-Italian, being brought to Italy from barbarian lands or increasingly from the eastern Mediterranean.

This was not an exclusively Roman problem — indeed it was hardly seen as a problem at all so far — and there were pockets of intensive slavery in other areas, especially where working conditions were so bad that free men would not do the work. Mining was a particular case, and parts of the Aegean — Athens, Chios — had seen brutal slave revolts in the past, brought about by the evil conditions, usually in mines, and by large numbers of slaves concentrated in small areas. The general movement of slaves was from east to west, out of Asia Minor and Syria towards Sicily and Italy, or from the Balkans into Italy. It would be some decades before a king of Bithynia would complain that his kingdom was depopulated because so many of his people had been kidnapped and then exported to Italy. The crises of the years between 150 and 140 greatly contributed to the slave trade, with results evident in the west by the end of that decade.

The slave trade, mining, new and growing cities, intensive agriculture: these are all signs of the vigorous economic development of the Mediterranean area which had been going on since Alexander's time. This was fuelled in part by the release of large quantities of gold and silver, which had begun with Alexander's capture of the Akhaimenid stored treasure. Whatever was later acquired by governments was generally released when wars began, for wars in particular forced governments to spend money, which then re-entered general circulation. But the real source of wealth was in the existence and the growth of the many new and old cities, many of which had been founded since Alexander's time. In wars all states were involved, but in the matter of cities the Seleukid kings had been the inadvertent main agents of the world's increased prosperity. Their city-founding had been mainly for political and military purposes, to secure conquered ground, and to populate it with Greek-speaking colonists. The result had populated Syria with a couple of dozen new cities, had encouraged the growth of existing ones, and had spread others over much wider parts of the rest of the empire, as far as the Baktrian kingdom, where Seleukos I and Antiochos I had founded cities before that region's secession, and even India.

These cities were the great engines of economic growth, forming the markets for the food produced by the peasants and the Roman slave population, the consumers of raw materials and the producers of manufactures. Resources had been widely developed, and extensive trading networks had become organized which distributed goods widely, particularly by the seaborne networks in the Mediterranean. Barbarian regions were drawn into the Mediterranean economy, partly by the slave traders, or by the employment of mercenaries, partly by the barbarian taste for civilization's luxuries, and the exchange of goods by sale or by gift had its usual economic multiplier effect.

This was therefore a world of developing prosperity, at least for the urban populations, a condition obviously facilitated by the worldwide use of the Greek language. It was also a world in which there were many and various problems, largely but not entirely political, some of which were intractable – as Roman slavery proved to be. In particular the many, and often mutually hostile, states were almost all politically unstable. In the decade after about 150 the problems of these states ripened one after the other into a succession of major crises, and each of them set off the next until the world from India to Spain was engulfed in warfare. The process began at the centre of that system, in Syria.

Chapter 2

The Syrian Crisis

I n 152 a usurper landed at the city of Ptolemais-Ake in Palestine in the
Seleukid kingdom. He was Alexander, nicknamed Balas, and claimed
to be the bastard son of King Antiochos IV, who had died twelve years
before. Alexander had made this claim public in 159, when he had set himself
up as a pretender on the frontier of the kingdom, and had been sponsored by
King Attalos II of the Attalid kingdom in Asia Minor.

The king he was challenging was Demetrios I, who had himself seized
the kingship from Antiochos V, another, and legitimate, son of Antiochos IV,
whom he had immediately ordered to be killed.[1] Demetrios himself was the
son of Antiochos' elder brother Seleukos IV, and he had always insisted that
he should have been made king when his father died in 175. He had been
living in Italy at the time, sent there by his father as a hostage for a previous
agreement, ironically replacing Antiochos (IV), his uncle. So the clarity of the
succession, which had always gone to the surviving eldest son of the preceding
king for over a century, had been comprehensively muddied, and murder had
entered the royal family.

Demetrios' father Seleukos IV had been killed by his minister Heliodoros,
who had later been driven out, or more likely killed, by Antiochos IV;
Antiochos had later killed Seleukos' younger son (Antiochos' own nephew
and stepson); Demetrios had killed Antiochos' own son (Antiochos V), along
with his minister and guardian Lysias on his arrival.[2] One of Demetrios' early
actions when Alexander's enterprise began to prosper was to send two of his
own sons out of the kingdom for their safety.[3]

Alexander had been something of a nuisance to Demetrios since he had
set himself up as pretender. Opinion was divided – and is still divided – on
the merits of his claim to be the son of Antiochos IV. If his claim is correct,
his mother was probably the king's concubine Antiochis, with whom he had
also a daughter, Laodike, and to whom he granted for her support the tax
product of two cities in Kilikia. This had so incensed the citizens that they
had rebelled, a most unusual action by Seleukid cities.[4] On the whole it is
probable that Alexander's parentage really was royal, as he claimed, though
that scarcely gave him a serious claim to the kingship, given the century and

a half of the primogenital succession system of legitimate sons, which had surely hardened into accepted custom, if not law, after six generations and 150 years.[5]

The issue becomes more complex when the marriages of the kings are taken into account. Seleukos IV's first wife was Laodike, who was both his sister and the widow of his elder brother. When Antiochos IV seized the throne he married her. She was thus the wife of three of her brothers. The rationale for this was that she herself was royal and any man she married would acquire a claim to the throne. This was something which had developed in the Ptolemaic dynasty (a practice inherited from the Egyptian pharaohs) where brother–sister marriage had been the custom since the 270s. It was a practice which reinforced the succession of a son who was born to parents who themselves were both royal. It had entered the Seleukid family with the marriage of Laodike to her eldest brother, a match organized by their father, Antiochos III. When Demetrios I drove out Antiochos V and Lysias he immediately married his own sister, another Laodike, who was the widow of King Perseus of Macedon. (There is another aspect to all this, however, for the concubine of Antiochos IV had a typically royal name Antiochis, and it is possible that she was another of his sisters.)

Demetrios' capture of the kingship in 162 had annoyed King Attalos II of Pergamon, whose recently deceased brother, Eumenes II, had originally assisted Antiochos IV in his expedition to remove Heliodoros, which in turn had put Antiochos under obligation to him. Demetrios had escaped from Roman custody in Italy, leaving without official Roman permission – but very easily. Thereby he had deprived the Roman Senate of the only hold it had, weak though it was, over the Seleukid kingdom. To be sure, the Senate never seems to have made any attempt to exercise such power, though by detaining Demetrios the ruling Seleukid king was inevitably made uneasy. In fact Demetrios had been assisted in his escape by several Romans, and above all by the Greek hostage and historian Polybios, who was of the household of the family of Scipio Aemilianus, of the great Scipionic family.[6] It seems reasonable to assume that Scipio was also involved in the escape in some way; he certainly had a long-standing interest in eastern affairs. So eminent was this family that Demetrios could reasonably assume that his escape was likely to be approved later, or perhaps simply ignored. In the event it was not, so both Attalos and Rome were annoyed by his arrival in Syria and his immediate assumption of the kingship, though they could not do anything about it once Demetrios was established in power – Attalos was not powerful enough to do anything directly, and Rome was too distant.

But Demetrios also went on to annoy others. One of his first acts after eliminating Antiochos V was to marry Laodike, his own sister, the widow of Perseus of Macedon. Demetrios was the last living male of the royal family; marriage and the production of children were dynastic necessities, but this marriage had other resonances. Laodike had been widowed as a result of the defeat of King Perseus by the Romans, whose successful commander had been M. Aemilius Paullus, who was the natural father of Scipio Aemilianus. Perseus and his children had been sent to Rome and allowed to die; Laodike had been carefully returned to Syria, to her uncle, Antiochos IV – Rome had no wish to be involved in a quarrel at that moment. Demetrios' marriage was thus, besides being dynastically necessary and appropriate in Seleukid terms, an insult to Rome, and perhaps to Scipio Aemilianus and his powerful family.

Almost at once, still in 162, Demetrios was challenged from the east when Timarchos of Miletos, the governor of the eastern provinces, marched the forces under his command towards Syria in order to seize the kingship for himself. (He must have made careful diplomatic arrangements to prevent any eastern power taking advantage of his weakening of the forces in the east – a matter to be returned to later.) Timarchos' challenge was clearly one of the results of the internecine conflict within the royal family. Demetrios was the last male of the royal line (ignoring Alexander, of course), so if Timarchos could eliminate him, the kingship would be vacant. It was not the first time a governor in the east had attempted to seize the whole kingdom on the arrival on the throne of an obviously inexperienced king. He received some encouragement from Rome, but no actual help. His campaign lasted two years, and he secured control not only of Media, the province he governed, but also Babylonia and part of Mesopotamia, where he coined at Nisibis. Then he was defeated in a battle almost in Syria, where he was captured and executed by Demetrios.[7]

This was only the beginning, however, for his brother Herakleides vowed revenge. He had been a minister of Antiochos IV and his envoy to Rome in 170 and 168; Timarchos had been an official of Antiochos' and was appointed to his eastern government by Lysias, the guardian of Antiochos V, whom Demetrios had had killed.[8] By executing Timarchos Demetrios had involved himself in a family feud. Herakleides clearly resented Demetrios' success and the death of his brother, however justified it had been in political terms. He devoted the next years to a project aimed at Demetrios' overthrow.

Herakleides and Timarchos came from Miletos, and it was to that city that the former returned after his brother's death, and from there that he co-ordinated his conspiracy. He contacted Alexander, who may well have been living in that city, or perhaps Ephesos, and of whom Herakleides clearly already knew (which is another indication that Alexander really was a son of Antiochos IV). He then contacted King Eumenes II of Pergamon, who was amenable to the idea that Demetrios should be threatened, and who is said to have dressed him in a royal diadem, the mark of kingship, or at least of royalty. Weakening the Seleukid kingdom would be a policy any of its neighbours would be keen to pursue, and another dynastic civil war would help to that end. Alexander was set up with a chieftain called Zenophanes on the borders of Demetrios' kingdom in Kilikia as early as 159 (only a year after Timarchos' death – Herakleides worked fast), but he could make no progress. At the same time Demetrios was unable to remove him, though we may assume he tried.

Partly this was because Eumenes II died in 160/159, and his brother and successor, Attalos II, needed time to establish himself firmly in power before launching out on foreign adventures. Herakleides arranged for Alexander and his sister, Laodike, to go to Rome in 157. The Senate heard the boy make his case, and was sympathetic, but the senators were not interested in doing anything concrete to install a king at the far end of the Mediterranean. Roman sympathy for Alexander and for Herakleides was certainly encouraging, and presumably this helped Attalos to continue his support, limited though it was.[9] All this had brought no real support, however, and after five years Alexander was no nearer success.

Demetrios, however, played into Herakleides' hands. While in Italy he had met and become friendly with Ptolemy VI, the Egyptian king, who had been looking for Roman support in an internal dispute with his brother. Having secured the Egyptian throne (his brother was given Cyrenaica), Ptolemy had a major task on his hands in calming down the problems of Egypt, which had suffered a major rebellion and a devastating invasion (by Antiochos IV) while he was a child. Since 163, when he and Demetrios had met in Italy, he had worked to settle down the country, and had shown himself a careful and vigorous ruler.

Demetrios' friendship should have been a diplomatic asset to both kings, but Demetrios spoiled it by intriguing to acquire Cyprus, a Ptolemaic possession, though one which was disputed between the Ptolemaic brothers, and was a long-standing target for the Seleukids. Further, he failed in his intrigue, so he simultaneously suggested incompetence in his intrigue and alienated the only ruler in the Mediterranean who was anything like his friend.[10]

This intrigue took place in 154, five years after the cause of Alexander had begun to be promoted by Herakleides and Eumenes II, and was the crucial development in Alexander's story. The benevolent encouragement of Rome, the active assistance of Attalos II, and the sponsorship of both Zenophanes and Herakleides, were not sufficient to make him king in Syria in the face of Demetrios' control of the kingdom. The betrayed and annoyed Ptolemy VI was another matter, and the plotters were now able to enlist his support. Ptolemy's involvement was crucial since he had both the wealth to finance the decisive move, which would require a mercenary force, and, as it turned out, the money to lay out for bribes; he also had the ships needed to transport Alexander and his men to the decisive point for the invasion. This was to be Ptolemais-Ake, on the Palestinian coast.

The conspiracy had shown no real energy between 159 and 154, other than diplomatic; suddenly between 154 and 152 energy began to flow. No more is heard of Herakleides, and Attalos fades away, but the geographical location of the attack, the obvious requirement for ships (of which only Ptolemy in the region had any) and money, makes it very likely that Ptolemy had become the lead planner in the expedition.

Wealth was required because Alexander's own resources were few, as, no doubt, were those of Herakleides. He had the assistance of the Attalid king and of the chieftain Zenophanes, but these were no match for the Seleukid king. Ptolemy's money, however, would be sufficient to finance the recruitment of a substantial mercenary force – it is even possible that he supplied the mercenaries from his Egyptian forces, and he was as independent of Rome's opinions and pressure as Demetrios. (Indeed, one of the notable aspects of all this is the absence of any Roman involvement – it is a test for supposed Roman power east of the Adriatic, one which Rome failed; Rome had effectively no influence in these events.)

The region which Alexander attacked first, Palestine, was carefully chosen – the obvious military move would have been to reinforce Zenophanes in Kilikia. But Palestine had been under Ptolemaic rule until half a century before, and it was familiar territory to the Ptolemaic government. This is not to say that there were still Ptolemaic loyalists in the region after all this time, but the Ptolemies knew the geography, and understood clearly that the area was already unstable. Ptolemy VI had his own agenda in this expedition, in which Alexander was, to him, merely an instrument. He was ambitious to recover southern Syria for his kingdom, and this was another reason for the attack to be mounted there.

The choice of Ptolemais-Ake as the point of attack was also a result of the situation in the region as it had evolved over the previous twenty years. One of Demetrios' major political successes had been to quell a nasty rebellion which had been going on for several years in inland Palestine. The Jewish people of the Judaean plateau had rebelled over their treatment by Antiochos IV in the matter of their peculiar religious practices. (The conflict had in fact originated in a series of mutual misunderstandings, but it had developed into a religious quarrel, rather to Greek puzzlement.) The fighting had begun in 166, and had continued for several years, until Demetrios had been able to suppress the rebellion in 161. A decisive military conquest was followed by the installation of garrisons in a number of forts, including Jerusalem, to hold the conquered region down. Demetrios had not appointed a new high priest for Jerusalem – it was the king's prerogative – and so had deprived the Jews of a political chief.

However, although the leader of the rebellion, Judah Maccabee, had been killed, his brother Jonathan had survived and had maintained a position within Judaea as the chief of the militant party. He had extended this position over several years into an unofficial chieftainship over much of the country, by persuasion and reputation in part, but mainly by terrorizing his (Jewish) enemies.[11] By 152, when Alexander and his men landed at Ptolemais-Ake, there had been formal peace in inland Judaea for several years, but in that time Jonathan had extended his grip over all the rural regions of Judaea, despite the Seleukid garrisons imposed by Demetrios. The situation was clearly difficult, but for Alexander and Ptolemy it was clearly a condition which could be exploited.

If one man may be said to have been the organizer of the whole affair, it was obviously Herakleides. He had found Alexander and Laodike, he had contacted Eumenes II, and then Attalos II, he had taken Alexander and Laodike to Rome and secured them a favourable hearing in the Senate. It was therefore presumably Herakleides who had brought Ptolemy VI into the plot. He is the only conspirator who had a personal motive; the kings had clear political aims, but these were hardly urgent. Of course Alexander would want to be king, though he had not put himself forward until Herakleides appeared. Eumenes II and Attalos II may have been annoyed that Demetrios had supplanted their friend Antiochos IV as Seleukid king, but neither of them had much to gain but a minor foreign policy advantage. Similarly Ptolemy VI may have had old family ambitions to regain control of Palestine and Phoenicia, but he had been king for fifteen years and more, ten of them securely, yet he had done nothing to realize those ambitions, and it was clearly not one of his political priorities. Rome was scarcely involved at all beyond the Senate's casual benediction towards Alexander. The overthrow of Demetrios was therefore to be attained for relatively minor political objectives by all of Alexander's backers – apart from Herakleides – and Herakleides has vanished from the story by the time of Alexander's landing. He had been a prominent official and plotter for at least twenty years before 164; he would be fifty or sixty years old by 152, and had perhaps already died.

It is the arrival of Alexander at Ptolemais-Ake which shows the extent of the conspiracy. He arrived in ships which were probably supplied by Ptolemy, and with soldiers supplied by or financed by the resources of Ptolemy and Attalos. The soldiers must have taken some time – months at least – to recruit and organize, and this will have involved frequent journeys for envoys between Alexandria and Pergamon and Zenophanes. (Eumenes' new port-city at Attaleia in Pamphylia may have been founded in connection with all this – at least it would provide a swifter entry for envoys into Asia Minor – and it could be a sign that some of Attalos' ships took part.)[12] All this is to be assumed, but the crucial point about the landing at Ptolemais-Ake is that Alexander's arrival at the city was welcomed. They knew he was coming. The commander and the garrison of Demetrios' soldiers in Ptolemais-Ake joined him without any fighting; there is no sign that the citizens were hostile. They may well have been cowed by the landing of Alexander's forces and the immediate junction of the city garrison with the invaders, though their behaviour in a later crisis does not suggest that they were easily intimidated. In other words, the political ground in the city had been well prepared in advance by the conspirators. The commander of the city garrison had been persuaded to join, and the garrison had been squared, no doubt by a donative.[13] Ptolemy's involvement was a guarantee of payment.

The gravity of the situation will have become clear at once to Demetrios. He was suddenly faced by a coalition of enemies: Eumenes and Zenophanes in the north, Ptolemy in the south, and now Alexander internally. Alexander also swiftly made friendly contact with Jonathan Maccabee in Judaea, and this eventually secured him control of all Palestine. Demetrios collected his forces and marched south, probably beginning at Apamea, the Seleukid military base. His army is described as 'huge' by the author of I Maccabees, but this is never a reliable source for military numbers.[14] More telling is the fact that Demetrios also made contact with Jonathan Maccabee. There followed negotiations. Demetrios needed the troops in the forts; Jonathan wanted the garrisons removed. By designating Jonathan as his 'ally', Demetrios could collect at least some of the soldiers, though he left garrisons in Jerusalem and in at least two of the forts. He also gave Jonathan permission to raise an army, which would count as a new garrison for Judaea, and allowed him to move from his base in the country into Jerusalem, with a concomitant increase in his prestige. Demetrios also released a number of hostages who had been held in Jerusalem, whom Jonathan supposedly returned to their families.[15]

Alexander was not yet involved in all this, but once Jonathan had made his agreement with Demetrios, Alexander made his own bid. This contest for gaining Judaean support implies that the contending royal armies were generally similar in strength, and that Demetrios, who had been in Palestine for the negotiations with Jonathan (and with other local authorities as well, no doubt), had not felt strong enough to tackle Ptolemais-Ake, a well-fortified city. Demetrios in fact was in a generally weak political position. He had become unpopular among his subjects, and rather than live in the palace in Antioch he tended to retire to a castle in the country for long periods. And he was reputedly drinking too much, though, again, much of this is from hostile sources or hearsay.[16] His unpopularity would help to explain his unwillingness to attack Alexander's forces, since he might well have doubts about the loyalty of his troops – the garrison in Ptolemaic-Ake's example could well be followed by others.

In Palestine, Demetrios put Jonathan in a stronger position, but, by failing to attack Alexander in Ptolemais-Ake, he had clearly shown himself to be vulnerable. Once Demetrios had left, Alexander could expand his control out from Ptolemais. We know that he came to control Ashkelon in the south, and so probably all the cities along the coast. And he also made a new offer to Jonathan, confirming the concessions made by Demetrios and adding an offer to make Jonathan high priest in Jerusalem.[17]

Demetrios' reaction to Alexander's landing and intrigues was therefore less than robust. He could not be certain where the next blow might fall, he had to gather troops, and most of his reinforcements will have had to come from the eastern provinces. He could not afford to reduce his military posture in Syria or in Palestine too much, given the hostility of the neighbours, particularly Ptolemy, and the activities of Alexander. He had therefore to mobilize his forces in Syria, whose garrisons will have formed his first reaction force, and then bring in troops from Babylonia and Iran. The latter, however, was territory which he also needed to protect in case the Parthians and others should take advantage of his preoccupation in the west. They seem to have supported Timarchos, perhaps because they were hostile to Demetrios. It was all confusing and difficult.

Alexander, of course, could afford to be more extravagant with his offers than Demetrios, one of whose priorities was to keep a proper military grip on the reconquered Judaean region. Jonathan wanted Demetrios' forces to be withdrawn from the dozen or so forts which they had occupied for the past several years, but this was the foundation of Demetrios' control, so he could not withdraw them all. Alexander, on the other hand, could offer to withdraw those forces, if he won, and could then bid for Jonathan's support, and the basis of a future mutual advantage. In the meantime the offer to make Jonathan high priest was accepted; Jonathan therefore placed himself and his followers on Alexander's side.

The record of military events fails between 152, the date of Alexander's landing at Ptolemais-Ake and Demetrios' abortive march south, and 150, when Alexander marched north in a decisive challenge to Demetrios. In political and diplomatic terms, however, several items advanced the usurper's cause. He gained control of all Palestine, partly by means of his agreement with Jonathan, for he was able to mint coins at Ashkelon as well as Ptolemais. He also extended his control into Phoenicia where coins in his name were minted during 151/150 at Tyre, Sidon, and Berytos, before his final success.[18] No doubt this extension northwards was partly the result of Demetrios' failed attack, but also perhaps because of the naval strength Alexander could deploy. Ptolemais-Ake was the Seleukid naval base, and he may well have secured ships along with the city.

How much material support Alexander had from Ptolemy is not known, but one might guess it would be fairly substantial, for by 150 Alexander was able to confront Demetrios somewhere in northern Syria. We know no details, but such a move does imply a great increase in Alexander's military and/or naval power; some of this was surely recruited in Syria, but the foundation must have been the troops he brought with him, plus the garrisons of the cities in the south he had won over.

Between Ptolemais-Ake and Antioch there are three land routes, as well as the sea route along the coast. Each land route – along the coast, through the Bekaa Valley, and through Damascus and along the eastern foot of the Antilebanon Mountains – had been used by conquerors in the past, though usually they had been moving from north to south. All three routes were therefore well fortified. To use any of these routes Alexander would need to capture, either by siege and assault or by subversion, several fortified and garrisoned cities. We know of no fighting on the way, which, of course, does not mean that none took place, but it rather seems as though the march of Alexander's army northwards was uncontested; probably he went along the coast road, judging by the record of his coin mintings at the Phoenician cities. Of course, it is possible that Ptolemy loaned him his navy to transport his troops to the north, or he had ships of his own, but the logistics of transporting a large army make such a move unlikely. The obvious conclusion is that the way north for Alexander's army was greased by well-targeted bribery.

However it was done, Alexander by 150 was in north Syria with an army powerful enough to meet that which Demetrios had gathered. We have indications of two battles, one a victory for Demetrios and the second a victory for Alexander. Another source maintains that there was only one battle, but this is probably the second of those mentioned elsewhere. There was clearly a good deal more campaigning and political manoeuvering than we hear about. The decisive battle took place somewhere outside Antioch. Demetrios' left wing defeated Alexander's right, but the reverse happened on the other wing. Demetrios himself was driven into a marshy area and there was surrounded with only a few of his men. He fought on until killed.[19] Perhaps to everyone's surprise, not least his own, Alexander had become king in the Seleukid kingdom.

When Demetrios had reached Syria from Rome in 162 almost the first thing he had done was to order that the child King Antiochos V and his guardian Lysias should be killed. Now Alexander, who, if he really was the son of Antiochos IV, was half-brother to the dead child, had Demetrios' eldest son Antigonos killed. He also murdered Demetrios' widow Laodike; she was clearly too valuable a dynastic property to be allowed to live in case she married again.[20] Demetrios had, however, sent his two younger sons, Demetrios and Antiochos, to Greece for safety when Alexander's invasion began. These two would ensure that the fight for the succession would continue for another quarter of a century.

Alexander's other reward, besides becoming king, came by way of a confirmation of the alliance with Ptolemy VI which had existed from the time the latter had joined the conspiracy. It was nonetheless a startling turn of events, for the method was for Ptolemy to give his daughter Kleopatra Thea to Alexander as his wife.[21] In effect this was the first time in a century that a Ptolemaic princess had been married outside the family.

The Ptolemaic practice was that the king should marry his sister. The first occasion for this had been when Ptolemy II married his sister Arsinoe II in about 278. Arsinoe had already had an adventurous marital career, including a marriage with her half-brother Ptolemy Keraunos when he was king in Macedon. She returned to Egypt after Keraunos' death and reputedly provided the energy and political will behind Ptolemy II's policies once they were married; this is extremely unlikely, and the theory seems to be based on general incomprehension and incredulity as to the marriage. But the purpose of the brother-sister marriage was eminently practical: it was to secure the succession. In Egyptian theory kingliness descended through the female as well as the male, but the male, the husband, was, so to say, the executive member of the partnership. So to marry a Ptolemaic princess was to gain a clear claim to the Ptolemaic kingship, and to marry the eldest daughter of a Ptolemaic king was to become his successor. Therefore the marriages of brother and sister confined the succession to the royal family and excluded outsiders. This obviated such matters as rebellions by non-members of the royal family, such as those by Seleukid opponents like Timarchos; there were no succession quarrels in the Ptolemaic family until the 160s and then the dispute was between brothers. (This practice had, of course, as noted earlier, spread to the Seleukid family.)

The decision by Ptolemy VI to give his younger daughter Kleopatra Thea to Alexander Balas as his wife (not, note, the eldest daughter – she was reserved for a brother) was therefore both almost unprecedented and a decisive political move. The only previous example of out-marriage was that of Ptolemy II's daughter Berenike to Antiochos II; this turned out badly when Berenike and her infant son were murdered when Antiochos died. This new marriage signaled that the full weight of Ptolemaic power and influence would be behind Alexander's tenure of the Seleukid throne now that he had won and secured his claim by victory. No doubt Demetrios had factored such a political alignment into his calculations from the time he realized the extent of the conspiracy against him, and Ptolemy's participation in it, but its formalization by a royal marriage was decisive as a means of affirming this new political link. It made any attempt to reverse Alexander's success all the more difficult.

The wedding was a display of political power, taking place at Ptolemais-Ake in 150, and attended by Jonathan Maccabee and probably by representatives of Alexander's other allies. It was a grand state occasion, a clear signal that both the Seleukid kingdom and Alexander were in effect Ptolemaic protectorates, and Ptolemy placed an Egyptian official, Ammonios, in post at Antioch as Alexander's chief adviser, to ensure that the protection was effective.

The effect of this conflict on Judaea was profound. With Alexander in power in Antioch Jonathan's position as high priest was confirmed, and some of the garrisons in the Judaean forts had been removed, and were not returned. On the other hand, Alexander did not remove the last of them, as he had perhaps promised, and thus was squarely placed in the Judaean centre, at Jerusalem. The effect of these changes was to render Judaea semi-autonomous, and less than amenable to the king's authority. It had become what the Maccabean insurgents had aimed for, an autonomous principality. But this was not the end of their ambitions: they aimed for complete independence next, and conquests, even empire, after that.

The necessary concentration by Demetrios on events in the west had been constant ever since his seizure of the throne in 162. Even the attack on him by Timarchos had been met by a battle not far east of the Euphrates. Since then the enmity of his western neighbours, in Asia Minor, of Rome, of Ptolemaic Egypt, and the threat from Alexander, had kept him virtually immobile in Syria. Unlike many other Seleukid kings Demetrios had never visited his eastern provinces. This was undoubtedly noted by his eastern neighbours, Parthia and Baktria. They do not seem to have taken any action to exploit his western preoccupations during his reign, but it soon became clear that this was a problem which affected Alexander as well. Alexander may well have benefited from the friendship of Ptolemy VI and Attalos II, but he was menaced by the sons of Demetrios I in very much the same way as he had menaced their father. (Ptolemy and Attalos were probably not concerned at this, since it reinforced Alexander's dependence on them.) As a result, Alexander, like Demetrios, was pinned down in the western parts of his kingdom.

Further, Alexander soon acquired a reputation for pleasure loving and partying. No doubt the acquisition of a new teenage wife encouraged his pleasures, though he is also reported to have frequented brothels and maintained concubines. Demetrios' unpopularity had partly been due to his reputed appetite for drink, though this had not diverted his attention from his governing responsibilities. Alexander, on the other hand, gained a reputation for laziness, and left much of the detailed administrative work to his ministers, of whom Ammonios was the most notable.[22] So, once again, but for different reasons, the king was in effect confined to the west of his kingdom, mainly, it seems, to Ptolemais-Ake rather than Antioch, and the government was in less than efficient hands.

Superficially, therefore, the kingdom continued, if under a rather more negligent ruler than before. It had lost no territory, and its king was accepted as a legitimate Seleukid (it was far too dangerous to say anything else) and had made a quite extraordinarily splendid marriage. This seemed to guarantee peace for the kingdom and support for the inexperienced king well into the future. In reality, however, the change of king was a new dynastic disaster. For the third time in a quarter of a century, the throne had changed hands by violence. The prestige and authority of the royal family was irretrievably damaged. Further, the concentration of the fighting in Syria will have weakened the outlying provinces and their armies. The next years would demonstrate this both in Judaea and in Media.

Furthermore, the success of one usurper was taken note of. What one pretender might attempt, another might also try. Alexander's success inspired imitators, both in his own kingdom and in others. One man had watched events in Syria and had decided he could do the same.

Chapter 3

Andriskos in Macedon

The example of Alexander Balas was infectious. Once he had shown that he could succeed in his pretence that he was the legitimate heir to the Seleukid kingdom – and by his success he legitimized that pretence – a rash of such adventurers appeared during the next few years. None of them (like Alexander, in fact) had anything more than a brief success, but perhaps only a brief period of power was what they really wanted. The Seleukid kingdom saw another Alexander, claiming to be Balas' son, and a pretender who, like Timarchos, at least did not claim to be Seleukid, during the next two decades; the Attalid kingdom saw an illegitimate son of the last king challenge Rome with some success for several years; in Sicily a former slave made himself king – and was copied by another slave later. But it was in Macedonia with a man called Andriskos that the most immediate follow-up came.

One of the inspirations of Alexander Balas' adventure may well have been the inheritance of the Macedonian kingdom by Perseus, the illegitimate son of Philip V. Philip had been king for four decades, but had then executed his son Demetrios, supposing him to have been treasonous. Having no other sons by his wife, he had invested another son by one of his many mistresses/ concubines as his heir, and Perseus succeeded to the kingdom with little fuss when his father died. Further, Perseus had made a considerable success of his kingship for some time, and his birth had not prevented him from marrying the Seleukid princess, Laodike, daughter of Seleukos IV, and later wife of Demetrios I. (she was the mother of Demetrios' three sons).[1] This story was, of course, familiar to Herakleides, who had been an official of Antiochos IV's.

Perseus, like Philip V, had collided with Rome. Between 215 and 167 Macedon and Rome fought three wars, a total of eighteen years' fighting. The first war, in which Philip was allied rather ineffectively with Hannibal, ended in a draw, perhaps with a little advantage to Philip. It had been fought mainly in Greece, where both sides had allies, and both had ruthlessly exploited those allies so that neither principal had suffered invasion by the other. Much the same could be said of the second war (200–197) but this time it resulted in a complete defeat for Philip, who lost considerable territories at the peace.

Nevertheless he used the subsequent periods of peace (between 197 and his death he was involved marginally in Rome's war with Antiochos III as Rome's ally) to rebuild his kingdom, encouraging enterprise and the growth of its population. It was, in fact, an object lesson in what a king could accomplish if undisturbed by wars.

So when Perseus inherited the Macedonian kingship in 179 he became the ruler of a flourishing kingdom. But what could a new king do with a rich and populous kingdom? Rome would not permit him to take the obvious course, which for Macedon was to campaign northwards to deter and control the constantly threatening Balkan tribes. Yet Macedonian kings were above all warriors, and it was necessary for Perseus to campaign somewhere as a means of legitimizing his kingship – despite his initial acceptance, his birth could all too easily be brought up in criticism; victory in war was the best way to prove his worth as king. The problem was that the only possible enemy was Rome. He made considerable efforts to gain allies in Greece and Asia Minor, with some success, for Rome was much disliked, but it is probable that even with the alliance of every power in the Mediterranean, he could not have won.

As it was, Perseus made a good fight of it, staving off invasions by a series of incompetent and arrogant Roman commanders, whose behaviour towards Rome's allies stood in stark contrast to Rome's pretensions of liberation and protection. It could not last, of course, for eventually the Senate chose men as commanders who were known to be competent generals. First Q. Marcius Philippus, consul in 169, broke through the southern defences of Macedon in the area of Mount Olympos, and at the same time exercised his considerable diplomatic skills in calming the agitated and resentful Greek allies and gaining their support. Then in 167 the consul M. Aemilius Paullus finally brought Perseus' Macedonian army to battle, while the praetor Cn. Octavius, in command of the Roman and allied fleet, threatened invasion from the sea. The defeated Macedonians were either killed in the battle of Pydna which followed, or, in many cases, they were killed in flight or when they took to the sea.

This time defeat brought political and economic destruction. The Roman vengeance which followed was a mark of the fright the city's rulers had had, and of their impatience at the repeated wars. The kingdom was thoroughly looted of its wealth, and even an ancient giant sixteener warship, which had been laid up and preserved for perhaps a century, was carried off to Rome, where it rotted away in a few years. The king and his children were carried off to Italy as well; Perseus died within a few years; his Seleukid wife was sent home. The children, if they survived, were never to be allowed home again – his son Philip died within two years. It is clear that the Roman Senate fully understood the loyalty of the Macedonians to their Antigonid dynasty, and had determined that its members should not be permitted near their old kingdom ever again.[2]

Not only that, but the kingdom itself was destroyed, not merely by having bits given to other states, or made into independent cities, though that certainly happened. The real destruction was that Macedonian unity was abolished. The kingdom was broken into four units, which had the semblance of city states on the Greek pattern but, of course, they bore no real resemblance to such states.[3] They had no tradition of operating as independent states, though the various cities and towns in the kingdom had always enjoyed a good deal of local autonomy. The real trouble was that they were quite unable, indeed were forbidden, to co-operate, and this destroyed the historic function of Macedon, which was to act as a military shield for the Greeks of the peninsular states. They were not disarmed, but their forces were restricted to a militia whose basic function was as a border guard.

For nearly twenty years these artificial, unviable, quasi–city–states struggled to function. They had little success. The gold and silver mines which had produced much of the royal revenue were closed. The republics were ordered to pay to Rome in tribute half of the taxes paid to the king. This might seem generous, but with the mines closed and commerce in salt and ship timber banned, even half the previous taxation was a heavier burden. The republics were to be reduced to a society of peasant farmers.[4]

The republics were supposed, according to the Roman decisions, now to be free and autonomous, ungarrisoned, and to live under their own laws. But within a few years they were quarrelling, and one set of councillors had been assassinated.[5] Rome sent a commission to investigate, but we do not know what resulted – probably nothing. After ten years the Senate allowed the mines to restart operations, presumably so that the tribute could be paid; generosity towards the Macedonians is highly unlikely.[6] These are the only interventions we know of, but there were probably others – repeated interference from Rome was, of course, profoundly disturbing. As usual, no final answer to the difficulties came from the Senate, and in 151 the republics were still internally disturbed. This time they asked Scipio Aemilianus to help them sort things out – he was the son of their conqueror Aemilius Paullus, adopted into the Scipio family, and so should have had a hereditary interest. He refused to help, having better things to do. In other words, neither the Senate selectively nor a prominent individual senator would help.[7]

The republics were hobbled in their government from the start, by poverty, and inexperience, and the chance of becoming stable entities was sabotaged by a toxic mixture of Roman interference and neglect. What was needed was either a constant Roman supervision or a deliberate absence of interference. The failure to do either made it impossible that the states should ever develop their own traditions of independent and competent government.

The problems faced by this artificial state system brought its collapse in 149. This was the result of the Roman decision not to extend its own direct rule forty years before. No substantial annexations to Roman territory had been made since the conquest of Cisalpine Gaul in the 190s, apart from odd bits of northern Italy which had been overlooked then. The Po Valley had been conquered as an aggressive defence for peninsular Italy; Spain was a constant battleground where some annexations had resulted but there the wars continued. Even so, a good deal less than half of the Spanish peninsula was Roman, not much more, indeed, than the Carthaginians had ruled when Hannibal set out for Italy in 218. There had been plenty of opportunities to acquire more lands – in Africa, in Greece and Macedonia, and of course in Spain – but all had been spurned.

This is certainly a curious matter. Rome was a self-consciously proud military state. Its armies had beaten every other army of every state within reach, even those of the skilful Hannibal, even that of the Great King Antiochos III. It was clearly possible for Rome to have expanded wherever it wished (though the failure to make progress in Spain was revealing). Yet the defeat of Hannibal and Carthage in 202 did not lead to the annexation of any of its territory (apart from the Spanish colony, which had already been conquered) and the successive defeats of Macedon did not lead to the acquisition by Rome of any territory in Greece.

On the other hand, the terms of peace after each of these wars did contain obligations on the part of the defeated to pay indemnities or tribute, and to pay heed to Roman wishes as a Roman ally (sometimes, with no hint of irony) as a 'friend and ally'. As a result, Rome was surrounded by lands which were technically allies of some sort, and who were paying sums of money into the Roman treasury. There was no need to annex these lands. If they had been taken over, and made into provinces, they would need to be garrisoned and governed. This way the only trouble Rome had was the constant series of envoys from the dependent territories that turned up asking for decisions on local problems.

For example, when Sparta wanted to escape inclusion within the larger league of Achaian states, it was to Rome it appealed, and when Carthage suffered raids by the horsemen of King Massinissa of Numidia, Rome was appealed to. And when the Macedonian republics could not cope with their problems Scipio Aemilianus was asked to help. And so on. Every Greek city, every Asia Minor city or kingdom, at some point between 202 and 150 appealed to Rome over some issue, and, worse, had to accept Roman decisions, some of which were, to the recipients, simply perverse. Of course, it was not justice or fairness which guided the decisions of the Senate, but the interests of Rome. It is not clear that the appellants ever fully understood that, wrapped up as they were in their own problems, but, even if they did, they had no alternative. And the prime Roman interest was to reduce the strength of any state which was within its range.

Hence, Massinissa's raiders were ignored, and Carthage was left to suffer from them – and Scipio Aemilianus would not help Macedon. When the loyal Roman ally Eumenes II of Pergamon headed for Italy on a diplomatic mission whom the Senate did not welcome, through sheer embarrassment at its earlier perverse decision, he was barred from landing by a hastily passed law which said that kings could not be admitted to Roman territory – a law never enforced against any other king. The Senate was thus quite unscrupulous. King Demetrios I of the Seleukids had annoyed senators by a skilfully contrived escape from Italy; when he was threatened by Timarchos' rebellion the Senate professed to 'recognize' Timarchos as king, but having thus encouraged him, did nothing to support him. Rome's interest decreed that the Seleukid kingdom be weakened, no matter who suffered. But Rome's interest did not extend to elementary courtesy towards its allies.

Yet Rome wished to enjoy the fruits of its victories. Having won a war, the Roman armies were generally withdrawn back to Italy, but the defeated state was presented with the bill. So Carthage paid an indemnity every year between 240 and 220 and between 200 and 150, Antiochos III's kingdom paid 15,000 talents over ten years – which stretched to fifteen – Macedonia paid a tribute every year between 166 and 148, and so on. This was a variation on another theme. The Italian states conquered in the fourth and third centuries had paid a different form of dues, in the form of soldiers called up for service whenever Rome went to war. This was highly successful in reducing the strength of the cities of Italy and at the same time reducing the burden on Rome. At the same time it tended towards making the peninsula into a political unity through shared sufferings and shared victories. In other words Rome's empire was being conquered by armies which were manned by a majority of non-Romans, and, when the tribute collected changed from men to money, its wars were financed by the tribute of the defeated states – and the tribute went exclusively to Rome. So not only were the armies less than half Roman in personnel, the taxes of Rome at home were reduced because of the inflow of tribute money. Rome had no need to annex more lands, they were being milked efficiently enough already.

It was this attitude which had brought the Macedonian kingdom to destruction and division. If Macedon was annexed, as was obviously to be expected after Perseus' defeat in 167, then a Roman magistrate and a Roman army would need to be stationed there for the foreseeable future. And this would be a fighting army, not a mere garrison. It would face an open and active barbarian frontier, just as did the praetors who governed the Spanish provinces. The army would need to be of at least two legions of Roman citizens and an equivalent force of Italian allies — perhaps 20,000 men in all. The governor would be of praetorian rank, his office prorogued for a year, and he would be assisted by a quaestor, but this would inevitably expand the number of magistrates. Further, if a serious war threatened it would become a consular command with a bigger army, where glory and fame and wealth accrued to the victor, which would probably intensify internal political feuds at Rome. With its long barbarian frontier it would be an ideal place for the governors to go triumph-hunting by picking a quarrel with a Balkan tribe and then fighting it. It was easier and more acceptable to the Roman Senate to destroy the kingdom and extract a tribute from the ruins.

The four republics had been left with an army each for this very purpose, to be able to defend themselves against barbarian attacks without having to call on Roman assistance. There was a semi-circle of ancient enemies along the northern frontier, from the Dardani in the west to the Thracians in the east. The kings of Macedon had repeatedly fought these peoples for centuries, but only Philip II in the 340s had been successful in conquering them, and since then they had slipped out of Macedonian control once more. The apparent protection of Rome had made little difference; indeed one of the reasons for the troubles which developed in 148 was that the Thracians are said to have hated Rome. They only did so because Roman power might seem to prevent them from raiding into Macedon. The almost complete absence of records of Macedonian affairs prevents any judgment on this, but the continued existence of the frontier guards implies a continuing threat; enmity between the Macedonians and their neighbours continued.

This was the situation when Andriskos came onto the Macedonian scene. He was a mercenary soldier, a man who bore a certain resemblance to either Philip V or Perseus, and was jokingly called 'son of Perseus' by his fellow soldiers. This clearly appealed to him and he began to speak of himself as a member of the Antigonid dynasty, specifically as Philip, son of King Perseus, who had in fact died in Italy after only two years' imprisonment — and so a decade before Andriskos claimed to be him.[8] No one in Macedon or elsewhere knew what had happened to him in Italy other than rumours. His identity was thus a safe choice, though there were other relatives of his still alive who might have identified him if they chose.

His service as a mercenary soldier had clearly given Andriskos a certain military skill. He went to Macedon, perhaps in 153 or so, and announced his identity, hoping to rouse Macedonian support, recruit an army, and be accepted throughout the country. Evidently no one believed him, and he failed to recruit any following at all. On the other hand, whether he believed himself to be of royal birth or not, it is evident that he was stubborn and determined, and as it proved, inventive as well.

He now went to Syria, and apparently enlisted as a soldier in the army of King Demetrios I. This was in 151/150, at a time when Demetrios was fully occupied with the problem of Alexander Balas, who by this time was preparing for his invasion of northern Syria. Andriskos' purpose was less to fight for Demetrios and more to gain support from the king for his own purposes. But this was a very bold move, for Demetrios' wife was Laodike, Perseus' widow, and so Andriskos' claimed grandmother. He may also have claimed to be the son of one of Perseus' concubines – his maternal history is never referred to.

Antioch at the time was no doubt in a febrile state. It was a city liable to be attacked by the pretender Alexander, while the actual ruler, Demetrios, was unpopular. In such a situation Andriskos could hardly expect any royal help. Possibly that was why he publicized his claim among the population first, and only then approached Demetrios, with a crowd of followers at his back. What he wanted was for Demetrios to 'restore' him to Macedon. How he imagined this could be done is quite unknown, but Demetrios' relationship, as brother-in-law to the dead Perseus, must have seemed a useful tool. Demetrios, who was surely preoccupied with fighting his own pretender at the time, impatiently brushed him off. Andriskos gathered more supporters, no doubt including Antiochenes, who were using him to express their dislike of the king. (One wonders if he had support from Alexander, who would welcome anything which would weaken or distract his enemy.) What is curious is that Laodike was not apparently consulted, or if she was, her opinion was not published. Finally, Demetrios had Andriskos seized by night and sent away to Rome. The disturbances he had stimulated presumably died down, but Demetrios was soon killed in battle, and Laodike was murdered.

In Rome, when he got there, the Senate was equally disbelieving and dismissive of Andriskos' claim. After all, the Romans had rounded up all the Macedonian royal family in 167 and had then allowed them to die off in Italy – and the son of Perseus had died after only two years' detention. The senators knew this perfectly well, or could easily find it out. Andriskos was dismissed as the imposter he no doubt was, but was ordered to stay in Italy, either in a town or in Rome, probably the former.

His pretensions had begun as a joke among his mates, but by the time it had reached an audience with the Roman Senate, Andriskos himself had reached the stage where either he had come to believe them himself, or had decided it would be too humiliating to back down. While in his Italian semi-detention, it seems that he had elaborated his story. Quite likely he was inspired in this by the story of Alexander Balas, who had by this time succeeded in his adventure and become a ruling king, but also by the universal story of the hidden prince brought up in secret. His version was that he had been sent to Crete to be brought up by foster parents. The secret of his birth was contained in a letter (a 'sealed tablet'), which was only to be opened when he had grown up. It also contained directions for the recovery of two sets of treasure which had been concealed in Macedon as the Romans closed in on his 'father', by whom he meant Perseus. The various elements were clearly gathered from fairy tales, legends, and recent events − the treasure, for example, came from a story that Perseus had sent two men to hide his treasure by throwing it into the sea; when they did not do so he had them killed − but what became of the treasure? Andriskos was clearly ringing a series of bells in his story, though how plausible it all was to the people of the time is less obvious. It is clear that those historians who recorded his story did not believe any of it – though they were all writing after his failure and death. It is this disbelief which makes it likely that they were telling the story as they understood it after his death, and not necessarily as Andriskos had retailed it, without much in the way of varnish or interpretation − though Polybios certainly puts a personal interpretation on the end of his version. The several sources each give part of the story; they can be linked more or less satisfactorily into a whole.

He escaped from his detention in Italy and turned up with his newly elaborated story in Miletos. When they heard of him and his story, the city magistrates threw him in prison. In the city there were some 'envoys', who in the circumstances are assumed to be Roman. They took their cue from the Senate, laughed at the story, and told the Milesians to let him go. (Note that both Demetrios in Syria and the Milesians were anxious to please the Romans in this, even though in both cases they were, to say the least, sceptical of his story.)

The fact that he went to Miletos is another of the clues to understanding his story. His original home would seem to have been Adramyttion, where he was brought up by a Cretan who worked as a fuller − hence the Cretan connection. This city was north along the coast from Miletos, and Miletos itself was the home of Herakleides, the sponsor of Alexander Balas, and it also had a substantial Cretan, or Cretan-descended, population. Then, in the Attalid kingdom, inland from Miletos, to which Andriskos went next, a considerable number of refugee Macedonians had settled, having left their ancestral kingdom in the aftermath of its defeat by Rome. These people were clearly anti-Roman; he soon linked up with a Macedonian harpist called Neolaus, who gave him information for the next stage in his journey. Whether Andriskos went to Miletos deliberately because of all these factors, or simply because he was heading to his home region, is not clear, but he did seize creatively on the opportunities which appeared before him.

When released from his Milesian jail, Andriskos, advised by Neolaus, went to Pergamon, where a former concubine of Perseus, called Kallippa, was married to Athenaios. Kallippa may have been the daughter of one of Perseus' generals, Kallippos, and so part of the old Macedonian elite; her husband Athenaios was a cousin of Attalos II, the Pergamene king; he is known from letters of the king as a priest of Dionysios, and is so recorded in 142 and in 135, and his son-in-law Sosandros was a prominent man of the Pergamene court.[9] The point is, of course, that Andriskos was once again putting himself into contact with a woman who had some knowledge of the Macedonian court twenty years before, as he had at Antioch. Recognition was out of the question after such a long time, for Andriskos was now adult whereas his earlier (probably non-existent) self had been a child at most. But the audacity he displayed might well convince others of his genuineness.

This actually was a clever move on Andriskos' part. Whether Kallippa or Athenaios believed his story is unknown, and probably irrelevant, but they played along, kitting him out with the appropriate clothes, putting a diadem round his head, and giving him funds and two slaves for his journeys. This is all the more appropriate in that it was exactly what Eumenes II and Attalos II had done ten years before in promoting the pretensions of Alexander Balas. (All in all Andriskos shows himself fully aware of the many royal nuances of the time.) It appears that he now went on to visit several of the places in Asia Minor in which Macedonian refugees had settled and was able to recruit a force from amongst them.[10] And, supposedly from Kallippa, he now heard of yet another royal Macedonian lady, the wife of the Thracian King Teres who was the daughter of Philip V, and so the sister of Perseus, and therefore Andriskos' 'aunt' or 'great aunt', depending on who he claimed to be his father.

Kallippa and Athenaios must have had some motives of their own in directing Andriskos to Thrace and presumably encouraging him to recruit followers. Their actions, in fact, have a strongly anti-Roman flavour. Kallippa, of course, was presumably Macedonian, and could be expected to be at least nostalgic for the independent kingdom. Together the two were prominent in the Pergamene aristocracy; it is evident that there was a strong current of anti-Roman feeling in the kingdom's politics even as the pro-Roman Attalos II was king. Twenty years later the prospect of becoming a Roman province led to an outbreak of fighting which was aimed at maintaining the kingdom's independence – and that war was led by Aristonikos, an illegitimate scion of the royal house; Alexander Balas was such, Andriskos claimed to be another, and Andronikos was fighting to rescue his kingdom from Rome.

The welcome he received in Thrace was all that Andriskos can have wanted. On the way he had been received at Byzantion as at least an important figure, though perhaps not as king; a fairly substantial armed entourage of refugee Macedonians may have been just as convincing. In Thrace proper King Teres, the husband of Philip's daughter, put a diadem on his head, so proclaiming him king, and gave him a hundred soldiers. Other Thracians contributed another hundred men; another chieftain, Barsarbas, agreed to assist in his invasion. The motives of the Thracians were probably fairly simple. At least one historian simply calls them anti-Roman, but they were also anti-Macedonian, and it is probable that the main motivation of many of them was a chance to raid and loot Macedon. (One aspect of this whole story is how often Andriskos was used by those he contacted as a means of advancing their own projects – but he seems to have played them at their own game quite successfully.)

The ancient enmity of the Thracians and Macedonians ensured that, commanding his Thracian troops, Andriskos was not welcomed in his invasion of Macedon. He adopted the throne name Philip, and together with his Thracians this was a clear threat to those who were running the Macedonian republics. His invasion was likely to cement Macedonian opposition – except that the republics were expressly forbidden to co-operate. He was defeated by the Macedonian frontier guards on his first attempt (suggesting that this Macedonian militia was a competent force), but he tried again, perhaps with reinforcements, and campaigned for some time – three or four months, says Polybios – in the land of the Macedonian First Republic, the easternmost one, which was mainly east of the Strymon River. When that republic was defeated, the others fell to him with ease, domino-like. At Pella, the old royal capital, the conqueror was enthroned as king – 'Philip VI'.

This sequence of events had largely been ignored at Rome until Andriskos' victory and crowning. In part this was due to the Senate's preoccupation with the developing crisis over Carthage, together with bad news from Spain; the victory of Alexander Balas and Ptolemy VI in Syria must also have drawn attention. And, of course, for some time the soldiers of the First Republic had been successful in fending Andriskos off. Polybios comments on the astonishment felt at Rome when the news came that the four republics had all fallen to the pretender, but he goes too far in claiming that the Macedonians should have been grateful to Rome for freeing them from the kings. (He was also, of course, commenting in this on his own theory of Roman imperial inevitability.) He remarks that Andriskos became busy in executing numbers of Macedonians; no doubt these were the prominent officials of the republics, whose vested interest was clearly in opposing him.

The first Roman reaction was to treat the problem as a local quarrel, on the pattern of the dispute which had erupted in 151, only a couple of years earlier, which was attended to by a Roman commission. If there had been intermittent Thracian raids on the republics, it would be easy to dismiss the attack as just another one. P. Cornelius Scipio Nasica Corculum, who had twice been consul and was the current *pontifex maximus*, was sent to conciliate, which could mean negotiating peace between Macedon and the Thracians. This suggests that his despatch was agreed before the Macedonian collapse, but also that eventually the problem was seen to be reasonably serious, for it is difficult to find a more distinguished and experienced Roman in 149/148 than Scipio Corculum. It also implies that the problem was seen as amenable to solution by diplomacy.[11] It was still not seen as a major political and military matter.

When he investigated, however, Scipio discovered that it was no longer a situation which could be solved by talking. The crowning of Andriskos as King Philip precluded the restoration of the republics and required a military response – unless, which was clearly out of the question – Rome could accept the restoration of the monarchy. Scipio had probably travelled by way of Corinth, sailing along the Corinthian Gulf. By the time he arrived in Greece Andriskos was invading Thessaly, traditionally part of the Macedonian kingdom since the days of Philip II. This news arrived by way of Thessalian messengers bearing appeals for help. Scipio gathered up a force from the Achaians and sent it north, and also sent an urgent report to Rome on the situation.[12]

The news finally shocked the Senate into paying attention. The praetor P. Iuventius Thalna took an army to invade Macedon and remove the pretender. We are not told how large the army was, but it was probably a single legion with an equivalent force of Italian allies, perhaps 10,000 men. Livy notes that it was met by Andriskos' army in Thessaly, where the Achaians had been helping to defend the country against Andriskos' attack. No doubt the Romans were over-confident, especially if the despised Greeks had been successful in their defensive. Andriskos had already displayed a certain military skill in defeating the Macedonians, and now he showed more in the battle against the Romans. Thalna was killed, and considerable Roman casualties were inflicted. In the night the Roman forces were withdrawn.[13]

Andriskos, still faced by Thessalians and Achaians, and probably also by the survivors of Thalna's defeated forces, pushed further into Thessaly, camping eventually near the battlefield of Pydna. Rome sent another army, a larger one this time (and so perhaps two legions), under another praetor, Q. Caecilius Metellus, and called up a fleet from King Attalos to institute a blockade of the coast. (Given the involvement of his cousin in the promotion of Andriskos, no doubt Attalos was all the keener to assist.) This combination was sufficient, aided by Metellus' cunning. He induced the Macedonian cavalry under the general Telestes to change sides, then defeated the infantry. Andriskos fled to Thrace, pausing only to wreak his revenge on Telestes' family. He was able to give battle once more, but was again defeated. He took refuge with a Thracian chieftain, Byzes, who handed him over to Metellus.[14]

The Roman decisions on what next to do about Macedon are unknown. Quite likely nothing was decided for some years, for the successive and simultaneous crises over Carthage and Greece followed on quickly. Two years later Metellus was still in Macedon, and he had to suppress another attempt at restoring the kingdom, by a man referred to as 'Pseudophilip' or 'Pseudoperseus'. This in fact may have been a Thracian raid headed by a Macedonian, or even a fake-Macedonian, which would have been particularly appropriate. But that it happened at all indicates that the disturbed condition of the region would continue.

The rapid collapse of the Macedonian republics made it obvious that Rome's original method of informally controlling all those states within reach was no longer viable. Even if other crises had not followed quickly on that in Macedon it was probable that the Macedonian crisis would have compelled a new, or rather a reversion to the old, method of empire. The imperial problems of Rome were thus highlighted all at once.

Chapter 4

Rome's Problems

In 151 when some of the Macedonians felt that a problem they faced was too difficult to solve they turned to Rome for help, as every city in Greece and Asia Minor had done for the previous fifty years. They contacted the son of the man who had emplaced the political system of republics in place of the old monarchy, P. Cornelius Scipio Aemilianus, the natural-born son of M. Aemilius Paullus, who had been adopted into the family of the Cornelii Scipiones. But this was a bad time to ask him for his political help, for he had become involved in a political problem at Rome over the wars in Spain, which looked much more politically advantageous for him. No Roman went to help the Macedonians, and two years later the pretender Andriskos succeeded in conquering and reuniting all Macedon, thus initiating the Fourth Romano–Macedonian war. Instead of one man, the Romans had to send two armies.

At Rome this was a time when a whole series of imperial issues, not just Macedon, developed into major crises. In that same year, 151, the Senate decided that the remaining hostages from Achaia who had been held in Italy since 167 should be released, but when, two years later, Kallikrates, the one politician in the Achaian League whom Rome could trust to hold down the league's hostility, died, relations descended into acrimony and two years later again the league initiated a war against Rome.

In 151 and 150, the Roman commanders in Spain, L. Licinius Lucullus and Ser. Sulpicius Galba, were victorious in a fight with the Lusitanians, but only succeeded by means of massacres, brutality, bad faith, and disobedience of the Senate. The behaviour of commanders in Spain had periodically become so unpleasant that it had produced protests both in Spain and in Rome, but in the case of Galba it was so heinous that it led to his prosecution; his escape from condemnation, by a theatrical legal performance, was followed by a new law which opened the way to greater control over such men's activities.

One of those involved in Galba's prosecution was the old political warrior M. Porcius Cato. For several years he had campaigned to persuade the Senate that Carthage was dangerous, claiming it had become too powerful. In the year of his death, 149, Cato's policy finally met success: Rome's unscrupulous diplomatic campaign led to a declaration of war; the year after that Massinissa also died.

These several events, in Macedon and Greece, Spain and Africa, all parts of Rome's imperial system, had serious repercussions in the political system which had been developed by Roman politicians over the previous half century. They all, of course, also produced a series of more or less simultaneous wars, with Macedon against Andriskos, with Carthage, with the Achaian league, as well as continued fighting in Spain, thereby demonstrating even to the Roman Senate the complete failure of that imperial system.

That these problems all came to a head at the same time is hardly an accident or a coincidence. The one common element in them all was Rome, and it is Rome's imperial problems which are the subject of this chapter.

The Roman imperial system had emerged as a viable and permanent method of government first in the 340s. The Roman scheme allied the city with a series of minor Latin cities. The two partners of the alliance, Rome and the Latins, would contribute more or less equally to their joint army, which was to be commanded by Roman officers. Rome was already one of the greatest cities in Italy, and with the Latins associated with her, the system acted as a military multiplier. Rome became the most formidable military power west of Macedonia.

After seventy years of almost continuous warfare the Roman–Latin confederacy controlled all Italy. In the process Rome had annexed a large part of the peninsula as its own territory, while the Latins had expanded by establishing − under Roman direction − colonies in other areas. Each of these, like the original Latin cities, was allied individually to Rome. As a result Rome controlled about a third of the peninsula directly, and the Latins and other allies the rest, though the whole was governed in effect by Rome. It was this state − for this is how it operated with regard to the rest of the world − which fought and beat Carthage twice, Macedon twice, and the Seleukid empire once between 246 and 189, and which had acquired subject provinces throughout the western Mediterranean as a result.[1]

The strains and challenges of war with these other great powers acted to hold the confederacy together from its origin to the second century BC. Only occasionally did the allies complain of the burden of the wars, and in each case the Roman Senate was able to deal with the complaints fairly easily. But the Latins found that they contributed their men disproportionately to the Roman armies, yet received a disproportionately small share of the proceeds. The loot, the indemnities, the tribute, went to Rome; the allies provided the troops. The complaints, which had emerged in the Hannibalic War, centred on the constant demands of the Senate for manpower, which many of the smaller allied cities were finding it increasingly difficult to provide.

The period of relative peace from about 190 onwards should have enabled a recovery to take place, but warfare in Spain continued for some time, broke out again from 154, and so tended to prevent such recovery. The Latin cities in central Italy lost manpower to Rome by migration, as well as to the army. The practice of founding colonies in conquered land slowly declined and ceased by 177 apart from occasional cases. The obvious reason for this was lack of demand – the last foundations had very generous land allocations. By the 180s therefore the balance between Rome and the allies in the confederacy had shifted decisively in favour of the former.

The supremacy of Rome as the controller of the confederacy had been overwhelmingly confirmed by the wars. After the Hannibalic War power had been concentrated above all in the Roman Senate, one of whose achievements during the war had been to reduce the democratic element in the Roman constitution in its own favour. All the envoys from Greece, from Carthage, from the eastern kingdoms, from Spain, went to Rome and were interviewed in the Senate, which then made decisions for the whole confederacy.

When the wars ended with the Treaty of Apamea in 188 Rome's empire had expanded, but in direct rule only into Spain. Neither Carthage nor Macedon were annexed, though both were decisively reduced in power; the 'informal' empire therefore spread over North Africa, Greece, and into Asia Minor. The result for the next forty years was continual fighting in Spain and frequent minor crises in the east. In both regions the system which Rome had developed operated poorly, and eventually broke down in the 140s. Here it will be convenient to concentrate first on Spain, then, more briefly, to look at Carthage and Greece, both of which will be considered in more detail in later chapters.

Having acquired Carthaginian Spain by conquest, Rome then had to fight a series of wars and campaigns, first to establish its control, and then to push the frontier forward to the middle of the country. In 179 C. Sempronius Gracchus finally made a durable peace with the Spaniards in and around the Ebro Valley.[2] Roman Spain then consisted of the Mediterranean coastlands from the Pyrenees to the mouth of the Guadalquivir at Gades – perhaps as long a frontier line as could be devised. Perfunctory attempts to establish colonies had taken place, and the old Carthaginian and Phoenician towns had a certain autonomy, so the two Roman provinces had a superficial similarity to Italy, but the Spanish tribes of the north and west remained independent, and many of those within the provinces were subdued but hostile.

Gracchus' achievement was to make 'precise treaties' with several of the tribes – a term suggesting that earlier agreements had been vague and were therefore easily broken by both parties. The peaceful period which followed was probably in part due to the precision of his agreements, but also to the reduction of the Roman forces from two legions in each of the provinces to one.[3] This made it more difficult for the praetorian governors to initiate wars. In a quarter-century after these treaties there was only one triumph and one *ovatio* from Spain.

In 154 the Spanish wars began again. The Romans, unhelpfully, called it a 'rebellion' because they had made earlier treaties with the enemy tribes, while the Spaniards no doubt felt that they were fighting for their independence, or at least for loot. And loot was one of the aims uppermost in the minds of the Roman commanders who were sent out to conduct the fighting. The Lusitani in the west began the war with raids and the successful ambush of a Roman force, and this early success stimulated the Celtiberians in the centre to join in when the Lusitani sent their trophies to be displayed.[4]

This is a crucial moment in Roman Spain. The Roman system in Italy relied on alliances between Rome and individual cities. In Spain the rudiments of a similar situation had existed, with cities in the south, in the Guadalquivir Valley, and along the coast. Many of these cities were Greek or Phoenician in origin, others were Spanish. All of these could be accommodated into the Roman system as allies. The interior did not have cities of this type, though Gracchus had founded a colony in the Ebro Valley which might be an example to the rest. Then came Segeda. This was a new city, founded more or less spontaneously by the people of two Spanish tribes, the Belli and the Titthi in the hills between the Ebro and the upper waters of the Tagus.

Here should have been an opportunity for the Romans to entice this new city into their system. Instead hostilities developed. The Roman commanders apparently saw the city as a threat; the Segedans by contrast were determined on independence. The Senate resolved on war, and sent out the consul Q. Fulvius Nobilior, with a two-legion army, to take Segeda. Meanwhile the Segedans gained the alliance of another tribe, the Arevaci, and so this war quickly involved the people of a large part of north-central Spain. Nobilior's army, said to be 30,000 strong, was ambushed on the march and it is said that 6,000 Roman citizens were killed (which probably meant that even more non-Romans died).[5]

The story of the Celtiberians being roused to war by the sight of the trophies of the Lusitani seems unlikely, and may best be assumed to be a Roman invention to excuse their own initiation of the war. Nevertheless there were now two Spanish wars going on. In the Ulterior province the

Lusitani defeated two praetors, killing supposedly another '6,000 Romans' and a quaestor. The next praetor, L. Mummius, was also at first defeated, but quickly recovered to ambush the Lusitani as they returned encumbered by their booty from their raid. Appian, our source, quotes unlikely figures for casualties, but the war seems to have been one of raids and ambushes, in which no Roman unit was safe from attack. Another Lusitanian group joined in with a raid on the southwest and then crossed to Africa; Mummius chased and defeated them, and recaptured their booty.[6]

The casualties reported by Appian may be inaccurate and exaggerated, but the war was regarded in Rome with some horror. The Celtiberian war in particular was called 'fiery', from the savagery employed by both sides, and that against the Lusitani cannot have been any the less disliked. The Senate turned to its most distinguished commander, M. Claudius Marcellus, who became consul for 152 and took out reinforcements to fight the Segedans. He also brought out a new attitude, offering terms of peace to those interested, but unleashing devastation on recalcitrants. This combination of tactics succeeded, and he brought about an agreement. The three tribes sent envoys to Rome, but there the Senate rejected Marcellus' terms. Indeed *deditio* — unconditional surrender — Nobilior's original demand, was required.[7]

The consul for 151, L. Licinius Lucullus, was assigned to continue the Celtiberian war, but had much difficulty in collecting a sufficient force of reinforcements to take with him, disputing with the tribunes over the fairness and extent of the levy. It is said that he and his colleague were even imprisoned by the tribunes for their harshness. The problem was, of course, that the wars in Spain, especially this latest one in Celtiberia, had acquired an evil reputation and that those men eligible for the levy were evading it, by legal and illegal methods.

Lucullus, failing in his recruitment, had the mortification to be upstaged in his conduct of the levy by Scipio Aemilianus, then a young senator from an inimical political family. When the levy was at a standstill he stood up in the Senate and announced that he was willing to go and fight in Spain as a military tribune; at this others are supposed to have been inspired to volunteer as well. It is more likely that Scipio chose a moment in the dispute when it became clear that Lucullus' methods were about to be replaced, and he was therefore able to capitalize on his errors. Scipio always did have an uncanny sense of political timing.[8]

As a result of the delays in Rome the news of the Senate's rejection of his peace terms reached Marcellus before Lucullus' belated arrival. Marcellus reacted by warning the Celtiberians that the war would be resumed, unless they proffered *deditio*. This they eventually did, Marcellus received a large sum of money, and in return he released his captives – in effect a compromise peace.[9] Deprived of his war Lucullus then attacked another tribe, the Vaccaei, who had not been involved in the earlier fighting. Lucullus claimed to be operating in favour of the Carpetani, enemies of the Vaccaei, and the Carpetani are known to have been friendly to the Romans. On the other hand, Lucullus had not been authorized to make war on the Vaccaei by the Senate.

He attacked the town of Cauca, where he carried out a massacre of the male inhabitants. He got into the town by making a series of successive demands: having defeated a sortie, he agreed terms which required the payment of an indemnity and the surrender of the town's cavalry (which probably meant the majority of the leading men); these terms having been carried out, he demanded that the town receive a garrison. This force, entering the town, occupied the walls, and the rest of the army then carried out the massacre.[10]

This method of warfare may work once, but it warns others to fight all the harder. Lucullus' campaigns against other Vaccaean towns were unsuccessful. At Intercatia only the intervention of Scipio Aemilianus persuaded the citizens to make terms; at Pallantia, as at Intercatia, the Roman army suffered severely from shortage of supplies, and failed to make any impression on the town.[11] On the other hand, it seems that the fighting in the region now ceased, probably because Roman forces became much reduced.

Lucullus took his army south to assist in the Lusitanian war. Mummius' successor as praetor, M. Atilius Serranus, had indulged in some fighting, and then made a treaty with those he had fought.[12] He was succeeded by Ser. Sulpicius Galba, praetor for 151, who found on his arrival that the war had restarted, either because the Lusitanians had broken the treaty or because a different group had joined in. It suited Galba, another hunter of triumphs, to believe the former.

He fought unsuccessfully at first, having to retire to Carmona, well south of the Guadalquivir River, though he was able to move forward later to winter in the lands of the Conii in the southwestern corner of the peninsula. In his second year, 150, he was joined by Lucullus, fresh from his Vaccaean campaign, who wintered in Turditania, north of the river. They conducted separate but apparently co-ordinated campaigns into Lusitania, where Lucullus captured a set of prisoners. Galba received envoys asking to renew the treaty earlier agreed with Atilius. Feigning to agree he promised them land, disarmed them, then massacred some and captured and sold others.[13] Whether because his conduct was even nastier than Lucullus', or because Lucullus was more careful, or from some other reason, such as personal unpopularity, Galba's massacre became the point of departure for another Roman attempt to compel provincial governors to conduct themselves properly.

The wars in Spain had had an increasingly destabilizing effect on the conduct of affairs at Rome. Right from the start they had compelled change in the city's constitution. The erection of two new provincial commands, Hispania Citerior and Ulterior, in 197 had required an increase to six in the number of annual praetors, and then, from 192, these praetors were regularly prorogued to serve a second year.[14] There was an experiment in about 180 to reduce the annual praetors to four every second year as a result of this prorogation policy, which was thereby intended to be permanent, but it was soon abandoned; quite possibly the senators liked the larger number of praetors, since it gave them more chances of advancement.

The outbreak of the Lusitanian war provoked more fiddling with the constitution. The despatch of Q. Fulvius Nobilior as consul to Spain in 153 was not quite an innovation, but it was a matter which bothered the Senate – having one of the two consuls so far from Rome for his full term of office was, at the least, awkward. But matters soon became much worse. Next year, Nobilior having failed, the choice of Marcellus to succeed him was in violation of a law, dating from 180, that required a ten-year gap between iterated consulships, for Marcellus had been consul only three years before, in 155. It is not clear how this legal requirement was evaded, but straining the constitution in this way set a precedent – which, in another way, was followed within six years.[15]

Marcellus' peace treaty with the Belli, the Titthi, and the Arevaci was the next occasion for manipulation. After the rejection of the first treaty by the Senate, Marcellus went ahead and imposed the same terms by a subterfuge, accepting the *deditio*, but then releasing the prisoners, reinstating towns, and so on. This time the Senate accepted his treaty, where it should clearly have repudiated him for his defiance.

These cases indicate that the Roman constitution was coming under serious pressure because of the wars in Spain. It was no longer a matter of flexibility and innovation. After Marcellus' third consulship (in 152) a new law was passed barring second (never mind third) consulships altogether; this purported to solve the unlawful election problem, but it was itself broken within fifteen years.[16] It is evident that the old constitution had become too rigid, and innovation of any practical sort was to be rejected. Evasion and fracture were to be the only way forward.

On the other hand, the prorogation of the praetorian commands proved to be a very useful device, so much so that it was used also for the extension of consular commands when consuls were sent to Spain – thus Lucullus' command was extended for a year, which he spent helping Galba, the praetor in Ulterior, against the Lusitani. In 148 the command in Macedon was a new praetorian post which was prorogued so that Q. Caecilius Metellus, the conqueror of Andriskos, was in Macedon until 146. It soon proved to be possible to prorogue provincial commands for more than a year – in Spain D. Iunius Brutus governed the Ulterior province for six years (138–133) as proconsul.

The purpose of prorogation, of course, was essentially to keep a man in post for long enough for him to become efficient. It had been widely used in Hannibal's war to keep the few effective commanders in post; now it was being used because of the distance consuls had to travel to reach their commands. Consuls especially had a myriad of duties to perform in Italy before they could set out for a province, and usually – at least in Spain – they could only get there about the end of the campaigning season. Prorogation gave them time both to investigate the situation when they arrived, and then set to work in their second year.

At the same time a two-year term of office, which most praetors in Spain could now expect, gave them extra time to gather the wealth they felt was their due. The province was expected to pay the governor's expenses, a requirement which was eminently, even infinitely, flexible. One of the incentives for warfare was to gather loot, part of which would then be distributed to the soldiers (those who survived), with the larger part going to the governor himself. Galba was said to have been especially greedy, keeping a much larger share for himself than was customary. The capture of prisoners could be turned into cash by selling them as slaves – both Galba and Lucullus did this to their Lusitanian prisoners, to their profit.[17]

This was all normal procedure, though it did make it all too easy for the governors to go to war, though this was not the real trouble. Warfare was one of the activities expected of provincial governors, and the victims were, by definition, enemies of Rome, on whom no pity was to be lavished. The difficulty for Rome was that the governors found it even easier to compel the provincials, Rome's subjects and allies, to pay up. In 171 a group of Spanish peoples had complained about praetorian extortion. The timing is instructive, for during the past several years Spain had been peaceful, and the praetors had only had command of one legion, which was not a large enough force to be able to start a war. The complaints were directed against three of the praetors who had held office since Gracchus' peace settlement in 179 – M. Titinius Curvus, praetor in 178, P. Furius Philus (174) and M. Matienus (173). These men had clearly felt it necessary to fleece their provincial subjects, being unable to loot their enemies.

The three men faced trials of a sort at Rome, but only by a temporary procedure devised for occasional problems by the Senate. Titinius was acquitted, though he was never elected to any office again; the other two were allowed to go into exile in nearby Latin cities. The real result came in a decree of the Senate which laid down rules for the requisitions the governors could make, and prohibitions to be observed – the governor was not to insist on his own valuation of the crops supplied, or impose officers on Spanish tribes and towns to forcibly extort money. It is particularly the Roman allies in Spain who complained; quite possibly abuses continued amongst others, and the decree was scarcely much protection for anyone.[18]

It has been supposed that the violent conduct of Lucullus and Galba was the trigger for the next step towards increased regulation. Galba was certainly the subject of an accusation of having unlawfully enslaved and sold Lusitanian prisoners. It became notorious that he escaped by invoking pity among his hearers – a political assembly, not a court – by displaying his young children, but the essential fact is that he was neither found guilty nor punished. His election to the consulship, which he might have expected by 147, did not take place until 144, which might be because of distaste at his Lusitanian methods. More likely his career advancement stalled because of the intervention of the Carthaginian War and the irregular election of Scipio Aemilianus as consul.

Nevertheless it is a fact that his accusation and the adoption of a new law against extortion coincided in time, and it is difficult to avoid making the connection between them. Perhaps the failure of the prosecution and the tale of his and Lucullus' misbehaviour were sufficiently unpleasant to bring about the determination among the senators to apply a more permanent system to the regulation of provincial administration, though the measure, the *lex Calpurnia de repetundis*, was hardly onerous. The misdeeds of Lucullus and Galba would not have been affected by it, for it applied, as with the earlier problem of extortion, to Roman subjects and allies, not to Rome's enemies. Its significance is that it set up a permanent procedure by which a governor, after retiring from his post, could be tried for extortion on the accusation of the provincials. He would be judged by a jury of senators, and could be compelled to restore those of his acquisitions which were judged to be ill-gotten.[19]

It is the permanence of the procedures which is the main point, for it began the process by which Roman law became less oppressive and more open to exploitation by provincial groups.[20] In fact it was little used for a generation, and only began to operate to control governors later. With reference to Galba, therefore, it seems that his attempted prosecution was less a Roman concern for the fate of his victims, and more a matter of internal Roman politics.

Spain was a constant problem for Rome from the time the Hannibalic War began with a dispute over Saguntum. By contrast the issue of Macedon seemed to arise out of nowhere in 149, and it was to be followed by a crisis over Greece which also seemed to arrive suddenly.[21] Of course, this is only from the perspective of Rome; neither Macedonians nor the Greeks would have agreed with such unexpectedness. The problems of Macedon have been discussed already, in the previous chapter. Those of Greece centred particularly on the main state which now existed there, the Achaian League. The crisis which developed there will be looked at in detail in Chapter 9, but it is worth commenting here on the overall Roman problem.

It was never easy for the Senate to persuade the Achaians to accept Roman authority. The league regarded itself as an independent state and as a voluntary ally of Rome. In this it was formally correct, but in practical political, strategic, and military terms this was a deliberate ignoring of reality. This was proved in 146, but until then the league could make that assumption and yet use Rome to pursue its own problems, because it relied on an Achaian politician, Kallikrates, to intercede, as the league's envoy, with the Senate. It also helped that Rome had removed a thousand prominent men from Achaia in 167, and these men included the most vocal anti-Roman and pro-independence politicians.[22] As a means of silencing, or at least a muffling of opponents, this was successful – except that regular embassies turned up in Rome asking for their return. However, to Rome this did not seem a major issue. What made it so was the final agreement by the Senate to let the exiles go home, and, shortly after, the death of Kallikrates. In combination these events fired up Achaian resentment at Roman policies. Until then, Achaia was generally supportive of Rome, if only because Rome was often willing to help. In 148, for example Achaian troops held the line in Thessaly against Andriskos.

In Asia Minor this role was taken by the Attalid kingdom. The disputes between the Asian kingdoms were generally filtered to Rome through the Attalid king, who was also always willing to send forces to assist in any war Rome fought within the region. And yet, just as opponents of Achaia could turn up in Rome with complaints, so enemies of Eumenes II (until 160) or his successor Attalos II could also arrive. Most of these disputes were militarily minor and could be settled by the dispatch of a group of senators to mediate. But in 154 a particularly serious quarrel developed between Attalos II and King Prusias II of Bithynia. Its solution shed particularly revealing light on the Roman methods, in all their unpleasantness.

Attalos and Prusias II, King of Bithynia, were old enemies. Prusias, in the latest of several wars, attacked Pergamon in 154, campaigning as far as Pergamon itself, though he could not take the city. Only slowly and reluctantly had he accepted orders from the Senate by way of several squads of envoys to desist and make peace. Eventually he complied, but with a very ill grace. It was obvious he would try again.[23]

Prusias left himself open to reprisal. He sent his son Nikomedes to live in Rome, since they did not get on, and Nikomedes had considerable popular support, whereas Prusias was disliked fairly comprehensively. At Rome Nikomedes became the centre of a plot, involving Prusias' ambassador, Attalos' ambassador, a contingent of Prusias' soldiers whose original task had been to kill Nikomedes, and a group of Roman senators. Prusias was driven to take refuge in the city of Nikaia, where he appealed to Rome. A weak embassy, sarcastically derided by Cato, came out to organize a ceasefire. Prusias trusted that this meant he had Roman protection, but he was wrong, and he was murdered in the temple of Zeus in Nikomedia by his son's soldiers. Nikomedes thus became king courtesy of a Roman plot conducted by a group of junior senators with a set of traitorous subjects of the king.[24] (It took place in the same period as Herakleides' plot to seize the Seleukid kingship, and Andriskos' plot to reunite Macedon. Rome could not claim the moral high ground.)

Then there was the issue of what to do about Carthage. This was a chronic problem for Rome. The peace treaty finally agreed in 201 did not remove the city from Roman concerns, but the approach of 151 made the problem increasingly urgent. In that year the obligation of Carthage to pay annual instalments of its indemnity would cease, and to Carthage (and to most states of the time) this would end its political obligation to accede to Roman wishes. In other words, from 151 Carthage would cease to be a dependent of Rome, and recover its power of independent action.

The Romans did not accept this interpretation, claiming that, once a state submitted to Rome, it remained in that condition thereafter. In fact this was a version which tended to be deployed whenever it seemed advantageous, and neglected at other times. It was not used, for example, in regard to the Seleukid Empire, which had paid off an indemnity in 173, several years late. Rome had not complained of the lateness presumably so as to be able to go on claiming dependence. The spectacular way the indemnity was cleared off implied that the Seleukid King Antiochos IV was actually reclaiming his independence and demonstrating it very publicly.[25] So the approach of 151 was seen by Carthage as a liberation, but by Rome as a time for decision. If Carthage acted as an independent state, Rome would complain that it was repudiating its obligation, and this was a cause for which Rome would fight. A new Romano-Carthaginian war was clearly in prospect.

The issue which the Carthaginians would probably tackle first, if they had the chance, was that of their relations with King Massinissa of Numidia. He had been given the right in 201 to 'reclaim' territory taken from his kingdom in the past by Carthage. He had used this quite shamelessly to nibble away at Carthaginian territory for the past fifty years. Forbidden to fight back by Rome, Carthage therefore looked to its ally (Rome) for assistance in the recurring dispute, but Rome had repeatedly favoured Massinissa. Even before the expiry of the indemnity, or perhaps in anticipation of it and so of possibly losing Roman support, Massinissa had made a grab for still more territory. He was resisted, and Carthage once more appealed to Rome.[26]

A deputation arrived to mediate, or at least to investigate, led by M. Porcius Cato. Predictably it came down in favour of Massinissa. It also investigated conditions in Carthage, and when he returned to Rome Cato was loud in his emphases on the wealth he had seen, the large and vigorous population, and the apparent preparations for war in the city. The report of a large stockpile of ship timber suggested the possibility of a revival of Carthaginian sea power.[27]

Not all of this was mere scaremongering and invention. There was a growing party in Carthage which was conscious of the threat of Massinissa, whose power had now come much closer than ever to the city itself. Massinissa himself was in his eighties and could not live much longer; when he died it was likely that the Numidian kingdom would collapse – he had a dozen sons, each of whom had been given an estate, and each of whom could be expected to wish to be his sole successor. To Carthage this would spell an opportunity to recover what had been lost from the quarrelling heirs and possibly more; to Massinissa this meant that he had only a very short time in which to complete his conquest; to Rome the likely collapse of Numidia might mean a sudden growth of Carthage, so that it went from being a beleaguered if wealthy subordinate city to a much larger and threatening power. So Massinissa's anticipated death was one of the factors everyone had to bear in mind.

During 151 and 150, therefore, opinion in the Roman Senate swung behind Cato's advocacy that the best way out of the dilemma was to see that Carthage itself was destroyed. This would simultaneously remove the potential that the city posed as an enemy, and eliminate the other possibility in everyone's minds, that the ultimate victory of Massinissa would see Carthage and the king at enmity replaced by a combined Carthaginian-Numidian union which would be an even greater threat. The victory or the death of Massinissa would compel Rome to intervene; Cato's suggestion that the city be destroyed was a brutal, but hardly un-Roman, way to solve the problem. It was also a highly self-centred Roman view on the matter.

The Carthaginians, who no doubt made all these calculations as well, could not wait. Once the indemnity obligation ended the anti-Numidian party gained power in the city and mobilized an army, said to be 25,000 strong (which only confirmed the rearmament which had been detected by Cato's mission) and campaigned to recover its lost lands. The Carthaginians won some preliminary fights, but then the campaign moved into difficult territory. As it happened Scipio Aemilianus was in Africa, sent there by the consul Lucullus in Spain to acquire war-elephants. He was asked by the Carthaginians (who had surrendered fifty years earlier to his grandfather) to intervene and to compose the differences which had led to the war. This was, of course, a sensible political move by the Carthaginians which was intended to suggest their reasonableness; it failed, the Carthaginian army was defeated and many of the men were massacred by a force led by Gulussa, one of Massinissa's sons, with or without his father's connivance. Massinissa kept his gains.[28] Scipio had once again displayed his uncanny ability to be on the spot when decisive political events were happening.

Scipio had, however, made no serious attempt to mediate. He may well have shared Cato's anti-Carthage policy, though his cousin Scipio Nasica Corculum had long argued that Carthage's continued apparent threat was a necessary element in keeping Romans alert and vigorous. In a way, this Carthaginian military expedition proved his point, but at the same time it helped push Rome into war. In Rome's view the expedition was an insult, since Rome had not been consulted. This was, it was realized, hardly an argument that would convince anyone else, but the attack on Massinissa, a true-blue Roman ally, was sufficient. On the whole it seems likely that Rome would have attacked Carthage anyway, but the Carthaginian expedition provided a convenient pretext.

Roman warlike preparations went on through 150. The Carthaginians realized this and sent envoys to offer apologies and ask for terms. The replies were evasive and confusing, deliberately so.[29] When another embassy arrived, this time from the city of Utica, a member of the Carthaginian confederacy, offering *deditio* in the full knowledge that this would give Rome the necessary landing place for its army of invasion, the way was clear for the declaration of war, and this came early in 149.[30]

The news from Macedon of Andriskos' success was therefore all the more shocking and alarming, though the ending of the Celtiberian War a year earlier had at least temporarily reduced the number of Rome's enemies. Galba's and Lucullus' violent and unprincipled wars against the Lusitani in 150 had done the same. One cannot help wondering if this was a deliberate atrocity designed to free Roman forces and attention for the greater war. Altogether it was clear to those who watched that the Roman diplomatic and military behaviour was deeply unpleasant. Even as the dominant military and political power in the Mediterranean Rome found it necessary to resort to deceit and evasiveness in achieving its ends. Its imperial system was without principle, bore little regard for its subjects, either Italian allies or provincials, and was bending and creaking in Rome itself under the strain. The collection of wars which engulfed the republic's empire in the 140s had steadily widened from 154 onwards; it was quite possible that the whole gimcrack structure would collapse. At the very least substantial changes in its constitution and its imperial system would be needed.

Chapter 5

Baktrian Problems

Alexander the Great, Seleukos I, and Antiochos III all invaded India and in the end all of them turned away from it, not without regret, but with due caution and an appreciation of the difficulties it presented to any invader. The kings of Baktria in Central Asia did not turn away, but then they had much better information on the country and they could seize a momentary chance of conquest, and so from about 180 there was a kingdom in northern India ruled by Greek kings.

Baktria had been the northeastern province of the Persian Empire, but then of the empire of Seleukos. It had resisted the Persians, Alexander, and Seleukos, and so now it was a region which was always ripe for rebellion and independence. This was achieved, without too much fuss, soon after 250, when the Seleukid governor Diodotos usurped Seleukid authority. His son, also a Diodotos, then made himself king. The problem with such a procedure is that it can be replicated by someone else with an equal ambition. Diodotos II, the first king, was thus removed by the same process by which his father had achieved power, by being overthrown by his rival Euthydemos.[1] The Seleukid King Antiochos III fought him in 208–206; his son Demetrios I was probably the invader of India.

The Baktrian kingdom was able to hoist itself into independence early and easily because it was cut off from its parent Seleukid Empire by the conquests of the Parthians to its west. Diodotos II therefore ruled a kingdom bounded on the west by the independent Parthian kingdom, on the east by the Pamir Mountains and on the south by the Mauryan Empire's provinces of Paropamisadai, Areia, and Arachosia. These limits were more or less clear, but the northern boundary is much less so. Alexander and Seleukos I had been able to campaign north across the Iaxartes River, and so presumably they had controlled Sogdiana (and Seleukos' wife came from there), which was essentially the valley of the Zerafshan River and the land to the north as far as the Iaxartes, though it is also sometimes claimed to include the upper valley of the Oxus.

The history of this region is highly complex, obscure, beset by contrasting and contradictory interpretations, with very few firm chronological stepping stones to provide a firm crossing. The main basis is a variety of documented Greek, Latin, Indian, Chinese, and numismatic sources, not to mention archaeological. It has, accordingly, even greater fascination than most regions. But the absolute basis of understanding must be to comprehend something of the geography. (Recent wars since 1979, combined with the ravages of the illegal diggers and treasure hunters, have prevented much work, and ruined many sites.[2])

Out of the complex of highlands called by geographers the Pamir Knot, mountain ranges spread in all directions. Those on the west and south are like the four fingers of a spread hand. To the south run the successive ranges which form the western border of modern Pakistan, the old Northwest Frontier of the British Indian Empire, pierced above all, but not only, by the Khyber Pass. The great Hindu Kush is the next range towards the north, spreading and descending south-westwards to beyond Kandahar. The third range is the Alai or Hissar, reaching as far west as about Samarkand. North again is the Alexandrovski Range, somewhat shorter than the rest, but reaching about to Tashkent. (The fifth of these ranges, a stronger, longer, massive thumb, is the Himalaya, going eastwards for thousands of kilometres.)

These are great mountain ranges, among the highest and most rugged on the planet. They are separated by areas of lower land in which comparably great rivers run, and which are cultivated by irrigation agriculture. From the north, the Iaxartes (now Syr Darya) flows westwards between the Alexanderovski and the Hissar ranges; the eastern part of this region is perhaps best called Ferghana, and is now divided between Tadzhikistan and a prong of Uzbekistan; from the eastern end of this valley a route leads by the Tungburan Pass, the least difficult, though they are all difficult, towards Sinkiang and China.

The Hissar range on the north encloses the valley of the Zerafshan River. This is the least of these rivers, but on its banks are two of the great cities of the whole region, Samarkand (also Afrasiab and Marakanda), whose origin predates Alexander and even the Akhaimenids, and the much later Bokhara. The river eventually loses itself in the Kyzyl Kum desert, much of its water having been diverted into irrigation channels. South of the Hissar range and north of the Hindu Kush is the valley occupied by the Oxus River (Amu Darya), which is fed by streams especially from the Hissar range to the north. The river was always a major obstacle to travellers, and even now forms the northern boundary of Afghanistan. Between the Hindu Kush Mountains forming the present Pakistani border is the heart of modern Afghanistan, including the cities of Kabul and Kandahar, a region drier and higher than the others, but wider.

These valleys formed the political components of which Baktrian history was composed: the Iaxartes area, plus the Zerafshan Valley, was Sogdiana; the Oxus Valley was Baktria; the Kabul region was the Paropamisadai, being the route along the southern edge of the Hindu Kush leading to the Khyber Pass and India; the Kandahar-Ghazni region was Arachosia. And the Paropamisadai and the Khyber was the route to the great plain of the Indus rivers, another five-fingered area, this time five rivers, flowing south to join together into the great Indus which flows all the way into the Indian Ocean.

The mountain ranges are penetrated by passes, but not by many, and all are either high or difficult, or both. The Khyber is lower but is also narrow, can be easily blocked, and can flood. The passes through the Hindu Kush are up to 13,000 feet high. Through the Hissar there is just one major pass, up to 8,000 feet high. To the east the pass towards Sinkiang is at 12,000 feet above sea level. There is an even more difficult route out of Sinkiang and into the Wakhan (Afghanistan's narrow eastward prong), high, narrow, and difficult. Finally, there is the possibility of evading all this difficult climbing, for those coming from the east and north. A route leads north out of the Sinkiang by way of the Issyk Kol (a lake) or the valley of the Ili River into the steppe lands north of the Alexandrovski range. This is more open country; by following the foothills west most of the mountain ranges can be outflanked – but beyond the hills is the desert. Nothing is ever easy, but if climbing has to be avoided, this will do.[3]

This geography made the region extremely difficult to control; its default political organization was division. The only successful way so far had been from outside, by dominating by sheer military power, and by installing governors – satraps to the ancient Persians and the Macedonians – in the several regions, all with substantial military strength. Seleukos I and Antiochos I had satrapies in Sogdiana, Baktria, Arachosia and in the Paropamisadai. From within the region, however, localism, and the vertical geography, indicated that a ruler in one part would find it very difficult to control any or all of the rest. When he made himself an independent king Diodotos I controlled only Baktria and probably Sogdiana; Arachosia, the Paropamisadai, and even Areia to the west had become part of the Mauryan Empire for half a century. Maybe the near presence of this great power persuaded the Baktrians and the Sogdians to stay together, but as the Mauryan state crumbled and its provinces became independent kingdoms – the king of the Paropamisadai was the Indian Sophagasenos – so the links between the Central Asian valleys weakened. There is numismatic evidence for an independent Sogdian kingdom from about 200 BC onwards.

This date is during the reign of Euthydemos, Antiochos III's enemy, who by the usual calculations continued to rule in Baktria until about 190. The only visible indication of Sogdian independence is the issuance of coins, which was still at first in Euthydemos' name and struck by the moneyers who had worked for him, but on the 'Persic' weight standard of the old Akhaimenid Empire rather than the 'Attic' standard used by the Seleukids and the Baktrian kings. But soon the moneyers' monogram disappeared from the Sogdian coins and re-appeared on Baktrian. The artistic standard of the inscribed images then deteriorated, as did the inscription in Greek, but an inscription in Aramaic appears on the reverse. From about 180 the inscriptions say 'King of Sogdia', or 'King of Kings', and then two later kings are named, Kagaha and Hasa. Coins in this series become steadily debased in style but they continued to be issued until perhaps 130 BC.[4]

Antiochos III attempted to recover control of the region in a great eastern expedition, which culminated in a two-year siege of the city of Baktra in 208–206. In the end, to break the siege, Euthydemos threatened to call in an invasion by nomad forces.[5] Antiochos made peace. The nomads Euthydemos was in contact with must have lived in Sogdiana to the north, or perhaps the west, where the Kyzyl Kum and Kara Kum deserts were the homes of such people. In that region a nomad kingdom, capable of producing coinage, had existed from at least Alexander's time, and perhaps earlier – we only know of it by the coins produced, which began about 330 BC or so.[6] The name on the coins identifies the people as the Dahai, a people whose young men were recruited by Antiochos III and others as mercenaries (whence came, no doubt, the silver which was made into the local coins).[7] The centre of the kingdom, if it had one, was east of the Caspian Sea and north of the Parthian kingdom; the people could easily come into contact with Baktria and Sogdiana. One result of the long siege was clearly the independence and sovereignty of Sogdiana, which had slipped out of Euthydemos' grip during his fight for survival.

Baktria was described in one ancient source as 'the land of a thousand cities', which has focused attention on these cities.[8] The results have been both startling and disappointing. The number of cities is nowhere near a thousand, not surprisingly; indeed it is difficult to find ten which existed in the Greek period.[9] At the same time the one city which has been examined in some detail, Ai Khanum, in the upper Valley of the Oxus, is large, was clearly rich, clearly was Greek, and suffered a disastrous sack, since when it has been largely abandoned. Such a site was manna for archaeologists, and the place has been well examined, helped by the thin depth of the deposits. Such work ended with the Russian invasion in 1979, but the beneficial result of the interruption has been that plentiful reports have been produced, though the site has been comprehensively destroyed since.[10]

Ai Khanum's ancient name is not known (the present name is Uzbek). Suggestions which have been made include Alexandria, Seleukeia, Antiochia, Diodotia, Dionysiopolis, and Eukratideia, which collection only emphasizes our ignorance. It appears to have been founded in the time of the first Seleukids, perhaps in or soon after 300 BC. It was developed into a major but local political centre, with substantial fortifications, temples, and a large administrative building, which is referred to as a palace. In the normal style of a Seleukid city it was surrounded by a wall, but the interior was dominated by a fortified acropolis set off to one side, so the garrison had independent access to the surrounding land. Indeed the acropolis also contained an inner citadel, which was separated from the rest by a ditch, with two other ditches crossing the acropolis below it.

It also has been considered to be a 'capital' city, or perhaps a 'royal' city, but it was sited rather too much out of the way for such a function when it was founded. Its geographic location, however, at the junction of the Kokcha River and the Oxus, is significant. Higher up the valley of the Kokcha the world's only lapis lazuli source is located, and there were other minerals in the region; the city was thus in all likelihood founded to supervise access to the region; it also blocked a possible invasion route from the east; the nearby land was cultivated and watered by irrigation canals.[11]

It is therefore best to see the city as a locally important garrison-and-administrative centre placed to control traffic along the Oxus and to supervise the mining region; that is, it was a provincial capital, though the later enlargement of the palace suggests that it became a royal seat eventually, perhaps that of a local king – Baktria had plenty of minor rulers later. Assuming that the acropolis was mainly military, and taking into account the large areas occupied by public buildings – the palace, the gymnasium, the theatre, temples – the population living in the city cannot have been large. The theatre is said to be capable of seating 6,000 people, but the city can scarcely have held a quarter of that number. The more one looks at it, the more it looks like a bureaucratic creation.

There were other urban centres of the same sort. Baktra was the main city of the kingdom, well enough fortified to defy Antiochos III for two years (and Demetrios II – of Baktria – for several months). Qunduz is reported to have had major fortifications, including a citadel the size of that at Ai Khanum. The crossing of the Oxus at Termez was fortified with a rather smaller citadel – and so on. There were never a 'thousand' cities, of course, but the land was certainly populated with them, and a substantial part of the people was urbanized.

This was in contrast to Sogdiana. The major urban centre there was Samarkand (Marakanda in Alexander's time), which, like many of the cities of Central Asia, had its origins in or before the Akhaimenid period. But this was a region close to the nomads in the steppes along and north of the Iaxartes. It had been fortified in the time of Darius III, Alexander's immediate (and brief) predecessor, presumably to defy nomad hostility – which broke out powerfully when Alexander attempted to found his own new city at Alexandria-the-Farthest. During the campaign which followed Alexander systematically destroyed the population and buildings and agriculture of the Zerafshan Valley, and it was occupied by nomads during the third century. Alexander's efforts to deter nomad hostility were thus ultimately in vain, and of course it was the kings of the Sogdians who minted their coins in succession to and in imitation of those of Euthydemos.

Euthydemos had therefore 'recovered' control of Sogdiana for a time, but must have lost control again when he came under pressure from Antiochos. He built a wall which controlled the passage through the Sogdian Iron Gate at Derbent, which was a fairly clear sign that he had abandoned the lands to the north. (The name comes from later when the Kushan kings (who ruled the region after the Greeks) installed a gate literally of iron to control the passage – it was their northern frontier too.[12]) When the Mauryan Empire, controlling the lands south of Baktria, disintegrated, it was more profitable – easier – for Euthydemos' son Demetrios I to seize control of the land south of the Hindu Kush rather than to attempt a long and difficult fight for Sogdiana.

Demetrios marked his conquest by issuing coins showing himself crowned with an elephant scalp, complete with tusks and trunk. His conquests were nevertheless limited, and no part of India proper seems to have become his – that is, he did not take over the Paropamisadai, which presumably remained under the control of whoever had succeeded Sophagasenos, the king encountered by Antiochos III in 206. But it seems that his preoccupation with the south provoked a usurper, Antimachos, to seize power and proclaim himself king back in Baktria.

Antimachos' coins suggest an affinity with the Diodotids, the predecessors of Euthydemos and Demetrios, so his usurpation may have been in part aimed at reversing Euthydemos' seizure of power.[13] (However, caution is required in interpreting coins in this way.) His coins are found almost exclusively in Baktria proper, but he also produced coins of Indian type, which implies either that he had moved south himself, into Indian provinces, perhaps in emulation of his rival, or less likely, that he was promoting trade in that direction. He also used the epithet '*theos*' (god), which implies a fairly high opinion of himself. Alternatively he was following the lead of Agathokles, who was probably of the Euthydemid family, and Demetrios II's rival.

There were now two rival families, both apparently ruling parts of the Baktrian kingdom. Antimachos' son Demetrios II became renowned as 'King of the Indians', and seems to have taken up his father's Indian interests (or ambitions) by conquering the Paropamisadai and the Kabul River Valley as far as the Indian city of Taxila. He is also supposed to have conducted a great raid south along the Indus as far as the Delta and even into Gujerat.[14] Of course once he was through the mountain barrier such a careering raid was quite possible, and the Mauryan state no longer existed to stop him. But this is exactly the sort of adventure which had provoked Antimachos to detach himself from Demetrios I's kingdom. Sure enough another Baktrian usurpation occurred, though this one was not necessarily the result of the Indian campaign, at least not directly.

The new man was Eukratides. All of these usurpers are supposed by modern commentators to have been satraps or provincial governors of some sort, but we have exactly no information about any of them before their usurpations, and little enough about their rule as kings. For Eukratides, however, we are told that he fought many wars. He did seize control of Baktra, where he was besieged for five months by Demetrios II.[15] This civil war spread into India, or perhaps, more likely, having eliminated Demetrios, Eukratides had to campaign to establish his control over all Demetrios' former territories.

For once we have an apparently convincing chronological link, for the later historian Justin states that Eukratides and King Mithradates I of Parthia came to power at the same time. And yet this link proves as slippery as all other chronological indications of this place and time. Mithradates' accession has long been dated to c.171, but is now thought to be c.165.[16] This in turn means stretching the reign of Demetrios II to at least 165 and maybe 160 – since he and Eukratides obviously overlapped, being active enemies. At the same time it pushes Eukratides' whole reign somewhat later. He was certainly in power in 162/160, for the Seleukid usurper Timarchos, active in those years, copied his coins.

One of the reasons for Eukratides' many wars was no doubt the continued existence, with power, of rival Baktrian and Indian royal families. It took some time to eliminate Demetrios II, and there are indications that descendents of his survived – there is another king named Antimachos sometime later, who presumably descended from the first of that name. Eukratides we know had to campaign into India, but he perhaps did not succeed in establishing full control there.[17] For a new king emerged in the Indian territories, Menander,

who was married to Agathokleia, the daughter of Agathokles, of the
Euthydemid dynasty. There were thus four separate royal families competing
for the throne of the Baktrian kingdom by about 150, though Menander
may perhaps be reckoned as founding an Euthydemid branch. Menander
is reckoned to have become king about 155, and probably overlapped with
Eukratides, just as Eukratides earlier overlapped for a time with Demetrios II.
Menander may well have emerged as a successor-cum-avenger of Demetrios.
Perhaps, since he married a Euthydemid princess, he was originally another
of those supposed satraps.

It will be clear from all this that little is certain about the Greek history
of Baktria, and the wide scope for the interpretation of the exiguous sources
has been taken full advantage of by those who work on the subject. The final
emphasis, however, must be on the deplorable willingness of the Greeks to
indulge in dynastic warfare. These several, successive, and/or contemporary
kings were clearly able to gather support from their subjects; had those
subjects wished to remain at peace, they could probably have smothered the
fighting. As it happens, we know relatively little of the events in the wars, and
much of what is stated, here and elsewhere, is padded out with a good deal of
conjecture.

North of the Hissar/Alai range an unrelated series of conflicts was about
to impact disastrously on Greek Baktria. In 162 BC the Yuezhi ('Yueh-chih'
in older accounts), a nomad confederacy in Sinkiang was defeated in war
and moved westwards to evade their enemies. They settled in the Ili Valley
where they displaced the local inhabitants, a Saka nomad people, some of
whom escaped south through western Sinkiang and ended by establishing a
kingdom in Kashmir, while others moved southwest and reached the Sogdian
kingdom. Their arrival stimulated much disturbance and this spilled over into
attacks on the Baktrians, and a little later, on the Parthian kingdom as well.[18]

The Baktrian kings had faced this issue before. Euthydemos, back in 208–
206, claimed to be able to use nomad groups as he wished. He seems to have
had some authority north of the Hissar, though he had lost it by about 200 BC,
when the local coins began to be produced, marking the area's independence.
The inhabitants of Sogdiana even then were Sakas. So the arrival of more
Sakas no doubt re-awoke thoughts of southward invasions. The internal
conflicts within the Baktrian kingdom can only have encouraged them, and
it may well have been a particularly atrocious deed, the death of Eukratides,
which tipped the balance.

Eukratides is described as returning from India. On the way he was
murdered by his son, who then celebrated his patricide by driving his chariot
over the dead king's body and refusing it burial.[19]

Clearly the son hated the father. Eukratides' violence and usurpation, his constant warfare, will no doubt have created similar feelings in others, Baktrians and Indians, Sogdians and Sakans. But he had also been a vigorous and largely successful commander. In resisting Demetrios II's siege of Baktra he is said to have used a force of just 300 soldiers. If this was his own chosen bodyguard, he may well not have had a very large force at his command at the beginning of his rule. But he reigned for at least a couple of decades and had campaigned in all directions. There are signs that he succeeded in re-establishing suzerainty over the Sogdian kingdom to the north for a time, perhaps until the refugee Sakas arrived, and that as a result the fortifications of the Iron Gate were neglected (though they were not demolished). So the death of such a king is quite likely to have been greeted with relief, even joy, by substantial numbers of his subjects as well as his son, and by his external enemies.

We do not know the name of the murdering son, though two kings, Plato and Heliokles, have been suggested as Eukratides' children. (Eukratides' father was another Heliokles, and it was a Greek custom to name sons after grandfathers.) Which one was the murderer is not known, but it is all but certain that the family's reputation, and so its power, abruptly waned.

This disputatious internal situation attracted the Sakas, already under uncomfortable Yuezhi pressure from the north. In the next few years the Sakas very successfully spilled over the Hissar range through the Iron Gate. By the early 130s they were in occupation of the land between the Hissar and the Oxus River, had raided over that river, and enforced their suzerainty over the remnant Greek kingdom south of the river.[20]

It is in this period that the city of Ai Khanum was captured and sacked. Once again chronological uncertainty besets the issue. The link of the sack with the death of Eukratides is not established, but it is claimed that the coins discovered in the excavations contain none produced later than that king's reign;[21] then again, it is also stated that they were a couple of later coins, of Heliokles and of Eukratides II, who were probably related (perhaps Eukratides II was the son or brother of Heliokles) and, of course, there is no clarity as to the date of Eukratides' death.[22] Yet the two coins of later members of his dynasty do not invalidate the apparent connection of the sack of the city with Eukratides' death suggested by coin finds. It is hardly claimed that the death of the king caused or was followed instantly by the sack of the city; there would certainly be a period of time, long or short, between the two events. The pattern of finds in the city has suggested that it was abandoned by its inhabitants before the sack, which therefore happened to a deserted city.[23] One suggestion is that Heliokles and Eukratides II reigned together, either in partnership or in enmity, in immediate succession to Eukratides I, and so there was probably time for someone to lose these kings' coins in the city before the Sakas overwhelmed it. So if only two such coins were found, the sack clearly did follow on Eukratides' death fairly quickly, say within at most a couple of years.

Eukratides' dates are, as pointed out, and as with the dates of every single Baktrian and Indo-Greek king, uncertain. The link stated by Justin with the beginning of the reign of Mithradates I in Parthia is only superficially precise,[24] and now that Mithradates' inauguration has been moved later, from 171 to 165, so Eukratides' *coup d'état* must be shifted as well.[25] Not only that but the length of his reign is variously put at between sixteen and thirty-six years, with many settling for a mid-point of twenty-five years. The issue is bedevilled further by the inscription on an *ostrakon* from the 'treasury' of Ai Khanum which bears the date 'Year 24'.

The era – the starting date – to which this date referred is not known, nor, if it was a king, which king. Various proposals have been made, of which an era of Eukratides is the one favoured by the excavator Paul Bernard.[26] He has a good case. The *ostrakon* clearly was left in the building when the city was destroyed, and had been inscribed not long before (since it was clearly one of the items held in the treasury when the palace burned); Eukratides, as a vicious usurper, would be as likely as anyone to instigate his own era – the Seleukids, the Parthians, the Kushans all did so. Yet even if it was an era beginning with Eukratides' usurpation it does not tell us either how long the king reigned (for eras were designed to continue after their inventor's deaths, so he could have been already dead when the ostrakon was inscribed), nor does it tell us when the city burned.

There is no doubt that the city was captured and destroyed. The 'palace' was burned, the rafters collapsing, and then the ruins were covered by bricks from a falling wall.[27] In the suburb outside the wall a villa was destroyed in the same way, the owners leaving a cache of coins in a pot in the rear (the '1973 Hoard'). Investigations elsewhere, however, have not confirmed that the whole city was destroyed in this way, and it has been theorized that it continued to function for a time but was then captured and definitively decommissioned by the next conquerors.

Where the attackers came from is not known. It was long assumed that they were the Yuezhi, but this group did not penetrate south of the Hissar for another decade or so, until about 132/130.[28] So the Sakas have been given the blame, and they certainly reached the north bank of the Oxus about the right time (145/135 approximately). Yet there are other possibilities. One is an approach from the east, along the Wakhan out of Sinkiang.

It is known that part of the Sakas reached Kashmir by way of the 5,000 metre-high pass called by the Chinese, evocatively, the Hanging Pass, roughly on the route of the present Karakoram Highway. This migration took time, perhaps three decades, with the Sakas repeatedly splitting into separate groups and reuniting along the way. Some stayed in the towns of the eastern Tarim Basin, which they occupied or captured on their passage; the group which reached Kashmir, perhaps about 130 BC, set up a kingdom which lasted almost two centuries.[29] On the way, however, there was another possible route for some of them to escape from their pursuers – over the Wakhjir Pass, which leads west from the route of the Karakoram Highway and into the Wakhan. Travelling along this route would bring the Sakas to the Kokcha Valley, the lapis lazuli mines, and Ai Khanun. Given that the Sakas in Sinkiang split into several, even many, groups during their journey, such an invasion seems quite possible.

Another possibility is an internal upheaval in the city and/or the surrounding country stimulated by the possibility of support from outside, from, that is, the invading Sakas, from wherever they arrived. The architecture of Ai Khanum has been increasingly recognized to contain much influence from Akhaimenid practice, in its houses, temples, even the palace, and in many of the details of architectural decoration. It was therefore a city built by and for the Iranians as much as the Greeks. Yet what we know of the ruling group of the kingdom shows that, apart from a few Iranian names, none of which were of people in the elite, the rulers were very largely Greeks.[30] It is not difficult to see a basic antagonism here, fuelled by the normal Hellenistic practice of laying a Greek colonial presence over an existing non-Greek population, who supported the colonists by providing rents and taxes. The destruction in the city seems to have been fairly selective, with the 'palace' suffering most; as the administrative and tax collecting centre it would be an early target in any uprising.

Then there is the apparent chronological connection between the killing of Eukratides and the end of the city. If it was suddenly abandoned, as is theorized, it could be that it was because it had been a favourite residence of the murdered king – work had been going on to renovate and enlarge the palace to the very end – and so we have to accept that it is possible that the destroyers were Baktrian Greeks. It must be admitted that this was more a Greek (or Roman) practice than one of the nomads. The nomads in Sogdiana did not destroy any other city, so far as can be seen.

Whoever was the enemy, the city was destroyed. A population, suggested to be 'indigenous', occupied the site for a time, which means that Greek and royal Baktrian authority had been removed. But even that residual local population was eliminated, or left of its own accord, after a relatively short time, perhaps one or two decades. It seems possible that without the Greek administration, and perhaps a royal subsidy, the city was not viable, and judging by the size of the palace and of the specifically Greek elements, such as the large gymnasium, the administration was top-heavy.

Ai Khanum is a spectacular site, and its excavation has been revelatory, yet one must not assume that it was necessarily, even in its heyday, politically important. It is not surprising that western classical archaeologists excavating the place saw it as necessarily an important city – some even regard it as the capital of the Baktrian kingdom – but it was in fact by no means as important a place as Baktra, or even as Qunduz, the next major urban centre to the west (which did not submit to the invaders). Ai Khanum was a frontier fortification, placed to administer a local region and to block an invasion route from the east. When it fell, the frontier post retreated to Qunduz, which held out successfully. The fall of Ai Khanum did not signal the end of Greek Baktria, though the destruction of the city is a clear sign of approaching domination by others.

For Greek Baktria was nonetheless on its last legs. In 128 the Chinese diplomat Zhang Qian (Chang-kien in the older books), having (not surprisingly) failed to persuade the Yuezhi to return to Sinkiang to fight their old enemies on behalf of the Han Empire, crossed the Oxus and visited the city of Baktra. He called the country Daxia (Ta-hsia), bounded by the Oxus on the north and the Hindu Kush on the south (and so without that part north of the river). It had, he guessed, a population of about a million, but his estimate of its military potential was very low. The men were unskilled in weaponry and were fearful of fighting, he said. They had cities and stone-built houses, but the land had no king, only chiefs in the several towns. By then it was subject to the suzerainty of the Yuezhi, who had conquered the land between the Hissar and the Oxus, further displacing more Sakas.[31] No doubt the Yuezhi had disarmed the Baktrians and appointed the city 'chiefs'. (This may explain the plethora of almost unknown kings in the last phase of Baktria's history.)

Conquest by the well-led and tough army of the Yuezhi was no doubt an unpleasant experience, but it is clear from the envoy's account that Baktra was a flourishing city, with a market where goods from many areas were on sale. But as a political organization it is clear that the kingdom of the Greeks in Baktria had foundered. Further, the Yuezhi, like their Sakan and Greek victims, eventually split into five semi-independent groups. (One of these controlled the Wakhan region.) As an international power Baktria was no longer of any real significance, and had not been since the death of Eukratides.

This inevitably had its effect on its neighbours to the east (in India) and to the west (in Parthia).

One of the reasons for its fall was the split between Baktria and nearby part of India, both with Greek kings but who were antagonistic. The siphoning away of Greek strength into India after about 190, together with the subsequent civil war, even if it produced a new region for Greek enterprise, spread Greek strength very thinly. And in India the most spectacular Greek achievement was the sack of another great city.

Chapter 6

The Sack of Pataliputra

T he Far East of Greco-Macedonian activity under Alexander and
Seleukos I was the Indus Valley. Alexander had campaigned through
the Khyber Pass and into the Punjab, where he had beaten King
Poros in battle, but had then been deflected from his proposed invasion of
the Ganges Valley by his army's mutiny. He marched that army south along
the Indus to the delta, brutally crushing any presumptuous Indian state
which stood in his way. From the delta he turned west, but he left a sort of
administration behind in the form of several kings, including Poros and the
Taxilan king, and two satraps with their attendant clerks and guards. How
many Greeks or Macedonians remained is not known. He is supposed to have
founded at least two cities in the region, but whether they survived for very
long seems doubtful.

The civil wars of the Macedonians which followed Alexander's death had
a disastrous effect on these Indian conquests. By 317 King Poros had been
murdered, and next year the last Macedonian satrap pulled out to join in
the fighting in Iran, and did not return. Eventually the victorious Seleukos
came east to recover these abandoned territories, but found that the Indian
emperor Chandragupta Maurya had beaten him to it. After an indecisive
conflict, Seleukos also withdrew. He and Chandragupta made a treaty by
which Seleukos confirmed Chandragupta's possession of Arachosia, Areia,
and the Paropamisadai; in return he received a corps of elephants, 400 or 500
in number, with which he later won the decisive battle of Ipsos in Asia Minor.[1]
In this, by defeating and killing Antigonos Monophthalamos he confirmed
the permanent division of Alexander's empire and his possession of a great
part of it. No doubt he considered his Indian treaty a good bargain.

Again it is by no means clear that any of the Greeks or Macedonians who
had stayed in India remained there after Seleukos' withdrawal, but by sheer
probability we may surely assume that some Greeks stayed on, whether
Alexander's cities continued or not. Some will have expected the return of
the Macedonian forces, some will have been too lethargic to contemplate with
any pleasure the long journey west, some will have liked living in India. They
were tough and capable men, usually literate, skilled in various ways, and

warriors; to Indian rulers they would have been valuable and employable. And in the western lands ceded to Chandragupta, Greeks were still living in his grandson's time, for Asoka made a point of inscribing his edicts at Kandahar in Greek (and in Aramaic, for the Persians). The names of a fair number of Greek in that region are known, but none in any detail.[2]

The Indian territories, including Arachosia, may have been relinquished by Seleukos, but those in Central Asia were not. The independent Greco-Baktrian kingdom emerged there soon after 250. This land was certainly well populated by Greeks, and ruled at first by Greek governors and then by Greek dynasties and a bureaucracy which included Greeks and local recruits.[3] It was to be expected that communications existed between Baktria and India, both by travellers and by diplomatic messages. One man who combined both of these roles is the ambassador Megasthenes, sent to Chandragupta by Seleukos. Other envoys turned up later: Daimachos visited Chandragupta's successor Bindusara, and Dionysios was sent by Ptolemy II, presumably in an attempt to outflank his rival Antiochos I. All three of these envoys were in India between 300 and 270 BC.[4] It is highly unlikely that they were the only Greeks to visit, but they are the only ones we know of. The visit of Daimachos may well have been made on behalf of Antiochos I in order to renew the treaty Seleukos had made with Chandragupta by making a new one with Bindusara.

When Antiochos III campaigned in the east in 209–205 he was successful in establishing his suzerainty over several kingdoms in that area: the Parthia of Arsakes II, the Baktria of Euthydemos, and the Paropamisadai of the Indian King Sophagasenos. It seems he also took control of Arachosia. These latter two provinces had been handed to Chandragupta by Seleukos I; now that the Mauryan Empire had lost control of them, Antiochos reclaimed them. Antiochos also came away with prizes as an indication of his supremacy over each king: land from the Parthian king, and squads of elephants handed over by both Euthydemos and Sophagasemos.

When Antiochos marched off again, in 206/205, he had therefore increased his own kingdom by these annexations, and he had left a balanced network of a group of states whose rulers were all linked to him by subordinate treaties.[5] This scheme, by the usual practices of diplomacy of the time, would last as long as the individual rulers lived. It was perhaps not the solution to his eastern frontier that Antiochos would have preferred – that would no doubt have been the re-annexation of all these states to his kingdom – but he had spent five years on this eastern expedition and had to attend to accumulating problems in the west as well.

The weakness of the balance of power he had created in the east was that the subordinate rulers were linked only to him, and not to each other. The system would therefore break down as soon as one of the rulers in the east died. The Parthian king certainly lived on until after Antiochos himself died (in 187), but Euthydemos died in the decade of 200–190. He was succeeded by his son Demetrios I, who was not bound by the linked series of treaties, though he was not careless enough to mount a direct attack on Antiochos' kingdom. His first victim in fact was the ruler of the Paropamisadai, who may still have been Sophagasenos.

Sophagasenos' Indian name seems to have been Subhagasena, though this is only a backwards reconstruction.[6] It is possible – indeed it seems to be generally accepted – that he was a member of the imperial Maurya dynasty, but there is no real evidence for this, only another assumption. That dynasty's empire had broken up after the death of Asoka about 230. His heirs first divided control between them, and then several areas gained their independence. Sophagasenos may thus have been a cadet of the dynasty, but he was certainly an independent ruler. When Antiochos was in the region he met only that one Indian king; the situation in Arachosia is not known, but it may also have had an independent ruler.

The centre of Mauryan power was Ganges Valley, and there the last Mauryas of any power were displaced two decades after Antiochos' campaign. The last Maurya to rule in the imperial centre of Pataliputra was Brihadratha, three or four generations after Asoka. He is reported to have been a weak ruler, though this may be later black propaganda. He was deposed and murdered by the army commander Pushyamitra Shunga, who seized power in Magadha in about 186 BC.[7] Magadha, the kingdom around which the Mauryan Empire had been built, occupied a large part of the Ganges Valley, with its capital at Pataliputra (the modern Patna), and was the wealthiest and most agriculturally and commercially developed region of the sub-continent. Possession of this land was the essential basis of any kingdom whose ruler aimed to build an empire, but Pushyamitra's dynasty, the Shungas, did not succeed in expanding their rule, and many of the former Mauryan Empire's outlying territories remained free of their control. Fragments of the Mauryan dynasty probably remained in power in more distant areas.

Arachosia, which Antiochos III had apparently recovered for his kingdom, was centred on the city of Kandahar. It was still in the Mauryan Empire under Asoka, fragments of two of whose rock edicts, by which he proclaimed his beliefs, have been found there; the Mauryan Empire's collapse probably released it. Asoka had published these edicts in Kandahar in both Greek and Aramaic, as well as an Aramaic-Indian version.[8] It is therefore reasonable to assume that Kandahar, where a garrison of Alexander the Great's had been put in place, still had a noticeable population of Greeks in Asoka's reign; the

Aramaic also implies an Iranian population was there, surviving from the Akhaimenid period, for Aramaic had become the literary and bureaucratic language of that empire.

The geopolitical balance established by Antiochos in 206 lasted until the rulers involved began to die off. We know nothing of Sophagasenos, but Euthydemos died between 200 and 190. His son Demetrios I may or may not have been a party to the original treaty with Antiochos. There is a story in Polybios in which Antiochos suggested that Demetrios be given a Seleukid princess as his wife, but it is unlikely this marriage ever took place.[9] Such an alliance would, of course, have tied Demetrios down, and he was ambitious enough not to wish for that; it is also likely that the Euthydemids wanted as little connection with the Seleukids as possible, though Euthydemos himself could not avoid becoming a subordinate of Antiochos by their treaty. So it is fair to assume that when Euthydemos died, so did the subject alliance with Antiochos – and Antiochos himself was busy in the west almost until his death. Demetrios could assume he had a free hand.

And Demetrios had a wide-open field before him. With Antiochos in the west fully occupied first with Ptolemaic Egypt and then with Greece and Rome, and, on the other side, the disintegration of the Mauryan Empire in India, he had little trouble in conquering the Paropamisadai from Sophagasenos or his heirs, and Arachosia, which Antiochos had probably seized in 206. This would, of course, give Antiochos an excellent reason to return to the east.[10]

Antiochos began a new eastern campaign in 187, after a series of wars in which he conquered Palestine and Phoenicia from Ptolemy but lost Asia Minor in a war with Rome. He died in attacking a temple in Elymais, but it is quite probable that his ultimate intention was to campaign into Baktria to recover his old position there, and perhaps to extend it, provoked by Demetrios' actions.[11] This was in 187, only a few years after Demetrios inherited Baktria. Antiochos' minimum aim will have been to renew the old treaty and re-establish his authority in the east. His death relieved Demetrios of any fear that the weight of the Seleukid kingdom would be brought against him.

Holding the Paropamisadai the Baktrian kings had partial control of the entrance to India, but the prospects of conquest in India must have seemed less enticing within a year or so, for in 186 the Mauryan king, Brihadratha, was murdered in the *coup d'état* of Pushyamitra Shunga. This action, by a military man, clearly revived the central authority of the empire, and it was obvious that this was Pushyamitra's intention. There are good indications that he held power in Pataliputra and Ayodhya, which probably means he controlled much of the Ganges-Jumna Valley, and at Vidisa, near Ujjain, just north of the Narbada River.[12] On the other hand, there are equally good signs that a local dynasty centred at Mathura in the western part of the Jumna, and another in the Pancala region between Mathura and Ayodhya, remained (or became) independent. There is no sign that Pushyamitra ruled in the Indus Valley, or in the Punjab.

The south, only recently taken over by Asoka had probably been largely lost since his death. At least two organized kingdoms emerged there about the time of Pushyamitra's *coup*. South of the Narbada River in Vidarbha (the later Berar), a Mauryan loyalist set himself up as a successor king; the Vidarbha king, Yajnasena, was defeated by a Shungan army and compelled to hand over half of his seceded state to a Shunga-loyalist cousin. Both accepted Shungan suzerainty, but both had nevertheless established quasi-independent kingdoms. On the east coast in Kalinga another kingdom was formed − though it might have developed earlier. Kalinga had been the scene of Asoka's most violent conquest, and could be expected to bolt for independence when it got the chance. It was certainly a powerful state a century or so later, which implies a period of recuperation, organization, and consolidation.[13]

Pushyamitra appointed two of his sons (at least) as governors of provinces distant from the centre. One son seems to have governed in Kosala, but much better known is Agnamitra, who was governor in Vidisa. Agnimitra made his brother-in-law Virusena commander of the crossing of the Narbada − it was he who conducted the war with Yajnasena of the Vidarbha. This pattern of provincial government replicated that of the Mauryas − in fact Agnimitra had been made governor in Vidisa before his father's *coup* − and it is a clear sign that the Shungas replaced the Mauryans as rulers but did not disturb the imperial system. But the emergence of organized kingdoms outside the empire was a clear sign that the old empire no longer existed in any serious way. Instead it had been reduced to one power among many, though it was clearly the strongest. In a system of competitive states, of course, and with a political ideology presumably aimed at reviving the old greatness, it was also the most dangerous kingdom. Its neighbours were therefore inevitably its enemies.

The situation in the Indus Valley as a result of this is quite unclear. It seems unlikely that Pushyamitra's authority reached so far west. It is known that Taxila had been an unwilling Mauryan subject, twice having rebelled against what was seen as mistreatment by Mauryan officials.[14] It is thus likely that, like Kalinga, it took its independence as soon as it could. It was also menaced by the advance of Demetrios into the Paropamisadai. This same search for independence might well have applied to the whole Indus Valley.

If the above account of the Indian situation looks relatively clear this is misleading. The sources for this period, as for so much of early Indian history, are extremely fragmentary and very difficult to interpret. There seems to have been no local tradition of narrative historical writing, and so there are only odd details which have to be extracted from other works, often much later than the events, to put together a history which is half-way convincing. Dynastic lists, coins, etymological dictionaries, plays, religious texts, all have been plundered for information, along with external accounts, the odd inscription, and some archaeology. All these, of course, are the normal historical sources for any place or time, but usually they are supplemental to a basic narrative and chronological grid. In this case this grid does not exist, so the reconstruction is much more vulnerable to criticism, interpretation, and re-interpretation than usual.

The major political power in India had retreated into the Ganges Valley with the decline of Mauryan power and its replacement by Pushyamitra. The Indus Valley was perhaps an area of confusion, much divided among minor rulers – as in fact it had been before Chandragupta came to control it a century and a half before in the aftermath of the disruption of Alexander's invasion. Taxila, from the point of view of the invader from the north west, was perhaps the key city, for once it was captured the land of the Five Rivers was open to attack, and if that land was much divided it was clearly vulnerable to conquest.

The comments made about sources for Indian history at this period apply equally to the invaders, of course, who were the Greek Baktrian kings. Pushyamitra's *coup* in about 186 coincided with what seems to have been a period of confusion in the Greek kingdom. The sources, of course, are unreliable, and interpretations vary considerably, as do the dates of the kings, whose names are the only more or less firm ground. It does seem, however, that in the 180s and 170s there were all too many kings in Baktria. Some can be linked to the family of Euthydemos and Demetrios I, others with Antimachos I, and then there arrived Eukratides and Menander.

The latest formulation of the dates of the kings puts seven in the period 190–170, and this is a revision of an even earlier list which had eight; an alternative formulation has six, but not always the same men.[15] In the absence of better, more precise, evidence, particularly for the chronology, it will not be possible to decide on this – though one might assume that none of the theories presently put forward are correct in all details nor perhaps actually in any. The sequence of kings, for example, is not by any means certain, and, from the point of view of India, the kings who conducted the invasions are not unanimously identified.

One of the major elements in the reconstructions of this history is the distribution of the finds of the coins of any particular king. This assumes that, if the coins of one king are found in some numbers in a particular geographical region it is assumed that the king ruled there.[16] Yet to an objective view, this does not necessarily follow. What counts also is the acceptability and quantity of coins produced. The more coins, the more likely they are to spread widely; their weight and beauty will also clearly affect their acceptability outside the lands of their origin. For example, the coins of Euthydemos are found in some numbers in Sogdiana and it is reasonably clear that he ruled there, at least for a time, but when the land became fully independent about 200 BC, some of his coins and some of those of later kings can also be found in the region. Of these men only one or two seem to have ruled the region. In other words coins circulated to regions outside the kingdom of origin. So the findspots of the coins, in so far as they can be known accurately, are only one indication of the regions of rule of independent kings. The most extreme case is a large find of the coins of Diodotos I and II and Euthydemos I found near Vaisali in the Ganges Valley; this can hardly be used to argue that any of these kings ruled there, none of whom ruled outside Baktria.[17] This, therefore, is a most uncertain method, which often involves ignoring some finds to concentrate on just a few which support a particular theory.

The existence of several kings in Baktria during the reign of Pushyamitra in the Ganges Valley would suggest that it was difficult for any one of them to invade India with any hope of lasting success. It seems clear, for example, that Demetrios I's conquest of Arachosia and the Paropamisadai was interrupted by the secession of Antimachos I.[18] This was neither the first nor the last time that such a move happened. The mechanism was perhaps that once the king was busy elsewhere, having taken his main military force out of his kingdom on a campaign, his rival seized power in part or all of Baktria. The rival is usually assumed to have been a provincial governor, which would make sense since such men necessarily had command of their own military forces, but it is an assumption only. The geography of Baktria favoured division, which will presuppose that the power of the central government was weak in the more distant regions. The net result was repeated civil warfare; presumably, since several kings seem to have exercised power at the same time, during the period 190–170, it was a multi-sided civil war.

Demetrios I is certainly credited with an Indian conquest, which was commemorated by the coins issued in his name depicting him wearing an elephant scalp headdress.[19] Add to this fact that his coins are found in Arachosia, though those of earlier Baktrian kings are not, and it may be assumed he conquered that land. His coins are not found in the Paropamisadai – the Kabul region – but for a conqueror out of Baktria to reach Arachosia he would need to move through this region, so we may take it that Demetrios had conquered that land as well. No doubt his coins will be found there eventually; indeed the chaotic emergence of ever more coins from ever more sites in Afghanistan and Pakistan may well have hidden the precise distribution of his (and ever more kings') coins.

The first invasion of India proper seems to have been due to the next kings in the Euthydemid line, Agathokles and Pantaleon. These two are sometimes reckoned to be successive and sometimes joint rulers, or at least contemporaries, and possibly even brothers. They issued Indian-style coins, which are square and often of copper (rather than bronze); the inscriptions on them were in both Greek and Indian scripts. They had been preceded in this innovation by coins of Antimachos I, though there is no other evidence that he had reached India. Coins of both Pantaleon and Agathokles have been found in the Taxila region and in the western Punjab. Given the evident interest of Demetrios I in India, and the connection which is apparent between him and Agathokles and Pantaleon, it seems probable that, excluded from at least part of Baktria by Antimachos' *coup*, they turned their arms outwards along the Kabul River valley and through the Khyber Pass. Having secured Taxila they had access to the Punjab. In fact, the initial move could well have been an achievement of Demetrios I, with these two merely his heirs.

The next push forward in India was probably the work of Apollodotos I, another of the kings whose dating tends to be moved around. He appears to belong to a separate family from both the Euthydemids and the descendents of Antimachos. His coins are not found in Baktria itself, but do turn up in the Paropamisadai, Gandhara, and the western Punjab, so it appears that he was another usurper, seizing control of the Indian conquests of Agathokles and Pantaleon. He was succeeded, probably, by the decisive figure in this entire story, Demetrios II.

In the written sources the two Baktrian kings called Demetrios tend to be combined, for both were involved in Indian wars, but on their coins they are quite different.[20] It is thus the second of them who was able to campaign widely inside India, supposedly as far south as the mouth of the Indus River, so repeating Alexander's route; possibly he went further into the region of Gujarat.[21] The exact nature of this southern extension of his activity is unclear; suggestions are a conquest which he held for a time, a single campaign, or just a raid.

In fact it seems likely that it was only a campaign, or perhaps a raid, whatever Demetrios' ultimate intention. For during his absence the predictable happened, and in Baktria a rival king arose, Eukratides. The two men fought for some time, with the eventual result that neither prevailed. Eukratides established his rule in Baktria; Demetrios may have held on to his conquests in the Indus Valley. Certainly he was able to fight back against the usurpation, besieging Eukratides in Baktra for several months. Eukratides is also recorded as having campaigned into India, presumably in pursuit of Demetrios or his successor, though he was also returning from an Indian campaign when he was killed, after a reign of two decades.[22] During his progress Eukratides also had to face hostility from the Parthians, whose power had revived. He handed over two small provinces to the Parthian King Mithradates, who was his almost exact contemporary, either as a result of defeat in war, or, just as likely, as the price for leaving him alone to concentrate on his war with Demetrios.[23]

This had provided one of the few chronological pegs to hang this whole story on. Eukratides' seizure of power is said to have taken place at about the time that Mithradates I succeeded to his kingship.[24] Originally dated c.171, Mithradates' accession is now put at c.165, and so this is the approximate date for Eukratides' *coup*.[25] Since he and Demetrios II fought each other, the latter must have had a fairly substantial reign of perhaps fifteen to twenty years into the later 160s. (It is odd that most students have separated the rule of Demetrios and Eukratides by several years, yet since they fought each other, they were clearly contemporaries.) Eukratides is also given a reign of about that length, down to the 140s. He was, of course, killed by his son as he returned from campaigning in India, an event which seems to have precipitated the major crisis of the nomad invasion.

By 150, therefore, the Seleukid kingdom in the west was becoming engulfed in the crisis caused by the growing success of the conspiracy of Alexander Balas against Demetrios I; meanwhile the Greek kingdom in the east had invaded India and was now on the vigorous control of Eukratides. It was separated from the Seleukid state by the intrusive Parthia, which was now under the energetic kingship of Mithradates I, who had been given two small provinces, Turiva and Aspionos, by Eukratides, and so the two eastern kings were at peace — this was clearly the result of their treaty. Mithradates' boundary with Baktria was pushed eastwards, and by this time he had also probably recovered control of the lands originally lost to Antiochos. In 150 Parthian power was at its greatest so far, and lay firmly astride the great road which runs through northern Iran between Babylonia and Central Asia and India. The Parthians now effectively separated the two greater kingdoms, both of which were under pressure from other enemies.

The two Greek states were by no means unaware of the potential threat from Parthia. As it happened, Parthia was to be the main beneficiary from the problems which simultaneously beset the Seleukids in Syria and the Baktrians in the east. The crucial condition, however, was that Eukratides and Mithradates, linked by their treaty, no longer needed to be concerned with each other; so Eukratides could campaign into India knowing that his international boundary on the west was safe and Mithradates could turn west with a similar confidence. When Eukratides was killed his kingdom came under such pressure that Mithradates could continue his western campaign without fears of attack from the east, at least for some years.

The Baktrians' difficulties have been considered in the previous chapter, and those of the Seleukids in several other chapters. Here the events of the Indo-Greek kingdom in the Punjab can at last be concentrated on. The sequence of kings is not at all clear, depending as it does (here and in Baktria) on the interpretation of their coins, but it seems very probable that about 150 the king in the Punjab was Menander, who is said to have been from Alexandria – though which of the many cities of that name is meant is not known. He was probably the son, or at least the successor, of Apollodotos I, and may have been married to a princess, Agathokleia, of the Euthydemid family. (These relationships, note, are not by any means certain, being based on interpretations of the coins.) He is well known in Indian history because of the survival of a Buddhist dialogue in which he is depicted as a participant, under the name Milinda. His exact dates are not known, but his accession is generally put at about 155. He was thus a younger contemporary of Eukratides, and could well be a successor, politically if not genealogically, of Demetrios II.

In Baktria the conflict between Eukratides and Demetrios had ended by 160 or so, though another man who was probably of Demetrios' family, Antimachos II, is recorded as king on his coins; he was presumably Demetrios' son (named for his grandfather), and, also presumably, continued his father's fight, though his coins are fairly few and are found in Arachosia and the western Punjab only. This might indicate that he was driven from one area to the other; his reign is thought to be short, and it probably ended about the time Menander became king. Who Eukratides had been campaigning against when he returned from India to face his assassin is not known – since it was in the 140s, his enemy was probably Menander.

Menander, apart from keeping one eye on the threat from Baktria, whoever it was who ruled there, was also necessarily concerned with his Indian neighbours. He was apparently a firm Buddhist, as his appearance in the Buddhist dialogue named for him indicates, but this did not prevent him from indulging in aggressive warfare.[26] And in about 150, early in Menander's reign, Pushyamitra died.

His reign had been long, thirty-six years according to the Indian dynasty lists. He was succeeded by Jyeshtha (or Jethamitra), probably one of his sons, but then, apparently fairly quickly, by Agnimitra, another son, who was the former governor in Vidisa. Given that Agnimitra had been an adult governor when his father seized power, both brothers were no doubt fairly old by the time they succeeded. (Pushyamitra must have been in his eighties.) Agnimitra had already employed his own son Vasumitra as his field commander; he was to have the opportunity to do so again.

Pushyamitra had also, not surprisingly, been a successful commander himself. One of the few things known about his reign is that he twice carried out horse sacrifices, an elaborate performance in which the designated horse travelled through the realm before being sacrificed.[27] The ceremony was a celebration of a victory of an especially noticeable sort, but when and where the victories took place and over whom they were gained, is not known. Vasumitra is said to have escorted one of the horses on its pre-death travels, so this was probably fairly late in the old man's reign.

It is during this journey that Vasumitra and his horse escort collided with a force of Yavana cavalry near the Kali Sindhu River. 'Yavana' is the Indian term for Greeks, derived from 'Ionian' by way of the Persian 'Yenona'; it later became a general term for westerners, and was eventually applied to Arabs.[28] It resembles the widespread medieval use of the term 'Frank' to identify anybody from Europe, and which largely replaced it in India. The river is generally accepted as being the Sindhu, which flows roughly northwards to join the Chambal River just before their joint waters flow into the Jumna – that is, the clash took place well to the east of the present city of Delhi. This puts Menander's military activities well east of the Punjab even before Pushyamitra's death. He is also said to have sent forces to besiege Saketa and Madhyanika, which are respectively on the Gogra River and north of Ujjain. Menander's forces were clearly capable of long-distance campaigns. These references, from a book on grammar in which they serve as examples, are not indicative of conquest, but at least they indicate the range of Indo–Greek military activity under Menander.[29]

However, there is more to it than that. The ultimate achievement of Menander in this easterly direction was an attack on the great imperial city of Pataliputra. The usual fragmentary Indian sources make it clear that the Greek forces involved were only part of those which took part in the attack. At least two other forces, from the Mathura and Pancala kingdoms, sent contingents. These were areas which had fairly recently become independent, having formerly been part of the Mauryan Empire. In other words the three states had formed an alliance, quite possibly to defend themselves against any attack from the Shunga empire, and now were mounting a swift raid on Pataliputra, no doubt with the aim of gathering loot in the great city, but also in order to humiliate the Shunga king. The exact status of this is not known, but soon after Pushyamitra's death would be the obvious time, when a rapid succession of kings weakened royal authority and created local confusion.

The raid was successful, to some extent at least.[30] Since the city had been the capital first of the Mauryas and now of the Sungas it was undoubtedly large, rich and populous. A theory surmises that urban development in India was relatively slow, and that, in the Ganges Valley it is only in the Maurya period that true urban agglomerations developed, though a survey of archaeological evidence as it was in the 1980s found an impressive number of urban centres along the Ganges-Jumna plain.[31] The Greek ambassador Megasthenes, who was in Pataliputra about 300 BC, reported that it contained palaces — plural — and powerful wooden fortifications. Its size is reckoned to be 6km along the riverside, and with a depth of 2km inland.[32] This certainly sounds like a major metropolis.

The precise effects of the raid on the city are not recorded. However, it was mainly built of wood, and its defences were a wooden palisade on an earthen rampart. This is not very formidable — it was probably the result of the long Mauryan peace during which war had not approached the city or the region for a century and a half or more. The place was undoubtedly sacked, possibly partly burned, but it continued to function as a major capital city afterwards. Perhaps the raiders were pressed for time, or perhaps they were already quarreling, for the aftermath of the raid was a dispute among the allies which led to fighting between them. This is a not uncommon result of such an enterprise, of course. The Yavanas withdrew.

The two Indian ally-kingdoms reverted to their usual condition. The Shunga Empire was not apparently too damaged, except in its prestige. The rapid succession of two brothers after Pushyamitra's death was perhaps almost as unsettling as the sack of their main city. Agnimitra's son, the vigorous Vasumitra, succeeded his father, probably still in the 140s or soon after; the empire continued to exist, but it also continued to decline.

Menander was remembered as the greatest of the Indo-Greek kings. His reign is reckoned at about quarter of a century, and with his (presumed) father Apollodotos and his (presumed) son, the long-lived Strato I, the dynastic rule of the three lasted almost a century. This long period of authority contrasts with the constant changes and conflicts in Baktria, where the result was the destruction of the Greek kingdom. This happened during Menander's reign in the Punjab. Zhang Kian's report that Baktria was reduced to a set of city states refers to about the time of Menander's death. His coins imply that his kingdom stretched right across the land of the Five Rivers as far as Sialkot (ancient Sagala, possibly his capital, or one of them), and perhaps down the Indus. It may be that one of the reasons for the vigour, and longevity, and increase in his kingdom was that he received Greek refugees fleeing from the Baktrian disaster.

Menander undoubtedly commanded a major Indian kingdom, which survived him either in part or in pieces for a century and more after his death. But his success was bought at the price of ignoring and weakening his parent kingdom in Baktria. No doubt he had to survive attacks by, at least, Eukratides and possibly the Shungas, and perhaps he understood full well the divisive politics of Baktria and did not wish to become involved. His choice is epitomized by the raid on Pataliputra, clearly a much more attractive venture than attempting the hard task of assisting his fellow Greeks in Baktria. This preoccupation with India had helped to weaken Baktria, which in turn had succumbed to Parthian pressure, and had then collapsed in the face of nomad attacks. It was therefore in no condition to resist, or assist, the Parthians. And meanwhile Parthia was taking advantage also of the collapse of Seleukid authority in Syria.

Chapter 7

The Dynastic War in Syria, 148–145

lexander Balas had a splendid time as king in Syria. If he really was the son of Antiochos IV, he had also inherited his father's capacity for enjoyment and pleasure. With a new teenage wife, and soon with a son, whom he called Antiochos, he seemed well settled. He had the international support of Ptolemy VI and Attalos II, and he had no trouble, so far as we can tell, in extracting recognition of his accession from the rest of the kingdom.

He does, however, seem to have left much power in the hands of Ammonios, the Egyptian minister loaned him by Ptolemy. Diodoros relates a story whereby Ammonios was bribed by the island city of Arados to permit the suppression of the rival and competing city of Marathos, which lay across the narrow strait on the mainland. The Aradians are portrayed as impious schemers, but they failed. There had been a long history of Aradian attempts to gain independence, and Marathos was actually originally an Aradian colony, so the Aradians did have something of a case. The Aradian aim was not yet to achieve independence, but the result would have been a significant increase in the local power and autonomy. And the story does suggest a willingness on the part of Ammonios to contemplate the weakening of the Seleukid kingdom.[1]

How far he was loyal to Alexander or even to Ptolemy is not known. His name suggests an Egyptian origin, hence the assumption that he was Ptolemy's man at Alexander's court. It is perhaps most likely that Ammonios understood the instability of the ground on which he stood, and was most concerned to feather his own nest before the anticipated collapse came.

Alexander's rule, careless and dependent on such men as Ammonios, was clearly not of the most rigorous. In such circumstances any initial popularity will have soon waned. An earthquake which damaged Antioch in 148 will have also damaged Alexander's prestige.[2] His dynastic enemies, the second and third sons of Demetrios I, Demetrios and Antiochos, though the threat they posed was ever-present, were still very young. Their father had married almost as soon as he took the throne in 162, his wife being his sister (the widow of King Perseus of Macedon). The eldest son, Antigonos, was killed by Alexander; the second son, Demetrios, cannot have been more than eleven years old when he was sent away by his father to put him in a place of safety, at first in Asia

Minor. (The boys were sent to different places, as a further precaution.) The arrangements made by Demetrios I are not known, but the eldest boy was soon at the head of a growing mercenary force. The commander of this force was Lasthenes, a Cretan, and the majority of his troops were also Cretans, recruited by him. It seems likely that Lasthenes had been contacted by the old king before the end and had been given instructions as to what to do if the fight against Alexander failed. The boys had certainly been accompanied into their exile by a considerable quantity of treasure, which was used to recruit the mercenaries.[3]

It took two years for the mercenaries to be assembled (assuming Lasthenes began in 150). When they were ready, Lasthenes brought the elder boy, Demetrios, first probably to Kilikia, where Antiochos IV had been unpopular because of his assignment of taxes to his concubine – and where there was an easy line of retreat out of Seleukid territory into the wilds of Rough Kilikia or the Taurus Mountains.[4] Demetrios was the figurehead of the invading forces; Antiochos' whereabouts is not clear, but later he was at Side, just west of Rough Kilikia, in Pamphylia, and so was available as a replacement if Demetrios was killed; Alexander must have felt he was fighting a many-headed hydra.

Just as with Demetrios I's fight with Alexander, there was no quick resolution of this conflict. Alexander, who had lived mainly at Ptolemais-Ake, went north to face the invasion, and found that Antioch, recovering from the earthquake, was in an angry mood. And the provincial administration suddenly seemed unreliable. Many of the provincial governors appointed by Demetrios I had been retained by Alexander. At least two are known – Ptolemaios in Kommagene and Hyspaosines in Charakene – and there were surely others. This is a mark of Alexander's laziness and optimism, of course, but it was also a sensible political thing to do, utilizing their expertise and implying his confidence in them and that he was not challengeable. Yet he was undoubtedly seen as a usurper, and many of these administrators had also served Demetrios I for up to a dozen years; their loyalties could not be changed so easily.

The situation in Palestine is the one area where we have some detailed information on this. There the governor, Apollonios Taos, came out for Demetrios almost at once, presumably as soon as Alexander went north.[5] He may have been contacted earlier, which would be poetic justice after the betrayal of Demetrios I by the governor of Ptolemais-Ake. (It is also curious that he was originally from Miletos, like Alexander's sponsor Herakleides; he had been one of Alexander's appointees, possibly because of his origin.) But there was also Jonathan Maccabee, the high priest in Jerusalem and effective governor of Judaea, whose position depended entirely on Alexander's continuation in power. The result was a minor war in Palestine, one in which Jonathan pursued his own local ambitions. But he was available to whichever side would reward him best, and he would need to be sure that any reward he was given was concrete.

Alexander appealed to Jonathan when Apollonios rebelled. The Judaean army was mustered. He had recruited this in the past two or three years, and he brought it out of the Judaean hills to lay siege to the port of Joppa. In a sense this was a legitimate civil war target, since it was held by a garrison of Apollonios' troops, but Jonathan's attack was more to do with his own ambitions than the support he was offering to Alexander. Control of Joppa had long been an aim of the Judaeans, since it was the most convenient port for trade out of Judaea. Jonathan was using the Seleukid conflict to pursue his own aims, as ever.[6]

Apollonios, most of whose soldiers had presumably been taken away by Alexander, was unable to intervene in the attack on Joppa. Once the town was taken Jonathan moved south against the governor. In a battle near Ashdod, in which the most notable feature was the ability of the new Jewish army to stand firm against a long archery bombardment, Apollonios was defeated, though most of his forces survived. He took refuge in Ashdod, but the city was captured and sacked by Jonathan's army.[7] As a reward Alexander transferred the town of Accaron (the biblical Ekron) to Judaea.[8] In itself it was only a minor place, but it was the first town in the lowland which had been added to Judaea — and, of course, Jonathan now held Joppa as well.

In the north neither Lasthenes with Demetrios nor Alexander could prevail and Jonathan's victory in the south was not sufficient to bring Alexander any serious help. He was clearly very reluctant to bring Jonathan's Judaean forces to the north, just as Jonathan, fully occupied in holding on in the south, was unable to come north. The Jews had an unpleasant reputation for anti-Hellenism. In the war of terrorism waged by Judas, Jonathan's older brother, more than one city had been scoured to expel non-Jews. There was more danger to Alexander in using the Judaean army amid a Greek population than he would gain from its rather limited numbers and military prowess. Jonathan stayed in the south. Significantly, he withdrew from Ashdod, leaving it to the surviving inhabitants.

It may be assumed that the fighting in the north was indecisive for the same reasons that it had taken so long for Alexander and Demetrios I to reach a conclusion in their original war, that the balance of forces was close. Possibly it was also because of the reluctance of the soldiers to fight. For many Seleukid subjects the choice of king was between a lazy usurper and an unknown boy, the son of a disliked king. Lasthenes' army, though largely composed of professional mercenaries, was relatively small – it was presumably reinforced by Demetrios-loyalty. Mercenaries were expensive, and, though they could be partly paid in promises of future rewards, they still needed some payment, so a large army was not affordable to the insurgents. Alexander, on the other hand, faced the same difficulty as had been faced by Demetrios I: he had to gather his forces from considerable distances, which took time, but he had also to leave much of his army scattered in distant provinces to deter any sympathetic insurrections or a foreign invasion. Apollonios Taos in Palestine, for example, had a force of a few thousand soldiers in the fight against Jonathan, probably collected from garrisons and militia, and he will also have left many in the several cities in his province, though clearly in the case of Ashdod and Joppa these garrisons were insufficient. He had also the responsibility for guarding the frontier against Egypt, though since Alexander was Ptolemy's son-in-law, it could not be regarded as a hostile frontier. Ptolemy had his own ambitions to recover his family's old lands, so trust between the two kings was probably minimal; the frontier cannot have been left unguarded.

Elsewhere we know of another governor, Kleomenes, viceroy of the eastern provinces (the 'Upper Satrapies'), for whom a commemorative statue of Herakles 'Glorious in Victory' was sculpted at the Bisitun Pass between Babylonia and Iran, celebrating a victory he had won. It is not said against whom he had fought, but the probability is that it was either the Parthians or a rebellious Iranian group; the main inference is that he, and therefore Alexander, was in control when that inscription was cut. The date is given as the summer of 148, exactly the time Alexander was coming under pressure in the west.[9]

Alexander obviously had to leave a substantial force in the east even while he faced invasion from the west. Babylonia was traditionally quiet, but it was also the essential tax-cow for the whole kingdom. There had been some trouble in Babylon during the war between Demetrios I and Alexander, during which it appears – the wording is incomplete and so not definitive – that the governor, who was probably Demetrios' man, fled.[10] So, with trouble in Iran, a strong garrison was also needed in Babylon, especially as raids by desert Arabs had begun. They are recorded in Babylonia in 145, but may have started earlier.[11] All the provincial forces in the provinces not immediately threatened would of course be thinned out so as to provide contingents for Alexander in Syria, but most of the troops must have been left in place – Kleomenes in the Upper Satrapies clearly could not spare any – and anyway the contingents would take time to make the journey to the west.

By 147, after over a year of fighting, it was clear that neither side in the war in Syria could prevail, and Alexander persuaded Ptolemy to intervene. There must have been negotiations setting terms for this move; we have no details on this, but we may perhaps judge from the results. Ptolemy was obviously in a strong position and could impose his own terms. He brought his army into Palestine, where Jonathan had already largely prevailed against Apollonios Taos, but where the cities along the coast – Gaza, Ashkelon, Ashdod, and as far as Ptolemais-Ake – were still mainly in the hands of supporters of Demetrios. There is no indication that Jonathan had been able to capture any of these places except for Joppa and Ashdod, which had been sacked; Ashkelon had negotiated submission and had been left alone; of these places only Joppa was still occupied by Jonathan's forces. Normally the Judaean army was unable to capture cities, and these civil war captures were exceptional, due no doubt to weakened garrisons and confused citizen loyalties.

The Ptolemaic army, however, was a fully equipped Hellenistic force, quite capable of capturing such places, and in fact had been doing so inside Egypt within the past few years, while suppressing rebellions. Further, Ptolemy could promise good treatment to the citizens, whereas capture by the Jewish forces was liable to end in a massacre of non-Jews. (The citizens of Ashdod made sure Ptolemy got a good view of the wreckage of their city, and made bitter complaints against the actions of an ally of Alexander to another ally of Alexander.) Any further attacks by Jonathan's forces would be fiercely resisted, while Ptolemy could present himself in the guise of a rescuer – so long as the cities surrendered. Certainly none of the places along the coast resisted his progress. Some may have been on Alexander's side already; others swiftly joined it in the face of the advance of Ptolemy's army. Apollonios Taos is not heard of again. He may have died in the sack of Ashdod. It seems that Joppa was one of the places Ptolemy took over as well.

Jonathan presented himself to Ptolemy at Ptolemais-Ake, and the two men and their armies marched on northwards together along the coast through Phoenicia. But at the Eleutheros River Jonathan and his Judaean army were sent back.[12] There had been no fighting on this march, and, if anything, Jonathan and his forces were a political liability. The story, of course, is generally presented through Jewish eyes, given that the source for these events is the first book of Maccabees, but it is clear that it was Ptolemy who was in control. He it was who brought Jonathan along, even if it was Jonathan who volunteered, and it was Ptolemy's decision to send Jonathan and his army back.

The explanation for this curious matter appears with the end of the march. (This is quite apart from the apparent earlier unwillingness of Alexander to employ Jonathan's forces in north Syria.) The Eleutheros River, which reaches the sea between Tripoli and Tartus, had formed the boundary between the Ptolemaic and Seleukid kingdoms from the time of Seleukos I and Ptolemy I until the conquest of Phoenicia and Palestine by Antiochos III in 200 BC. The message Ptolemy was conveying by sending Jonathan back at this point was that his march through these lands was in fact his re-annexation of Palestine and Phoenicia to his kingdom. In practical terms this had been accomplished by the garrisons he had left in the cities as he went along.[13] The most telling sign of annexation, however – for the garrisons might have been only a temporary wartime measure – was that the mints of Ptolemais-Ake, Sidon, Tyre, and other places, changed from minting coins on the Seleukid standard of weight to that of the Ptolemaic kingdom.[14]

This was the price Alexander had evidently been compelled to pay for Ptolemy's assistance in the war with Demetrios II and Lasthenes. And by bringing Jonathan along, and then sending him back before he crossed the river, Ptolemy was indicating to him that Judaea was going to be part of the Ptolemaic kingdom once more, or, at most a subordinate province. It seems clear that Jonathan did not understand what was going on until they reached the river, and once he returned to Judaea no doubt the humiliation will have burned. Had Ptolemy's plans worked out, it seems likely that he and Jonathan would soon have come to blows. Given that he was re-annexing Palestine and Phoenicia, Ptolemy cannot have been pleased to see that Jonathan's army had spent some of its energies on looting and ravaging – the citizens of Ashdod's point had been well taken. It is not known what the reaction in Syria was to Ptolemy's evident re-annexation, but one would suppose it would compel some of Alexander's people to turn to support Demetrios.

When Ptolemy crossed the Eleutheros River he entered the cockpit where Alexander and Demetrios contended. His reaction was, to say the least, curious. He already had his own men in the administration which had been set up by Alexander, in particular the Egyptian Ammonios, who presumably reported back to Alexandria regularly to keep Ptolemy informed on Alexander. Now Ptolemy marched to Seleukeia-in-Pieria, while Ammonios secured Antioch for Alexander, having presumably suppressed the earlier disturbances.[15] Demetrios was somewhere in the north, but it is not known where. It looked as though he would soon be driven out or caught.

But at this point Ptolemy announced that, while he had been at Ptolemais-Ake, he had foiled an assassination plot, and he blamed Ammonios for instigating it.[16] He never produced any proof of this, no doubt relying on his royal word to be believed, and it looks very much as though the accusation was a means of discrediting and removing Ammonios. Quite probably the whole story was Ptolemy's invention, though this only raises the question of what had happened to sever the link between the king and Ammonios. The obvious answer is that Ammonios was now personally committed to Alexander rather than Ptolemy, and that Ptolemy's annexations in Palestine and Phoenicia had annoyed both of them. It is, in that connection, telling that Ptolemy did not accuse Ammonios until he had reached Seleukeia, after his annexations, and when he had had a first meeting with Ammonios. It is also obvious that in occupying Seleukeia he had secured the person of his daughter, Kleopatra Thea, Alexander's wife, unless he had already done so at Ptolemais-Ake.

Following up, Ptolemy demanded that Alexander surrender Ammonios, presumably for instant punishment. Alexander refused, perhaps because he was implicated in the plot (if it existed), more likely because he was loyal to his minister. Alexander may have gained a poor reputation amongst the ancient historians, but this was the only honourable course; it was also the best response politically, and of course, when utility links with honour, the choice is easy. Ptolemy then announced that his daughter Kleopatra Thea was no longer married to Alexander. It seems probable that she had been left in Ptolemais or Seleukeia when Alexander headed north to confront Demetrios II, and that she had come under Ptolemy's control when he took one of these cities. But Alexander's son, Antiochos, had already, before Ptolemy's invasion, been sent by Alexander to an Arab sheikh, Zabdiel, for refuge – just as Demetrios I had evacuated his sons. One wonders if Ptolemy had intended to proclaim the child as king under his mother's regency. As it was the child was out of his reach. So Kleopatra Thea was offered in marriage to Demetrios.[17]

Alexander was justifiably outraged, but the move deprived him of so much support that he had to retire from the neighbourhood of Antioch to take refuge in Kilikia.[18] He was followed, no doubt, by those of his forces who were loyal to him, and he was also able to recruit more soldiers in Kilikia. Ptolemy's action also upset many of those who had invested much time and effort on behalf of Alexander, but who were also committed to Ptolemy. Ptolemy's price was presumably once again Palestine and Phoenicia, and Demetrios was evidently desperate enough to agree. The new marriage was then quickly arranged. (It will be noted that Ptolemy's tactics were not really very different, if on a larger scale, from those of Jonathan Maccabee.)

Alexander's withdrawal to Kilikia allowed him to recruit more troops, for which Kilikia was a fertile source. He left Ammonios in control in Antioch, but, difficult already, that had now become an impossible task without extreme measures being taken. Alexander returned with a larger force but Ptolemy foiled him by seizing the city, no doubt to the relief of its inhabitants.

Ammonios tried to escape, disguised in women's clothes, but was detected and murdered.[19]

Ptolemy now installed two new men to control the city. They were Hierax, a native of the city and a flute player (or at least so we are told) who was one of Ptolemy's protégés, and Diodotos, from Kasiana near Apamea in Syria.[20] To these men, both Syrian Greeks, it must have been obvious that both Alexander and Demetrios were disliked in Antioch, and probably elsewhere in Syria; it was also clear that neither had a hope of winning the civil war; further, it was Ptolemy who held the balance, for he had control of every city from Seleukeia and Antioch south to Gaza, and probably the persons of Demetrios and Kleopatra Thea as well.

The two men came up with a solution: that Ptolemy should take the Seleukid crown as well as the Ptolemaic and unite the two great kingdoms into one.[21] They faced an immediate problem in persuading the king to accept, for the project contradicted all that Ptolemy had been working towards for a year, which was the revival of Ptolemaic power in Syria, supplemented by his patronage of the Seleukid king (either Alexander or Demetrios – he probably did not much care which).

There is no doubt that Ptolemy was tempted, and he was in fact regarded as king of both states for about a month, which is long enough for him to have thought through what was involved, and long enough to show that he did not reject the idea outright. But the longer he considered it, the greater were the difficulties he could envisage. The wealth of the Akhaimenid Empire gathered by Alexander in his conquests no longer existed to finance the joint kingdom. To rule both the Ptolemaic kingdom and the Seleukid probably seemed too great a task for a man who had worked hard for twenty years just to control Egypt. The sheer size of the joint state, stretching from Cyrenaica and Upper Egypt to the borders of Central Asia, was daunting, but this extent also brought with it a host of further problems – the Parthians in the east, where Mithradates I had used the civil war in Syria to launch an invasion of Media which was in the process of succeeding, and where Elymais had rebelled and invaded Babylonia, which was also being harassed by raids by Arabs out of the desert (Chapter 11). All this was to be added to a resentful brother glowering at him from Cyrenaica, and the enmity of the rulers of the lands beyond the Nile frontier. If Ptolemy, as king of the Seleukid kingdom, went east to restore control in Media, there is no doubt his absence would be seized on by his western enemies. The several states of Asia Minor would necessarily feel immediately threatened by the new great power, and would become instantly hostile. They relied to some extent on balancing Seleukid and Ptolemaic power to retain their independence. Then there was the problem of Rome. Rome was even then in the midst of fighting two or three wars at once, and could only see the sudden emergence of a joint Ptolemaic-Seleukid kingdom as potentially hostile to it. And Ptolemy was familiar with Rome and its senators; he could see this.

On the other hand, Ptolemy could put up a fairly good case for holding both crowns, and no doubt Hierax and Diodotos did so in their advocacy. He was king in Egypt by hereditary right, and was married to his sister, who was the only person able to provide legitimacy to his throne other than Ptolemy himself. But he was also a son of Kleopatra Syra, a daughter of Antiochos III who was married to Ptolemy V as part of the peace treaty negotiations in 195. It could be argued that all the Seleukid rulers since Antiochos III and Seleukos IV had been usurpers – Antiochos IV had seized the throne from a child nephew, Demetrios I similarly, Alexander Balas was a bastard or an imposter, and if Demetrios I was a usurper his children could have no claim. This meant that Ptolemy VI could claim to be the last of the true Seleukids, inheriting through his mother, the sister of Seleukos IV. Given the disputable claims of Demetrios II and Alexander, Ptolemy's might seem just as good.

Such arguments would certainly convince some men, for the hereditary kingship was the basis of the political system. Further, the Greco–Macedonian kingdoms had been declining in power and effectiveness for a century. Both the Ptolemaic and the Seleukid kingdoms had lost territory, while on their frontiers non-Greek powers had risen. To the west Rome was an enigmatic menace, particularly now that Carthage and Macedon were being annexed. To the east Ptolemy had surely heard of the collapse of the Greco-Baktrian kingdom, and was aware of the conquests of the non-Greek Parthians. It could well be argued that the only future for the two remaining successor kingdoms of Alexander's empire was in union.

But arguments like this would not cut much ice in Rome. There the calculation would not be a matter of legal and family definitions, but of power. And this was 145, the year after Rome had finally bitten the bullet and made extensive new annexations in Macedonia, in Greece, and in North Africa. Rome's power now extended into the Aegean Sea, where it was the neighbour of, and ally of, the Attalid kingdom, whose eastern boundary was on the Taurus Mountains, which were the Seleukid kingdom's western frontier. In North Africa Rome was now the neighbour of Cyrenaica, where Ptolemy's estranged, angry, and ambitious brother was king. He would certainly be only too happy to let Roman forces into Egypt by way of Cyrenaica should Rome request it, probably at the same time as a Parthian war. If he made himself the joint Ptolemaic-Seleukid king, Ptolemy VI would have to fight a Roman war sooner or later. And Ptolemy knew Rome, he had been there, he had negotiated with those senators, and he understood – who in the Mediterranean did not? – the force of the Roman army. The Roman army was the decisive piece on the board.

Ptolemy VI declined the Seleukid crown after a wistful month, despite the offer by his Syrian ministers, and despite the encouragements of a crowd of Antiochenes which had clearly been whipped up by Hierax and Diodotos. Meanwhile Demetrios was married to Kleopatra Thea and Alexander was gathering his forces. The three kings eventually met in a confused battle not far from Antioch, close to the Oenoparos River, after Alexander, with his reinforced army, had spent some time harrying the land around Antioch. This finally succeeded in drawing Ptolemy and Demetrios and their armies out of the city. In the fighting Alexander was defeated, and fled for refuge to Zabdiel with some of his people. Ptolemy received a blow which fractured his skull, from which he died a few days later. Perhaps to his own and others' surprise, Demetrios II emerged as the new king. He was contacted by two of the officers who were with Alexander, who agreed to kill him in exchange for their own lives.[22] They had done so before Ptolemy died.

Despite his victory, Demetrios faced some particularly intractable problems. The fighting, for a start, had caused considerable casualties, so his available forces were much reduced; also anyone who fought for Alexander – and he clearly had a substantial army in the last battle – was unlikely to be willing to fight for Demetrios. The administration of the empire had largely remained loyal to Alexander, even though many of the men involved had originally been appointees of Demetrios I. Whether the administration needed to be purged of any or all of these men was one of Demetrios' early problems, yet his youth and lack of experience scarcely equipped him to deal with it. He relied therefore on Lasthenes, who had, after all, succeeded in the end in defeating the army of Alexander, even if the final victory was probably due at least as much to the Ptolemaic forces brought north by Ptolemy. The two major ministers, Hierax and Diodotos, rapidly disappeared. Hierax went to Egypt, where he soon fell foul of Ptolemy VII, ever suspicious of anyone who had served his brother, and was killed; Diodotos went home to Kasiana, near Apamea, the Seleukid military centre.

Lasthenes' Cretan soldiers were the only force Demetrios could rely on in the aftermath of the battle, at least for the present, until he became fully accepted by his subjects. The troops were concentrated, it seems, in Antioch, where they were used to root out the more outspoken of Alexander's former people. Lasthenes himself was appointed 'First Friend' of the king, and, since he commanded the Cretans, he became in effect dictator of Antioch.[23]

One issue which might have been difficult was quickly resolved. The Ptolemaic army in Syria, deprived of its king, disintegrated. The soldiers could have held on to their cities in Palestine and Phoenicia. After all, this had been the price Ptolemy VI had demanded for his help, and Demetrios was in no position, once he and Ptolemy had ended up on the same side, to demand their surrender. But the Ptolemaic soldiers did not wait; instead they went back to Egypt on their own initiative, after a nudge or two from Demetrios' troops.[24] The soldiers knew that Ptolemy VI would be succeeded in Egypt by his brother, Ptolemy VII, who was not interested in war, or empire, and was to have some difficulty in establishing himself. The soldiers therefore left Syria on their own initiative, appreciating that the new king would probably have ordered them out in any case. (He did order the evacuation of the last three Ptolemaic naval bases in the Aegean, at Itanos in Crete, Thera, and Methana in the Argolid; they were rather too close to Roman territory for comfort by then.[25])

Any fears the Romans might have of the emergence of a new Great Power (if they got to know much about what was going on in Syria) were dissipated by the withdrawal of Ptolemaic troops from Palestine and Phoenicia and from the Aegean. In Syria no doubt Demetrios was pleased. But he was now burdened by the presence of the mercenaries and Lasthenes, he had lost control of the Upper Satrapies, and during the year he had been negotiating and campaigning with Ptolemy, the situation in the rest of the Mediterranean had altered drastically. Roman power had advanced from the Adriatic to the Aegean, and from Sicily to the Sahara Desert. From two sides, the Seleukid kingdom was clearly menaced, by Rome and by Parthia.

Chapter 8

The Destruction of Carthage

T he final decision at Rome to make war on Carthage was made early in 149. The Carthaginians understood all too well the Romans' military efficiency, and did their best to avoid destruction. The Carthaginian envoys knew the procedure: Rome required an act of *deditio*, in effect surrendering the city to Rome to do with it as Rome wished. Normally this could be the cloak for negotiations – as with Marcellus in Spain a short time before, or with Utica, which had by a well-timed move surrendered just before the declaration of war, so providing Rome with a port of disembarkation for its forces in Africa. In neither case had the *deditio* resulted in serious damage to the enemy, though this was no guarantee of generous treatment for anyone else.

But Carthage was different. The determination of the Senate was that the city was to be rendered impotent, though it was appreciated that physically this was a major and difficult task. The chosen method of reaching that goal was to reduce by stages Carthage's ability to resist. The method had been used by Lucullus in Spain quite recently. There was to be a gradual sequence of escalating demands which was to end with Carthage, disarmed and demoralized, totally at Roman mercy. At that point 'destruction' could be accomplished. This need not necessarily mean a physical destruction: removing Carthage's self-government would be a political destruction.

It did not work. For a start the council in Carthage was not in full control of its people. Hasdrubal, who had commanded the army which had eventually been defeated by Massinissa in Numidia, had been condemned for his failure but had evaded punishment. He had since then collected a new army, and was camped about twenty miles from the city at Nepheris, a well-fortified hill. By definition, this force was composed largely of Carthaginian die-hards, and it would be very unlikely that Hasdrubal would give in, at least not easily, and hardly without a fight. In view of this, Rome's plan was impossible to implement from the start.

The Roman forces were transported to Africa in the summer of 149. The consul in command of the army was M. Manilius; his colleague, L. Marcius Censorinus, commanded the fleet. The fact that both consuls were employed overseas at the same time is both a mark of the seriousness of the expedition, and the Roman expectation that it would be a quick and easy victory. Neither man was much of a soldier – Manilius had been defeated in Spain as praetor – but this was not supposed to be a handicap, since the intention was to complete the campaign without serious fighting. (In fact, since they were elected late in 150 to take up office in 149, the Senate probably resolved on war with Carthage after the election, and so was stuck with these consuls.)

The Senate had been opaque in stating its requirements to Carthage, asking only that Carthage 'satisfy' Rome, and when asked how this was to be achieved, remarked that the Carthaginians knew very well.[1] And, of course, so they did – the requirement was for *deditio*. Beyond that, the actual terms to be imposed, once *deditio* was made, were kept from the envoys, partly because they were to be revealed in stages, and partly because this was the normal process the Romans adopted. The consuls gathered an army of four legions – both of the consular forces for the year were commanded by Manilius – and transported them to Africa in the fleet, escorted by fifty quinqueremes commanded by Censorinus.[2] It is noticeable that the prospect of an easy victory and plenty of loot revived the martial ardour of the young Roman males which had faded away two years before at the prospect of serious fighting in Spain's 'fiery war'. Scipio Aemilianus once again was present, as a military tribune in the fourth legion.

Once it was clear that the Roman army was on its way, the Carthaginian envoys at Rome offered to surrender. The Senate required as a preliminary gesture that three hundred sons of prominent Carthaginians should be surrendered as hostages and sent to Lilybaion in Sicily, where the consuls were making final preparations for the crossing to Africa. With understandable reluctance – for their own sons were specifically required – the Gerousia and the Council agreed. The other instruction given by the Senate was that Carthage, having put itself at Rome's disposal, must now obey the consuls' instructions.[3] The hostages were kept in the shelter constructed to house the great Macedonian warship confiscated by Aemilius Paullus – the ship had evidently rotted away by 149.

The fleet crossed from Lilybaion to Utica, and the army, having disembarked, made camp at Castra Cornelia, where Scipio Africanus had camped half a century before. This was undoubtedly a deliberate choice, both because it was close to Carthage and because it would remind the Carthaginians of their earlier defeat. When envoys came out of the city to learn of the Roman decisions, the whole army was drawn up intimidatingly in formation, and the envoys, having been led through the midst of the army, were placed in a roped-off area, symbolically imprisoned. They were then told the first condition, that they surrender any arms in the city, having been promised protection by the Romans against Hasdrubal's army.[4]

A huge amount of armour and weaponry was surrendered, making it clear the city could have been equipped with a large army.[5] It was at that point, with the city thought to be defenceless, that the final set of terms was pronounced: the city was to be evacuated, and a new city (or cities) built at least ten miles from the sea. Carthage would then be physically razed, apart from the temples and the tombs.

The Carthaginian envoys protested loud and long, of course. Censorinus gave the reasons for the decision, curiously speaking, at least according to Appian, as if reasoning over a minor point of law. He said that removing the Carthaginians from the sea would remove them from temptation to piracy, sea wars, trade, and foreign expeditions. The pursuit of agriculture would ensure a much more pleasant, less stressful life.[6] To a Roman senator, most of whom lived by the product of their estates and were prohibited from indulging in trade, this was how life should be. The North African region could certainly support the Carthaginian population, though learning to be farmers, for the sailors and the merchants, would be difficult, no doubt. To Romans, of course, the elimination of the city was the removal of a threat and a rival. To Rome the whole business seemed to make sense, and would avoid bloodshed. It also fitted in with Roman methods of conquest as they had been practised in Italy, for it was one of the tactics they had used, moving a recalcitrant population into new lands. It took absolutely no account of the attitudes, history, and politics of Carthage. It was also, of course, the typical attitude of a great power introspectively concerned only with itself.

The protests by the envoys who first heard the Roman plans were repeated in anguish by the people of the city. This was a far worse fate than had been anticipated. *Deditio* was very rarely followed by actual physical destruction, so presumably some sort of punishment which left the city in existence, perhaps under direct Roman government, had been presumed, no doubt with exile for prominent politicians, as had happened to many Greeks twenty years before. The envoys had asked to be able to send a deputation of protest to Rome, but had been refused; the Senate of the city asked again, and was again refused. Meanwhile the despair amongst the citizens gave way to anger, the city gates were shut, and the walls were manned.[7]

If Manilius and Censorinus were following the path laid out by Lucullus in Spain, they had omitted one crucial ingredient – between the surrender of arms and the order to evacuate, they should have occupied the city's walls, or at least the gates. By omitting this very obvious step they showed themselves complacent, and let their city in for a bitter war. They presumably expected their orders to be obeyed after the ritual of protest, thereby convicting themselves also of a failure of imagination, for to expect the citizens of the city which claimed to be even older than Rome quietly to give in was just silly.

Faced by resistance the consuls did the obvious thing, and attacked the city. It was built on a peninsula, and defended by an encircling wall, which was triple-strength across the Isthmus. Manilius launched an attack on this part, while Censorinus attacked the only really weak part of the defences, at the southern end, where a prolongation of the peninsula had not been so strongly fortified, and so gave a foundation from which to launch an attack on the single-width wall. Both attacks failed, partly because of Roman over-confidence, though it made sense to attack as soon as possible, while the city was presumably unprepared, and the consuls had certainly chosen the best places for their attacks.[8]

Diplomatically, the consuls made contact with old King Massinissa, but his offers of help were not taken up. Had his forces helped to take the city he would have had to be rewarded, and the Senate was not anxious for his power to grow even greater than it already was. The aim was to destroy Carthage's power, not to enhance Massinissa's. They also either persuaded, or compelled, several of Carthage's former allies in Africa to join the Roman side. Besides Utica, they could now count on Hadrumetum, Lepcis, Thapsus, and Acholla; they provided some supplies for the army, though not enough.[9]

Carthage had enlisted the help of Hasdrubal and his army at Nepheris, who could now feel that his intransigence had been justified. He had a quantity of cavalry, and a considerable force of infantry, who proved to be tolerably efficient when tested. This obviously restricted the range of Roman foraging, though Roman control of the sea allowed their ships to bring supplies in from overseas. Hasdrubal moved forward to Tunis, which restricted Roman movements even more. The Romans then had to fortify their own camps before the walls. Another assault brought some success when Censorinus' men broke through the walls on the south. The Carthaginians sortied in the night and damaged the rams being used to attack the walls, and when the Romans broke into the city next day, they found themselves bombarded from the rooftops and had to withdraw.[10]

The star on the Roman side, at least according to the sources, of which Polybios is the main origin of the others, was Scipio Aemilianus, serving as a military tribune once more. (But Polybios was Scipio's friend; it is unlikely he shone quite so brightly as depicted.) To him is attributed a series of actions and precautions which do suggest, however, that he was a natural commander.

He was also, it seems, a political ally of the consul Manilius, which may be how he was able to be present and prominent in several operations. Manilius had also asked Polybios to come to Africa to advise him; Polybios was on his way to Greece at the time, but turned round and obeyed the summons.[11]

In the summer the Roman forces were hampered by sickness, being camped rather too close to the stagnant lake of Tunis. The Carthaginians succeeded in a seaborne raid on the Roman ships which were blockading the approaches to the city; as a result they were able to receive supplies more easily, and were emboldened to begin raiding the land forces. Manilius was forced to spend more time and resources on fortifying his camps, and raiding for supplies. In other words a stalemate had developed.[12]

Censorinus went back to Rome to hold the elections for the next year – this was in the autumn – and Manilius' command was continued until his replacement arrived in the spring of 148. There does not seem to have been any question of proroguing his office. In Rome no doubt there was considerable disappointment that the war had not yet been won, and Censorinus' report when he got back would surely emphasize the difficulties he and Manilius had faced. In addition a command such as this would clearly excite much competition among those eligible to stand for election.

But there were other, wider concerns. By the time the elections arrived, Andriskos in Macedon had burst onto the scene, had overrun that country and made himself king. So one of the new praetors, P. Iuventius Thalna, was assigned the task of removing him with an army, probably of one legion and a legion of Latin allies. Meanwhile in Bithynia the king had been murdered by his son – another usurpation – and a commission of inquiry was to be sent, though since the murder plot had been hatched in Rome this urgency seems redundant. One man with a strong claim to the consulship in 148 was Ser. Sulpicius Galba, but he was damaged by accusations about his conduct of war in Spain. There seems to have been no sense at Rome that a competent general was needed in Africa, so the elections resulted, as usual, in the election of magistrates from among those whose turn it was. There was a move of opinion away from the group to which Manilius belonged. The new consuls were political allies: Sp. Postumius Albinus Magnus, whose family had produced two consuls already in the past few years, and L. Calpurnius Piso Caesoninus, whose family had not reached even the praetorship for two or three generations (apart from himself, of course). Albinus was clearly the senior of the two, but it was Piso who went to Africa, even though, like Manilius (and in fact in the same year) he had been defeated in Spain as praetor. Albinus took Cisalpine Gaul as his province – or was allotted it – and spent his year organizing the layout of a new road, the Via Postumia.[13]

Before being replaced Manilius made an attempt to secure victory. He had already dislodged Hasdrubal from his forward post at Tunis, and that Carthaginian force had returned to Nepheris. A series of foraging expeditions had achieved some success in collecting supplies and in wearing down the Carthaginian cavalry, which was commanded by Himilco Phaemeas, who had gained some early successes in cavalry fights. Once again Scipio Aemilianus distinguished himself in these raids by his care and professionalism.

Manilius brought part of his army – probably two legions – to attack Hasdrubal and Himilco at Nepheris. The initial encounter was successful for the Romans, and the Carthaginians retreated to their hilltop fort. The Romans broke formation to cross a wadi and Hasdrubal launched a counter-attack while they were in disarray. Once more Scipio is given the credit for covering the crossing and holding off the attack, though a group of four infantry maniples was cut off and left behind. When this loss was discovered Scipio took the cavalry back and attacked the besieging force from an unexpected direction, so rescuing the maniples. The retirement of the Roman forces was harassed by Himilco's horsemen, and by a sortie from the city. Manilius then took his army back to Castra Cornelia into winter quarters.[14]

A commission came from Rome to investigate the situation. It was supposedly met with praise for Scipio, which is no doubt the case, but not the whole case. A more practical result was that Massinissa was again contacted, and this time he was asked to provide assistance. Himilco's cavalry had been all too successful, and reinforcements of Numidian horsemen would counter him. Massinissa was found by the Roman envoys to be dying (though it seems more than likely that the Romans knew this already), and by the time the messengers had returned to the camp and another envoy had been sent out he was dead. Scipio, the grandson of the conqueror of Carthage, went to Cirta, Massinissa's city, to act as executor of the old man's will.

Most of Massinissa's many sons had been provided for already, having been assigned estates for their upkeep. These bequests Scipio confirmed, and supplemented their inheritance by a distribution of commemorative treasures from the king's hoard. Massinissa himself was replaced by a collective kingship of three of his sons: Micipsa, Gulussa, and Mastanabal. From Rome's immediate viewpoint Gulussa was the most important, since he was made commander of the forces. He was persuaded to contribute the horsemen Massinissa had been asked for, in order to search out Himilco's country bases.[15] (The Numidian kingdom was clearly considerably weakened by Massinissa's death. The tripartite kingship was unlikely to last long, and in fact Micipsa soon emerged as sole king, his colleague-brothers opportunely dying.)

Under the new pressure Himilco indicated in a chance interview with Scipio that he was amenable to be persuaded to desert – but not yet. Manilius came out of winter quarters to attack Hasdrubal at Nepheris once more. During the operations Himilco made contact again and then deserted with 2,200 of his men, though just as many remained loyal to Carthage. Between them Scipio, Gulussa, and Himilco then gathered up enough supplies by foraging to help the Roman army return to camp. Hasdrubal, though hurt by the loss of a large part of his cavalry, could claim a defensive victory.[16]

Manilius' replacement, Calpurnius Piso, arrived soon after. Manilius, presumably concerned that his achievement was being criticized, carefully sent Scipio off to Rome first, taking Himilco with him as an obvious prize. The army is said to have demonstrated loudly in acclamation of Scipio's prowess as he left – or at least part of it did – and no doubt news of this got back to Rome as well. When Manilius returned to Rome himself he could be sure that his own lack of achievement would not be held too much against him.[17]

Piso had much the same experience as Manilius. He was faced by a besieged city which had been much encouraged by the Romans' setbacks, to such an extent that there was talk of a Carthaginian victory. The commander in the city, another Hasdrubal, knew better, as did anyone with sense, but he was politically vulnerable in that his mother had been one of Massinissa's daughters, and Gulussa and his brothers were thus his uncles. In the febrile atmosphere of a city under siege, this sort of thing produced suspicions. In addition, the victories of the other Hasdrubal at Nepheris and in the field contrasted strongly with the less spectacular success of the city in resisting its blockade.[18]

Piso took up the same strategy as Manilius. He identified the main problem as Rome's inability to control the open country, which forced the Roman army into fortified camps and restricted supplies, making it impossible to exert the full force of the army on the city. So he concentrated on attacking these other places. He had some success, though the account we have of his activities deliberately emphasizes his defeats in order to highlight the previous and future achievements of Scipio. He is said to have failed to capture Aspis, on the eastern end of Cape Bon, but he did take Neapolis, along the coast to the south. An attack on Hippagreta, or Hippocritae, an old fort, turned into a prolonged siege. Meanwhile, though no mention of this is made, the city itself continued to be blockaded. It seems probable that some of Piso's successes have vanished from the record, for, combined with the earlier achievements of Manilius, the Romans now held almost all the coast, and dominated the interior with the help of Gulussa's horsemen.[19]

The minor successes of the Carthaginians at Hippagreta and Aspis, and the continued existence of Hasdrubal's army outside the city, had the effect in the city of heightening expectations of, at least, survival. Contact was made by the Carthaginians with the king of the Mauri, to the west of Numidia, probably in the hope that he would draw the attention of the Numidian kings away. Contact was also made with Andriskos – 'King Philip' – in Macedon. The desertion of a group of Numidian horsemen to the Carthaginian side encouraged an approach to Micipsa.[20]

None of these diplomatic initiatives had any result. It was only inside the city that the Roman campaign looked as though it was not succeeding. To everyone else it was obvious that Rome would persist until victory; the cities of Side in Pamphylia and Rhodes sent ships to assist the Roman campaign, and probably others did as well. None of these was significant in numerical terms – though the Sidetans were notably skilful in a later fight – but they were clear signs, if the Carthaginians could have seen it, that they had no support other than a few adventurous mercenaries.[21] The Numidian connections of Hasdrubal the commander in the city may have been the origin of the attempt to contact Micipsa and his brothers. His failure in this may well have been the signal for a *coup*, and he was accused of planning a betrayal, and then beaten to death by his fellow councillors. The command in the city was handed to the other Hasdrubal, who remained for the present outside the city with his army, clearly understanding that his authority depended on securing more minor victories.[22]

In Rome the claimed lack of success of Piso was exploited by Scipio Aemilianus. The elections for the officials for 147 were held late in 148. The presiding consul was Postumius, back from his Cisalpine command, while Piso remained at his command in Africa. But Postumius faced a tumultuous situation, in which crowds had been incited to demand the election of Scipio to the consulship, though he was in fact a candidate for aedile, and not legally entitled to stand for anything else. He had not yet been praetor, a legal requirement for a consular candidacy, and he was too young to be eligible anyway. Yet he was elected, after a popular campaign in which the Senate was overborne by a mass near-uprising. The legal requirements were repealed for a year, when a tribune interposed his veto on the whole electoral process. The Senate, faced by the threat that no magistrates would be elected, gave in.[23]

Scipio had, on the face of it, not intervened personally, and had certainly not put his name forward. His claim ever after was that he had been elected by the will of the people. On the other hand, he could clearly have stopped the agitation by simply refusing to become involved and stating publicly that he was not and could not be a candidate. He was, of course, behind the whole process. One of the arguments put forward during the crisis was that election lay with the people and that artificial limits – age and experience requirements established by law – should not stand in the face of the people's will. In fact, of course, it was a *coup d'état*, of a peculiarly Roman sort, carried out by and on behalf of Scipio.

He could certainly put forward some convincing qualifications – his military skills, about which some of the soldiers in Africa had written home, his family connections, his diplomatic ties with the Numidians – though other men had such experience and connections and were not elected – Galba, for example. And his *coup* was, to some of his opponents at least, justified by his later success in Africa. Yet it was nonetheless a *coup*, a seizure of office carried out in defiance of the laws. That the laws were a senatorial construction designed to restrict the public offices to men of whom the Senate approved and which were therefore anti-democratic and illogical, is not the point. The result, in the longer term, was to push on the destruction of the senatorial constitution as it had existed since Hannibal's War, a process, of course, already begun by the illegal re-election of M. Claudius Marcellus to the consulship five years before.

Scipio set out for Africa again in the spring of 147, no doubt as soon as he could sail with safety. The news of his election and of his coming seems to have stimulated Piso into further activity. The commander of the fleet, L. Hostilius Mancinus, made a landing from the sea at a place he judged to be less well defended than elsewhere. He got 500 soldiers and 3,000 sailors on shore, and broke through into the city, but his further advance was blocked. The improvisation now turned into a trap, for he had brought no supplies and had no reinforcements within reach. Messages went out to the camp, to Utica, even to Piso, who was in the interior, asking for help and reinforcements.

Scipio, as it happened, arrived at that moment. He arranged a relief expedition, carrying a large-seeming force by sea. By the time they arrived at Mancinus' breach, the invaders had been driven back to the shore; Scipio's ships took them off before they were actually driven into the sea. Later, Mancinus used this episode to claim that he had been the first into the city – ignoring the earlier failed attack by Censorinus in the south – and there was a dispute as to whether Scipio 'rescued' a failed attack, or prevented an exploitation of a glorious opportunity. The best conclusion was that improvisations in such conditions do not work, and that the Carthaginians were still fully capable of a vigorous resistance.[24]

Scipio tightened up on discipline in the army, claiming to believe that Piso had let it slacken off.[25] He sent Mancinus back to Rome and installed Serranus — probably an Atilius, a family which used that cognomen — as fleet commander. We know the names of a few others of his officers: C. Laelius was the grandson of the companion of the original Africanus, C. Fannius, and Ti. Sempronius Gracchus. Polybios was still in, or had returned to, Africa, as his friend and adviser.[26]

Hasdrubal and his outside army were still an effective force, and the city was still receiving supplies, in part because Hasdrubal was able to collect them and send them in by ship, and partly because he had established a second camp close to the walls of the city. Scipio, having the benefit of the control of a good deal of the coast and of the interior as a result of the campaigns of his predecessors — not acknowledged, of course — was able to concentrate on blockading and assaulting the city. A night attack on a part of the single-line section of the wall (as Censorinus had done two years before), seized a gate and got some troops into the city inside the walls.

The threat brought Hasdrubal and much of its force into the city, which had been Scipio's intention. His assault had been no stronger than that of Mancinus', and he would never expect it to succeed in taking the whole city. But it did cause a panic, and this is what brought Hasdrubal to move many of his men inside the walls. Scipio brought his assault force out, destroyed Hasdrubal's fort near the walls and spread his army out across the Isthmus.[27] To complete the blockade the men were set to dig a ditch and rampart facing the city, and another ditch in parallel behind him. The army then camped in this space between the lines.[28]

Inside the city Hasdrubal established his dictatorial control by killing opponents and directing the better part of the food supplies to the soldiers. Some food still arrived by ship, running the Roman blockade, and more was produced in the open areas of the city.[29] Scipio mounted an operation to block the entrance to the harbour by constructing a mole. This led to a complicated series of fights involving ships and men, a new canal and a new wall, but the net result was that the Carthaginians were finally completely blockaded, and all outside supplies were prevented from entering.[30]

The end was thus now inevitable so long as the Roman forces remained on the alert and blocked any breakout attempts. While waiting for the end Scipio led mobile forces to seize control of any remaining Carthaginian posts in the countryside. This included a siege of Nepheris, which was only taken after a series of assaults on the fort and the town. Then the only stronghold left to the Carthaginians was the city itself. They had no allies, no outside help, and no supplies.[31]

Deserters from the city provided regular information about conditions inside as they steadily worsened. An offer of life, liberty, and riches was made to induce Hasdrubal to desert, or perhaps to organize a surrender, but it was unsuccessful.[32] At last in the spring of 146, the final assault on the weakened population began. Scipio had plenty of time, for, unlike Manilius or Piso, his command had been prorogued, probably because it was at last obvious that the end was close, and a new commander would probably have nothing to do. The end of winter, before any supplies could be produced in the town, was the point at which the defenders were at their weakest. An assault on the damaged area near the harbour was eventually successful in getting some men onto the city wall. The defenders set the market area on fire to delay any further assault, and withdrew to the citadel, the Byrsa, defending the approaches to it by holding the tall apartment buildings lining the streets which led up to the gates.

There followed the most vicious part of the fighting, street by street, apartment building by building, floor by floor, an ancient Stalingrad. When the Romans had cleared the area it was burned to the ground, the fire lasting six days.[33] At that point the way to the citadel was open, and envoys came out begging to be allowed to surrender. Scipio agreed, and 50,000 starving people went into captivity. The last act was staged by a group of 900 Roman deserters who faced instant execution with no option if they were to surrender. They fought on. Even Hasdrubal surrendered, reviled by his wife and children just before they, along with the deserters, threw themselves into the fire.[34]

The fighting had lasted three years in place of the original plan to secure a bloodless, virtually immediate, surrender. In the process much of the countryside had been ravaged and many of the country towns destroyed. Utica and half a dozen towns did survive; they were the old Phoenician settlements along the coast, contemporary with Carthage, which had been subject allies in much the same way as the Latins were allied to Rome. The two states, Rome and Carthage, were in many ways mirror images; they usually communicated with each other in Greek. The Roman Senate now had to decide what it was to do with this ravaged land. And in the meantime a similar problem had developed in Macedonia and Greece.

Chapter 9

The Sack of Corinth

The reconquest of Macedonia by a Roman army under Q. Caecilius Metellus in 148 placed a potent Roman force in the Balkan Peninsula for the first time for twenty years. As in earlier armed interventions by Rome in the region, the army stayed on for a time after its victory. It was no doubt expected in Greece and Macedon that it would once more be withdrawn to Italy, though to do so would leave the whole region once more open to attack by the barbarian tribes to the north. The adventure of Andriskos had been distinctly unwelcome in Greece: the Thessalians had appealed for help against him, and the Achaian League had sent its forces north to oppose him, even if there had been a certain gloomy satisfaction at the early Roman discomfiture. All concerned had co-operated with Rome in suppressing Andriskos, yet this was done to protect themselves in Greece against the sudden revival of Macedonian armed power, not because the Greeks liked being subject to Rome, however light the burden. Indeed they may well have opposed Andriskos in the hope of obviating a new Roman presence.

The defining moment in relations between the Greek states and Rome had come in 167, when the last Romano-Macedonian War had ended. Having with great difficulty finally lined up the Greeks on their side by a mixture of threats and promises, Rome used its victory to turn on those Greek states which were deemed insufficiently supportive, which meant, in fact, almost every one. It was not even enough to point to a general attitude of friendship towards Rome to avoid punishment. Mere neutrality or lukewarmness was equated with enmity.

Roman actions were designed to cull and intimidate, and for a time it was successful in this. In Macedonia, the conqueror M. Aemilius Paullus (Scipio Aemilianus' natural father) received delegations of congratulatory envoys from every Greek state. They also came with complaints about fellow citizens whose opinions were anything from enthusiastic about Rome to bitterly hostile. All this saved the Romans the effort of investigation. Paullus obligingly had some of these men killed, but many more were ordered into exile in Italy.[1]

Some territorial changes were made as well as the destruction, looting, and dismemberment of Macedonia. Aitolia had been an ally of Rome in the war, but was shorn of several areas; its leaders had already massacred over 500 of their internal opponents; these murderers were now acquitted of any blame by Paullus, who had in fact no legal authority to do so – he also executed another Aitolian, Andronikos, whom he found in Macedon.[2] Boeotia had sided with Macedon and its league had already been broken up; now one political leader who was supposed to have induced the alliance with Macedonia, Neon of Thebes, was executed.[3] A town in Lesbos, Antissa, which some Macedonian ships had used as a base, was destroyed.[4] That is, Paullus was using his predominant military position to pay back those whose minor contributions to the war on the enemy side had, however briefly, impeded the Roman conquest.

But this programme of retribution was not, as the Aitolians had discovered, confined to Rome's enemies, major or minor. Virtually every Greek state, neutral, enemy, or ally, was visited with Roman wrath. But particularly it was neutrality which had annoyed Rome, since this had put Rome and Macedon on a basis of equality. So two major Greek states were punished, and another was deemed insufficiently enthusiastic and suffered even more severely.

The island city of Rhodes had eventually attempted to mediate, which again implied that Rome and Macedon were equal in moral and political terms. This suggestion the Romans could not entertain. So Rhodes was punished by being ordered to surrender control of a mainland region in Lycia which had been awarded to the city by Rome at the end of the previous war. This was less of a punishment than it seemed, since Rhodes had been having considerable difficulty in exerting control over that region. The city's real power lay in its commercial prosperity and its naval expertise, the second being dependent upon the first. To reduce its importance therefore the Senate gave the holy island of Delos to Athens, and designated it as a free port. It rapidly became the preferred host to the Aegean slave market, and a major entrepot for other goods.[5]

The Achaian League had remained neutral during the war, like Rhodes, and when Paullus examined the Macedonian archives nothing incriminating was found against any of the Achaian leaders, though evidence was found and used against other states. But the Roman attitude by now was suspicion of everyone who had not spontaneously and enthusiastically participated in the war on the Roman side. Two of the ten commissioners sent by the Senate to assist Paullus in the peace settlement were sent by him to Achaia. They had come from Rome at the end of the fighting, and had more up-to-date instructions from the Senate, which is undoubtedly where their actions originated.

The two men, C. Claudius Pulcher and Cn. Domitius Ahenobarbus, met the Achaians at a specially called meeting. They had been advised by Kallikrates, a prominent politician of blatantly pro-Roman leanings, and by others of the same persuasion, but apparently chose not to use the list of the names of the men they had presumably supplied. These were, of course, primarily political enemies of the Kallikrates group, and so the product of internal enmities. Instead the Roman envoys cast their net even wider, demanding that the Achaians condemn – either to death or to exile – all those who were suspected by the Romans. Not surprisingly the Achaians objected on various grounds, as a neutral state not subject to Roman authority, as a firm Roman ally even though they had not helped in the war, and that to vote blindly to condemn men without even knowing who they were was clearly wrong. Pulcher, who probably did the talking since he was the senior of the two Romans (consul in 177, censor in 168), then stated that all the Achaian generals were guilty – though he had not yet directly accused them of anything. One man got up and said he had been a general, and was willing to stand trial either in Achaia or at Rome, presumably daring the Romans to accept the offer. But this is exactly what the Romans did. They picked out a thousand prominent Achaians and sent them to Italy. There was no resistance in Achaia to this. Once in Italy, no trial was organized, of course; after all they had not been accused of a crime, therefore they could not be found guilty.[6] Alternatively, Rome said they were guilty, and therefore they were guilty. The 'crime' was implicit in the sentence.

Epeiros was treated to an even more unpleasant punishment. There, suspicion rested mainly on the Molossians, the most prominent of the several tribes making up the Epeirote Confederacy. The peace settlement had already been imposed on the region, and the political leaders had been exiled 'for trial' to Italy, but as the Roman army marched through Epeiros on its way to the Adriatic ports for shipment home, Paullus gave the soldiers permission to sack the whole country. The loot of Macedon, which they might have expected to share in, had mainly gone to the Roman state, and the sack of Epeiros was a sort of compensation for the men. They set to with a will; it is said that 150,000 prisoners were sold into slavery, for the benefit of the soldiers. The land was left desolate for the next generation.[7]

These experiences were obviously still in Greek minds when they faced the prospect of another Roman army stationed in Macedon from 148. It showed no sign of moving back to Italy while Macedon was still disturbed; it was still there in 147 when a new crisis in Achaia reached its peak, involving both the integrity of the league and its relations with Rome.

It had become the ambition of the leaders of the Achaian League to unify the whole Peloponnese. This had been achieved in 188 under the generalship of Philopoemon of Megalopolis, who came from a city which, while a member of the league, was also an old enemy of Sparta. The two least enthusiastic league members had been Messenia and Sparta, and while Messenia was more or less reconciled to membership, Sparta was not; indeed Philopoemon had forced Sparta to become a member. Several times between 188 and 160 Spartan delegations appealed to Rome to allow the city to secede.[8] The Romans were quite happy to be appealed to. The Achaians, of course, detested the practice, since it implied Roman suzerainty over the league, a status which the Achaians rejected. The Roman insistence on the exile of the thousand politicians in 167, however, was a clear demonstration of their power. The Achaians, of course, had legality on their side, since they had concluded an alliance agreement with Rome as between equals, and so technically had full control over their internal affairs. But in political terms, no alliance of these two states could possibly be between equals; Rome was simply too powerful. Yet Achaia could not accept the discrepancy in power without abandoning all pretence at independence.

Roman behaviour in Greece in 167–166, therefore, had been designed to make quite clear that Greek opposition would not be tolerated, and that even neutrality was not good enough. Its deliberate and calculated breaking of previous agreements – as with the Achaean alliance – was typical behaviour by a great power. In their days of power, both Athens and Sparta had behaved in the same way towards states inferior in power to themselves. This is clearly one of the explanations for the Achaian reaction to the collapse of the Roman organization of Macedon – not that this was remembered when the crisis came.

While Kallikrates lived he acted as the necessary contact and pipeline between Achaia and Rome, fending off Achaian resentment, mollifying Roman arrogance. The continuing irritant was the problem of the exiles, and Achaian envoys repeatedly asked that their missing men be allowed to return home – there never was a trial, of course.[9] At last in 151 the Senate agreed that the survivors could return – to be buried in Achaia, not Italy, as Cato joked.[10] Not all of them bothered – Polybios stayed on in Rome, though he was now free to visit Achaia, as he did in 146.[11] Probably not by coincidence the issue of Spartan-Achaian relations revived at the same time.

The Spartan politician Menalkidas was elected general of the league in that year, 151, the first (and only) Spartan to reach that position, which might be taken as a sign that it was thought that Sparta was at last reconciled to membership of the league. But he and Kallikrates became involved in a complicated quarrel over dividing up a bribe and Menalkidas escaped condemnation by bribing his successor as general, Diaios of Megalopolis. Then in the process of his struggle to escape the toils enmeshing him, Menalkidas raised the issue of Sparta's independence once more. In turn Diaios may well have been one of the returned exiles, but even if he was not, he was very strongly anti-Roman. Kallikrates had, in effect, been Rome's man in Achaia since 167, and had been partly responsible for the selection of those who were to be exiled. He is routinely execrated in the sources, which go back to Polybios, as 'the wickedest man in Greece' who had 'brought Achaians into an utter subjection to Rome'.[12] In this tangle of internal enmities it is quite possible that the story of the various bribes was invented, or at least exaggerated.

Certainly it seems that the bribery affair was a cover for an attempt to smear Menalkidas and solidify support behind Kallikrates. The underlying issue was always Spartan separatism, as it seems probable that Menalkidas had recently visited Rome to argue once more for this, but without result. (It was not a good time to attempt to contact the Senate on any subject but Spain or Carthage.) But the trial of Menalkidas, far from helping Kallikrates, only influenced Spartan opinion still more against continuing membership of the league. The trial could therefore be, and was, used by Kallikrates' local enemies to inflict a political defeat on him, led by Diaios. In other words, the return of the exiles had emboldened the Achaian opposition, while the Spartan separatists were also encouraged. But so far the dispute was essentially an internal political matter inside the Achaian League. Rome was not paying much attention.

Diaios, presumably feeling he had Menalkidas under control, then attempted to cut the ground from under the Spartan protests. A Spartan embassy went to Rome. At this Diaios, pointing out that this was illegal under the league's practices, mustered the league army and invaded Lakonia. Once there he demanded the exiling of twenty-four leading Spartans, including Menalkidas, thus taking a leaf out of Rome's book. The Spartan *gerousia*, until then a moribund institution, complied, but the exiles immediately set off to Rome as their own quasi-official embassy.

No doubt the Roman Senate was confused by all this, and the senators probably had no clear idea of what was going on in the Peloponnese. They relied for their information on the claims and counter-claims of the various embassies and exile groups. And now Kallikrates set out for Rome in order to answer this Spartan group's accusations, and to attempt to secure Roman support for his own position, which was being eroded by such men as Diaios. If anybody from Achaia was trusted at Rome it was Kallikrates, but he died on the journey.[13]

This was now 149, the year of Andriskos' success in Macedon, of the fuss in Rome over Galba's treatment of the Lusitani, of the declaration of war on Carthage, and of the despatch of the Roman army to Sicily and North Africa. So one Roman army was being sent to North Africa, and an intricate series of successive demands was being presented to the Carthaginians; then Andriskos' sudden appearance called forth another Roman army, which was quickly defeated. In the midst of all this the never-ending repetitive dispute between the Achaian League and its Spartan member was an irrelevant distraction for the Senate. The death of Kallikrates was perhaps in a way welcome, since it put off for a time the need to pay any attention to Greek affairs. Diaios took Kallikrates' place in the embassy to Rome.

Pre-occupied, the Senate gave an ambiguous response to both embassies, and both Diaios and Menalkidas went home believing that they had gained their point. But Menalkidas' version was the trigger for action, whereas Diaios reckoned that his actions had been vindicated. Therefore, persuaded by Menalkidas' interpretation of the Roman message, in 148 Sparta seceded from the league. This can hardly have come as a surprise to the Romans when they heard, since their replies to both delegations had been deliberately worded so that both would go away happy. To the league, of course, those words had given it the authority to suppress any Spartan move. So the Roman reply had merely brought both sides to the point of action whereas before they had merely been arguing.[14]

And yet one cannot entirely blame the Senate. It is clear that Menalkidas was pushing his secession agenda even when operating as general of the league. It is also clear that the return of the Achaian exiles had infused a much stronger strain of anti-Roman feeling into Achaian politics. It did not help that the Achaians tended to elect generals from Megalopolis − Diaios was only the latest − who arrived at the centre of power fully equipped with vigorously anti-Spartan feelings. The Spartans meanwhile not only aimed to secede from their unwanted status as league subordinates, but they also repeatedly picked quarrels with their neighbours over territories which had been Spartan in the days of its power centuries earlier but had been lost since, and were now wanted back. They quarrelled in this way with Argos and Megalopolis and Messenia, and eyed also the small ex-Spartan towns and villages east of the Parnon range.[15] To quarrel with every neighbour when one does not have the power to succeed in the argument is politically stupid, but this is what the Spartans did. They also − or some of them − believed that the way to recover their military strength was to reinstate the old Spartan social regime, which had been designed to produce fearless soldiers. This, naturally, was opposed by those neighbours, for their own self-preservation.

Into this dispute intervened the Roman campaigns against Andriskos. The precise timing of these is not certain, but Thalna's expedition and defeat seems to have happened in 149. The Thessalians appealed to Achaia for help, and an Achaian army went north, where it operated with the survivors of Thalna's force and then with the army brought over by Q. Caecilius Metellus in 148. (One wonders if any Spartans were part of the Achaian force.) The Achaians could be pleased with themselves in all this; they certainly garnered a good deal of goodwill in the rest of Greece as a result. The city of Herakleia-by-Oeta, in front of the Thermopylai pass, appears to have joined the league, perhaps at this point. It was an old Spartan colony, ironically, and did not stay a member for long. (We only know this because the league was ordered to release it in 147.[16])

Sparta's secession from the league took place amid all this uncertainty, quite possibly taking advantage of the absence of the league army in the north. The action posed a danger both to the league and to Sparta's neighbours. The league promptly declared war. An army commanded by the general for 148/147, Damokritos, invaded from the north and defeated the Spartan army, a defeat which cost a thousand Spartan lives. The surviving Spartans scampered rapidly back into the city. Damokritos, presuming that his task was achieved, and probably unwilling to waste Achaian lives in an assault on the city walls, took his army home.

Another reason for staying his hand was that the Roman commander Metellus now intervened. He had received a visit by a Roman commission which was heading for Asia. This is presumably the three-man commission which was going to investigate the death of King Prusias in Bithynia. Metellus persuaded them to go by way of Achaia (though it is likely that they would do so anyway, since the obvious route from Italy to Asia was through the Gulf of Corinth, with a passage through Corinth to the Aegean). The commissioners arrived after Damokritos had invaded Lakonia. They met with the senior Achaians and Damokritos, and presumably it was their warning which helped to deter Damokritos from attacking Sparta city, though it is reported that he paid them no attention and went ahead with the battle.

The anti-Spartans in the league, however, wanted more, and in particular they wanted military control of Sparta city. Damokritos was surely aware that this would not please the Roman Senate, which had repeatedly favoured the Spartans in the various quarrels. But the anti-Spartans had fused with the anti-Romans, and Damokritos was accused of 'betraying Achaian interests' by halting his campaign, and was fined heavily, at which he went into exile.

The Achaian army must have gone straight from assisting the Romans against Andriskos to the campaign in Lakonia. There was then a period of time – several weeks at least – during which Damokritos was prosecuted. Once he was condemned Diaios took over as general of the league and prepared to finish what Damokritos failed to do. However, when he mustered the army again with the intention of finishing Sparta off, he also was deterred by a Roman message, this time directly from Metellus. He, commanding a Roman army and reasonably close, had the authority to convince and insist. Diaios agreed to a truce, and to wait for the arrival of another Roman commission, but he did occupy a series of towns north of Sparta city in the meantime.[17] These Achaian expeditions had prevented the fields being sown, so starvation threatened Sparta as well.

Menalkidas was Diaios' opponent. He responded by attacking a place called Iasos, location unknown, but probably a border town somewhere towards Megalopolis. This paradoxically brought down on him the wrath of the Spartans, for his adventure seems to have been a private venture, which could be interpreted as a breaking of the truce, and so might leave the city open to attack. He committed suicide.[18] On the other hand, no doubt he would have been greeted as a hero had he succeeded.

At much the same time, the summer of 147, the Roman commission promised back in 149 finally arrived. At last it seemed that the Roman Senate was actually looking to solve the 'Achaian problem', as they may have regarded it. No doubt the three-man commission in 148 had sent a report before going on to Bithynia, and Metellus will have done the same, so the Senate at last had some information which was not tainted by partisan interpretation, probably for the first time in a decade or more, certainly for the first time since the return of the Achaian exiles.

The commission was headed by L. Aurelius Orestes; there were other members, probably two, but their names are not known. He was fairly familiar with the region, having been on an embassy back in 163; he had been consul in 157. He arrived after the Senate had had time to gain some understanding of what was going on in Greece, from the reports by on-the-spot commissioners and legates, and when it had become all but certain that Scipio Aemilianus would be able to finish off Carthage reasonably soon, while Metellus had already done the same in Macedon. The Senate therefore had had time at last to discuss Achaia. Roman confidence was no doubt riding high in the wake of these victories, and drastic measures were now to be taken to stop the constant bickering in the Peloponnese. The Roman solution, as in Africa and Macedon, was destruction, preferably political but, if necessary, physical.

Orestes called a meeting with Diaios, the general of the league, and the elected magistrates of the cities which were its members. This was intended to be an informal but semi-official gathering, and it took place at the house where Orestes was staying (its location is never stated, but it was probably not in any of the main cities). He told them what the Senate wanted to happen: that not only Sparta, but Corinth, Argos, Herakleia-by-Oeta and Orchomenos should be detached from the league into independence.

The ploy of beginning with a private meeting immediately backfired. Without waiting for Orestes to finish – and so probably never learning Rome's reasons, not that this mattered – his audience rushed out to spread the bad news. Diaios called a meeting of the league Assembly, by which time rumour and exaggeration had no doubt taken hold. When he explained what Orestes had told him the delegates exploded with anger. When the news spread there was an anti-Spartan riot in Corinth in which Orestes felt that he had been personally threatened. Spartans, or anyone looking like a Spartan, were chased, and those caught were murdered. Those who survived were jailed.[19]

Rather more constructively a new league envoy, Thearidas, was sent to Rome to protest and/or negotiate. By that time Orestes had himself returned to Rome, and had made his report to the Senate; Polybios says he exaggerated the danger he had been in. The Senate decided to send another embassy to insist, and chose Orestes' consular colleague in 157, Sex. Iulius Caesar, as the leader. On their journey, they met Thearidas, who turned back to accompany them. Clearly his message to the Senate was now redundant.[20]

Caesar reached Corinth after Diaios' term had expired, and so had to deal with the new Achaian general, a man called Kritolaos. The Achaian elections took place in the autumn, and Polybios points out that the fighting against Carthage was still going on (and so this is the autumn of 147). Caesar's message was conciliatory – Rome evidently had no wish to be involved in yet another war at that time. He largely ignored the insult to Orestes and worked hard to persuade the Achaians to accept his arbitration over the dispute with Sparta. But the order brought by Orestes to remove the four cities from the league was not rescinded, even if Caesar seems not to have mentioned it.

Kritolaos is regarded by the sources – principally Polybios, of course – as a determined anti-Roman. He held governing power for a year, and was only controlled by the six-monthly meetings of the Assembly, which took place in autumn and spring. He decoyed Caesar to a proposed meeting at Tegea in Arkadia, where Caesar was supposed to arrange the arbitration, but meanwhile Kritolaos organized that the league's delegates should absent themselves, and then said he could do nothing until the next Assembly chose more delegates in the spring. When Caesar finally realized he was being hoodwinked, he left for Italy in anger.[21]

The Achaians had thus ignored three Roman commissioners, the Roman commander in Macedon, Metellus, and two special envoys, who had been so angered by their reception that they had left in fury. This was scarcely sensible behaviour. No wonder Polybios heaped blame on the Achaians – though it was Rome which was the aggressor. There is, however, no doubt that the Achaians knew what they were doing, and Diaios and Kritolaos had strong public support. And they knew what was coming.

Having gained several months of breathing space, Kritolaos spent the winter of 147–146 organizing for war and conducting diplomacy. A stop on payment of debts was ordered, as was an extra tax levy on the rich.[22] The population was roused to enthusiasm in defence of their league, in part by a speaking tour by Kritoalos, and when the decision was taken on war, at the spring Assembly of 146, attendance was unprecedentedly high. Diplomatically the Boiotians, who had their own disputes with Metellus over fines he had imposed on them for attacking their neighbours, indicated that they were willing to join in, and so did the Lokrians and Chalkis in Euboia also.[23]

At the spring Assembly a declaration of war was made against Sparta. As Polybios says, it was 'in reality directed against Rome'.[24] This took place at Corinth, where a delegation of four Romans arrived, sent by Metellus in Macedon. This was the third time he had intervened, and once more he was unsuccessful. The four men spoke in the same terms as Caesar, that is, in conciliatory terms, but without withdrawing the Roman demand for the four cities to be separated from the league. They were hooted and jeered out of the meeting.[25]

In Rome meanwhile there had been elections. The new consuls for 146 were Cn. Cornelius Lentulus and L. Mummius. The former is more or less an unknown entity in the records, though he was from a distinguished family, but Mummius is an interesting man. In his praetorship in Spain, like almost every praetor, he met defeat, but then recovered, built up his forces again, and returned to gain a victory, which was clear and large enough to win him a triumph. For a *novus homo*, this was a very creditable record in Roman terms. As consul he would have expected to be allocated the command against Carthage, the only war the republic was then fighting, but it was impossible to prise Scipio Aemilianus away; his irregular appointment had probably been made by a special law, and replacing him would therefore need another law, which would likely be blocked by a tribune acting in Scipio's interest. In any case it was obvious by the time of the election (late in 147) that the Carthaginian war was almost over. This was not what he wanted, so a different war was his target.[26]

The Senate had received more reports about the situation in Greece, from Metellus, from Caesar, and it seems from some commissioners who had stayed on there after Caesar had left.[27] It was known that all through the winter the Achaians were building up to a new war. They had been forbidden already to attack Sparta, and had been ordered to break up the league. To neither of these instructions had they been obedient. Successive attempts by Romans – Metellus more than once, Orestes, Caesar – had been made to persuade the Achaians to comply with Roman demands, and all had been unsuccessful. The Achaians could not claim they had not been warned. By the spring of 146 Metellus could report that the war had begun. Here was the war for Mummius. The Senate authorized him to levy a new army, and a fleet to move the troops to Greece. He aimed to land close to Corinth.

The Achaian army, well accustomed by now to mustering and marching off to war, after three campaigns in the last three years, was first off the mark, probably soon after the spring Assembly meeting. It cannot have been a surprise that the order to muster was given, though the army did march off before all the troops had arrived – a contingent of Arkadians and another from Patrai, at least, were still marching well after the first battle had taken place.

The urgency was perhaps due to the news from the north. First the city of Herakleia-by-Oeta, one of those designated by the Senate to be separated, had taken this news as an accomplished fact, and, at least from the Achaian point of view, was 'in rebellion'.[28] Second, the insult to the four Romans Metellus had sent to the Corinth meeting forced him to react. The news of the declaration of war on Sparta had to be interpreted as a disguised declaration against Rome, and he had earlier warned the Achaians twice not to attack Sparta. He would therefore need to move against them.

The Achaians were fully aware that they were liable to be attacked both from the north by Metellus' army, and by an army from Italy. Their plan was thus to meet Metellus as far north as they could, given that they were allied with the Boiotians, and as it appears, some of the Lokrians as well. The earliest troops to muster were thus sent north to seize Herakleia, and were joined by Boiotians on the way. Some parts of the Achaian forces were retained, notably those of Elis and Messenia, who stayed in their homelands to guard against a possible Roman landing from the sea. Troops mustered later, or who had to march further, therefore followed the first contingents northwards. It is evident that the men from Patrai crossed to Lokris by sea, and the Arkadians will have marched by land. The earliest contingent was thus probably the men of Corinth and Sikyon and the old original cities of the league, and Argos and the Argolid – two of these were cities scheduled for separation.

Metellus' four legates had no doubt sent the news of their reception to him, but they remained in Greece. Presumably by pre-arrangement Mancinus went to Naupaktos, Cn. Papirius went to Athens and then on to Sparta, and the other two, Popillius Laenus and C. Fannius, went to Athens and stayed there.[29] These locations enabled them to exercise some control over their hosts – the Aitolians and the Athenians to remain neutral, Sparta to be reassured and to keep its troops at home. (Rome this time was determined to do the job with its own people; there would be no conciliation of allies this time; and neutrality was the required (in-) action of all.) They were well placed also to gather intelligence and to report. The men at Athens could report to Metellus by sea; Mancinus from Naupaktos could report to Italy. In addition, at Thebes was A. Postumius Albinus (consul in 151), a noted hellenophile. Metellus, of course, had had a full year and more to plan what he would do in the event of a war with Achaia; the movements of these men are clear evidence of his pre-planning.

What must have been unexpected was the participation of much of central Greece on the Achaian side, and the arrival of the Achaian army just to the south of Thessaly to attack Herakleia. Given the city's location it is obvious that the Achaians had set off first, no doubt hoping to defeat Metellus, or at least hold him off, before Mummius' army could arrive. On the other hand, Kritolaos, who commanded, felt he had to besiege Herakleia, to him a rebel city. It was also a good position from which to block an enemy advancing from the north. The city dominated the Spercheios River crossing, and there was the Thermopylai Pass close by. Yet neither the river crossing nor the pass was defended. Instead, when Metellus met the Achaians it was at Skarpheia, east of the pass. Clearly Metellus had got across the river and relieved Herakleia without fighting. Presumably Kritolaos retired to avoid being trapped between the hostile city and the hostile army, and had then retreated in order to gather up the Achaian contingents who were still not present. He did not choose to make a stand at Thermopylai, but by then the ease with which this pass could be outflanked was surely notorious (though more than one historian blames Kritolaos for not fighting there). Metellus therefore fought only part of the Achaian army at Skarpheia.

The size of the Achaian levy is not known, but later, after several defeats, the league could still field an army of 14,000 infantry and 600 cavalry. Kritolaos clearly had less than that at Skarpheia, and many men of his force were killed; a thousand were taken prisoner. Metellus marched on, catching and defeating the Arkadian contingent (a thousand men) at Chaironeia. Thebes was captured, and the Theban leader Pytheas, who had led the anti-Roman party, was found and executed.[30]

In Achaia Diaios resumed command, Kritolaos having vanished at Skarpheia, presumed dead. A levy of slaves was ordered – specified as 'home-born' since they were assumed to have some loyalty to the league, and a financial contribution from all was levied. The slaves were freed, and then conscripted as soldiers. Women gave up their jewellery, men were enlisted. He produced the army of 14,000 infantry, though whether this included all or many of the freed slaves is not clear.[31]

He was able to do this because, while at Thebes, Metellus discovered that another Achaian force had appeared to his north. This was the levy of the Patrai region, and was of some strength. The troops had crossed by sea, landing somewhere in western Lokris, and were marching north into Phokis (which was doing its best to stay neutral while the various armies marched through its territory). In Phokis this force was astride Metellus' communications, and he therefore had to turn back to deal with it. It appears that the Patraians were heading further north, possibly even to invade Macedon. The two armies fought somewhere in Phokis, the Romans finding it a much tougher contest than at Skarpheia – hence the assumption that the Patraian force was substantial. The Romans were victorious, and the Patraians were destroyed, though one must assume that there had also been Roman casualties.[32]

It was this doubling-back which gave Mummius the time to bring his forces to Greece. He will have collected his army – two legions, amounting to 23,000 infantry and 3,500 cavalry – as early as possible.[33] He had the power to collect ships, and so he could transport his army directly to Greece as soon as the sailors would set sail, probably in April. He himself sailed on ahead, having seen the fleets of transport started. He arrived in front of Corinth without his army just as Metellus' forces were also arriving. For once a Roman army had sailed directly to Greece rather than being taken simply across the Adriatic and having the soldiers march through Macedon and Thessaly. (This must have been Mummius' decision; he comes out of this as a notably independent commander.)

The near coincidence of the two Roman commanders arriving close to Corinth more or less simultaneously provoked assumptions that they were in a race. This seems thoroughly unlikely, if for no other reason that, though both were clearly keen to reach Corinth there is no sign that either knew where the other was. When Mummius arrived, his imperium clearly outranked that of Metellus; there could be no question of a conflict between them. It is not even known if Metellus knew of Mummius' appointment to command, or if Mummius knew what Metellus was doing. The concept of a race is nonsense, the only indication of any conflict is in the wording of Pausanias, that Mummius 'dismissed' Metellus' troops – though what he was doing was actually sending them back to Metellus' province, Macedon.[34]

Metellus had probably left a considerable part of his forces in Macedonia, so the army he took into Greece had probably begun as one legion-plus-allies, between 10,000 and 12,000 men; he had certainly lost some men in the fights and marches since he set out for the south. His primary responsibility was to hold Macedon, and he had to fight another pretender to the throne, a man called Alexander, at some point. The precise date is not known, but since Metellus did the fighting, Alexander must have invaded in 147 or 146, possibly taking advantage of Metellus' absence in the south.[35] Now at Corinth Metellus' one legion (less casualties) faced another numerically superior Achaian army, so when Mummius arrived, in advance of his own forces, he quite rightly ordered Metellus back to Macedon and took over the war. Knowing that the army he commanded was on its way and would outnumber the Achaian forces, so it was a choice between a certain victory by Mummius or an uncertain action by Metellus – whose province was simultaneously in danger.

Once Mummius' forces had arrived and landed the matter was effectively settled. His army outnumbered that of the Achaians by perhaps three to two, and he had contingents also from Pergamon and archers from Crete. Diaios attempted to delay the Roman advance by garrisoning Megara with 4,000 men, but when the Roman army approached the citizens surrendered their city and the Achaians escaped south.[36] At about this time there was a discussion among the Achaians as to the terms they might expect. An envoy had gone to Metellus some time earlier, probably after the defeat at Skarpheia, soliciting them. Metellus sent a Thessalian, Philo, with his reply. This approach appears to have been on the initiative of an Achaian faction which had been associated with the pro-Roman Kallikrates, and so was opposed to Diaios. But the terms Metellus could offer were only what Romans had offered before – separation for the four cities and Sparta. Diaios was able to have the initiative and terms both rejected.[37]

So Mummius' army met the last army of the Achaians in front of Corinth, at a place called Leukopetra. Roman over-confidence was perhaps justified by the Achaian record so far, but the Achaians did conduct a successful night raid which inflicted some casualties. Next day the Achaians launched a full attack, which was defeated when a Roman detachment circled round to threaten one flank. Probably standing and waiting to be attacked would have been too much for them, so the Achaian commanders utilized popular enthusiasm by sending the army to the attack. It did not work. Without much difficulty the Romans inflicted a decisive defeat, though the Achaians did fight hard.

The Achaian forces disintegrated. Diaios fled to his home city, Megalopolis, and committed suicide. Most of the people of Corinth fled from the city, fully understanding what the victorious Roman army would do. Mummius, careful and sensible as ever, waited two days before moving in. The city, as expected, was sacked.[38]

The Senate now had yet another country to dispose of.

Chapter 10

Roman Decisions

The city of Carthage fell to Scipio Aemilianus' army in the spring of 146; the city of Corinth fell to Mummius' army a little later, in the early summer of the same year. By that time Macedon had been under the control of the army of Q. Caecilius Metellus for two years or so. In Rome, all this had been seen as inevitable for at least a year, since the rupture of relations with the Achaian League, or even longer, for Macedon had fallen earlier; no-one in Rome had any doubt that Carthage would fall, even if the process was more difficult and was taking longer than had been anticipated. The defeat of the Achaian League was never in doubt. By the summer of 146 three Roman armies stood triumphant in all three lands, of which Macedon and Carthage had been great powers only a generation earlier.

The timing of all this implies that the decisions of the Senate on what to do with these new conquests were arrived at after a considerable length of time had passed in contemplating the answers, and that the senators were neither rushed into their decisions nor were they suddenly arrived at. When the Senate, therefore, set about selecting the commissions to be sent to Africa and the Balkans to implement its intentions into political reality, those decisions were presumably the result of exhaustive debate and consensus. We do not have any record of debates in the subject. Of our main sources, Livy is lost for this period except for the brief epitomes, Polybios is fragmentary, and Appian concentrates always on events in the field. It seems certain, however, that such debates took place; it is probable that the Carthage commission had been set up by late 147, indicating that the war was expected to end in the near future.[1]

We do not know either the personnel of the commissions or their instructions, but it is certain that the guidelines for their decisions were laid out in the Senate before they left; indeed it is quite likely this happened before the men were selected. The procedure was that the commissioners would agree on the details of the changes or decisions needed, taking into account the wishes of the Senate, and that the magistrate in command would then implement them. It might take the use of force to insist on whatever was decided, and the commander of the Roman army on the spot was the only man with the authority to direct the army into action. Therefore the commissioners gave instructions to Scipio Aemilianus in Africa, to Metellus in Macedon, and to Mummius in Greece – though it may be that Mummius had an authority overriding that of Metellus.

The basic decision, in both Africa and Macedon, was that the territories involved were to become Roman – that is, in modern terms, they were to be annexed. There were also certain preliminary measures to be taken which could more precisely indicate that all the territories were to be henceforth regarded as either Roman or held at Roman pleasure.

In North Africa there were several cities and kingdoms which had become Roman allies before or during the fighting. The disposition of the Numidian kingdom had already been decided, when, after Massinissa's death, Scipio Aemilianus had supervised the implementation of the old king's will. Massinissa had clearly drawn the will with one eye on Rome, possibly even after consultation with the Senate, and in it Massinissa had carefully avoided any hint of a challenge to that city. He had done this partly by dividing governmental responsibilities between three of his many sons, and allocating substantial estates to the other sons. The kingdom thus being sensibly weakened, Rome could be assured that no challenge was intended. The continued participation of Numidian forces in the Carthaginian war had further reassured the Romans; the Senate did not insist on any further changes.

The Numidian gains at Carthaginian expense in the last years before the outbreak of war were probably lost. (If so, this was Rome very effectively recognizing that the policy of constantly punishing Carthage was retrospectively repudiated.) The cities in Africa which had supported Rome in the war, first of all Utica, where the Roman army had landed from Sicily, but also a string of cities along the coast south of Carthage – Hadrumetum, Lepcis Minor and others – preserved their status and their lands and were accepted as Roman allies, free and untaxed. Utica, indeed, gained an extension of its territories, now holding the coast 'from Carthage to Hippo', and presumably a considerable area inland as well.[2]

The city of Carthage, burned and in ruins after the sack and the burning, was to be destroyed. This had two meanings in the context. The first, the obvious meaning, was physical. The surviving buildings were razed, and the population, if there was any left on the site, was driven out. Scipio had already taken perhaps 50,000 prisoners, who were sold as slaves, so there cannot have been many people still present. The other meaning of destruction in this case was that the political entity which was the city of Carthage was abolished. There was thus no city in the sense of a political and social community left in existence. The ruined area was to be left uninhabited, and a curse was laid on any who resettled it. (The land itself was not cursed, nor was it sown with salt; the targets of the curse were, quite correctly, the people who might reconstitute the city.)

This curse must have been partly directed at any Carthaginian citizens who had survived. There were at least 2,000 men who had deserted from Carthage's forces to the Roman side during the fighting and who were now settled, presumably with their families, on lands outside the city area. Towns, mainly in the interior, which had taken the Carthaginian side were destroyed – those that had survived so far. Most of the surviving rural population was left in place, and they were to pay annual taxes to Rome. A praetor was sent to supervise, basing himself at Utica. No garrison was felt to be needed.[3] This was annexation.

These measures were those which had been discussed in the Senate and carried to Africa by the ten commissioners. The commissioners' function seems to have been to sort out the details – the bounds of Utica, for example, and the settlements of the deserters, or in setting up the tax system – but it was Scipio who implemented everything. A constitution for the province – a *lex provincia* – was also probably drawn up by the commissioners as a guide for future governors, though in fact this is only an assumption. The commissioners returned to Rome fairly quickly.[4] They had probably been appointed before the final agony of Carthage and would have arrived quickly once the news reached Rome of Scipio's final victory. Scipio himself organized the implementation of the new measures after the commissioners had left and was still able to return to Rome to celebrate his triumph before the end of 146.[5] Clearly either any further details were left for the governors to sort out or much of the work had already been done before the end of the fighting.

Another ten-man set of commissioners was sent to Mummius in Greece, arriving in the late summer or autumn of 146 – the men returned to Rome in the next spring, having been in Greece for six months.[6] The measures they set Mummius to take are both similar to, and somewhat different from, those imposed on Africa, showing that the Senate was not imposing a defined pattern on its conquests, though it was certainly operating within a set of assumptions of what the provinces should be and have; yet the differences do show that local peculiarities were being taken into consideration. One basic difference in these treatments must have been that Greece was much better known to Roman senators than Africa. It was, apart from being visited frequently by the many senatorial delegations over the past forty years, a place to which Romans looked culturally. Even if many senators had not actually visited the place, they were often familiar with its cities by reputation.

The commissioners came with instructions that, like Carthage, Corinth was to be both physically and politically destroyed. It had been very badly damaged in the sack, which was accompanied by a fire; now the buildings, especially the public buildings which in a sense personified the city's existence, were to be physically overthrown, and the walls were rendered incapable of defending the site (though this was done by slighting parts of the walls, not destroying the whole). The land was not cursed, nor were any future inhabitants. Instead the land was handed over to the neighbouring city of Sikyon to rent out to farmers, it having been declared Roman public land.[7] The Corinthian community was also declared dissolved. This was much more necessary than the similar non-physical destruction of Carthage, for most of the Corinthian population had fled from the city before the sack to take refuge in other cities, and could well have returned after the Roman army had been removed and would then reconstitute their community. No doubt handing over the land to the Sikyonians was also a means of preventing the return of the Corinthians (though one wonders how many of Sikyon's new tenants were actually former Corinthians).

The Achaian League was also dissolved. Quite possibly this had already happened spontaneously as a result of the military defeat at Leukopetra. After that battle the defeated army collapsed and the soldiers scattered to return to their home cities. The Roman concentration on capturing Corinth assisted this, since Mummius waited two days before moving against the city (so allowing many citizens to escape), and the soldiers then spent several days enjoying the sack and collecting loot. By the time the Roman army had recovered itself all the Greek soldiers who survived will have reached their homes and the fleeing Corinthians were given refuge in other cities. Diaios the league general died by his own hand in Megalopolis.[8] He was already the replacement for Kritolaos, who had vanished in or after the Skarpheia fight.[9] The Achaians had made provision for the death of a general during his term of office by arranging that the general of the previous year should take up the office for the remainder of the dead man's term, but there may well not have been any provision for the deaths of two generals in a year. Diaios had already replaced Kritolaos, and it could be claimed that Diaios had deserted his post. (And Diaios' predecessor, Damokritos, had gone into exile.) It is likely that there would have been a nasty dispute as to whether the league continued; certainly there was no chance of an Assembly being convened to conduct a new election in the circumstances of defeat and occupation.

In the event Mummius cut through such arguments by accepting the surrender of the league's cities individually.[10] Thus the league dissolved through a combination of desertion and conquest. The same thing happened to the Boeotian League, if it still existed in 146, and to the Phokian, which had struggled to remain neutral during the fighting, but had become entangled in hereditary connections with Achaian cities – one Phokian city gave shelter to part of the Achaian army; this league too was dissolved.[11] Both Boeotia and Phokis had probably been dismantled by Metellus on his way south, when he accepted the surrenders of the cities individually, as Mummius probably did in Achaia. But the leaguing of groups of small cities was too useful a concept to fade away; all three leagues, suitably chastened and reduced, were able to reconstitute themselves 'a few years later'.[12] The Achaian League in fact reverted to its original members, the line of small cities along the southern shore of the Gulf of Corinth. Argos, Sparta, Messenia, and Elis all thankfully stayed out – and Corinth was destroyed, of course.[13] (Other leagues – Akarnania, for example, and maybe Aitolia and Thessaly – were never dissolved.)

The commissioners handed out punishments to other places as well, such as Chalkis in Euboia, but generally, despite the shock of the loss of Corinth – the city evoked mourning and memorials in the next century – the Roman settlement was welcomed, perhaps above all as a respite from the constant disputes.[14] The evidence for this is the existence of a variety of inscriptions and statues commemorating Mummius or the commissioners, or both. These existed at Olympia, Elis, Argos, and Eretria in Euboia, where he was honoured in various ways;[15] the general attitude was summed up by Polybios, who reported that Mummius 'was honoured in every city and received appropriate thanks'.[16] The sincerity of these commemorations, of course, may be doubted; Mummius had been brutal at Corinth, so a conciliatory memorial might have been deemed a worthwhile investment; on the other hand, many of the memorials still remained to be seen by Pausanias three centuries later – Mummius was in fact the founding father of Roman Greece. He also spent some time hearing and attempting to solve interstate disputes,[17] and may have made a triumphant tour of Greece in the same way as Aemilius Paullus had in 167.[18] He distributed some of the booty from Corinth to all the great sanctuaries of Greece, and many of the smaller ones.[19] He still had a vast amount to display in his triumph, and to keep for himself.

The commissioners and Mummius both returned to Italy in 145, but Mummius left in Greece one of the Greeks who had been advising him. This was the historian Polybios, who was an Achaian and who had been one of the thousand exiles carried off to Italy by Rome in 167. He had been able to return home since 151, but had not done so until accompanying Mummius' expedition. This was partly due to his position in the household of Scipio Aemilianus, with whom and Manilius he was in Africa. Now in Greece, after the sack of Corinth, he stayed on with some sort of commission from Mummius to sort out problems the consul had not been able to deal with. His task was to calm down disgruntled Greeks, and persuade them to accept Mummius' settlement. This must mean that he dissuaded them from appealing to the Senate, whom he must have known would have no patience with such appeals so soon after the commission and Mummius had left. He devised laws for some places, and one in particular, which he developed for interstate arbitration, evoked Plutarch's admiration two centuries later, so it was presumably successful.[20]

The commissioners sent to assist Mummius may or may not have been assigned also to Metellus to settle Macedon. On the whole it seems likely that either a separate group went to Macedon, or the Senate simply told Metellus what was required – after all, the commissioners were only required for intricate or difficult or large cases, and the solution for Macedon was straightforward. However, there is the presence in Macedon and then in Greece of five Romans who took part in Metellus' attempts to dissuade the Achaians from war: A. Postumius Albinus (consul in 151), C. Fannius, Cn. Papirius, A. Gabinius, and 'the younger' Popillius Laenas. Apart from Postumius, it is very difficult to identify these men. A Fannius was with Scipio in Africa, and another was busy in the Balkans, Greece and Asia in the years before 146. The man in Africa can be ruled out, but the other was possibly with Metellus. If so, including Postumius, this would have been a fairly high-powered delegation. This group of five could well be Metellus' commissioners. Pausanias, in fact, in a casual comment, remarks that 'the commissioners in Greece' in 146 sent reports back to the city.[21] These were presumably these five men who had stationed themselves in Athens and Sparta and Naupaktos and Thebes during the war.

Whoever made the decisions in Macedon, essentially very little was changed. The four republics which had collapsed so easily were restored, no doubt with a very different set of councillors in each of them.[22] There does not seem to have been much destruction during the fighting, though no doubt the soldiers were here and there allowed to sack, burn, and loot. Whatever they did was not spectacular enough to survive into the records.

What was different after 148, when Andriskos was driven out and killed, was that a Roman army was stationed in Macedon to take the place of, or reinforce, the local militias, and a praetor was sent out regularly to command it. The local forces had not done so badly in facing isolated raids – at least we do not hear much about them until Andriskos, which might be a sign that they had defended their homelands well. But once Andriskos was able to mount a much more sustained campaign, the militia of the eastern republic was defeated. Militias, by definition, could not stay mobilized and active for long, and the militias were probably not permitted to serve outside their republics – after all, the purpose of the republics, so far as Rome was concerned, was to keep Macedon divided. The militias could defeat and expel raiders, but could not stay in the field long enough to see off a determined invasion. So Andriskos' adventure made it clear to the Senate that a Roman army was needed to defend the Macedonian area, a conclusion reinforced by the appearance of another pretender in 146 which Metellus had to deal with before he returned to Rome.[23] The army in Macedon would be able to supervise Greece as well: an incidental benefit; this was another good reason for the appointment of a regular praetor.

Here therefore was another case of a senatorial dispensation which took careful note of the particular and peculiar local requirements of the conquered country. In Africa no garrison was needed, though no doubt the praetors had a personal guard, and there would have been a local militia, which would deal with the raids likely to emanate from the desert. There was no other enemy likely to attack since Numidia was obviously quiet and friendly – and remained so for the next generation. The praetor's work was thus largely civil, financial, and judicial, together no doubt with the supervision, in a very distant sense, of the Numidian kingdom. In Macedon, on the other hand, the praetor was required to be a military commander. The local government and the judicial system remained functional at a local, civic level, with the praetor presumably acting as a court of appeal when necessary. In Greece, there was to be no praetor and no garrisons. The cities there now understood full well that Roman orders were to be obeyed, and if there was doubt, they were to be solicited. This was the primary lesson taught by Mummius and his soldiers. Otherwise Greece was composed of a mass of cities who were well accustomed to ruling themselves, and so there was no need for the imposition of Roman authority on a continuing basis, or for the presence of a garrison. The army in Macedon acted as a defensive shield, and any trouble in Greece could be dealt with by a relatively small force sent from that army.

In fact Macedon was to be considerably disturbed in the following years. Not long after the return of Metellus to Rome and a triumph, yet another pretender, referred to by the historians as 'pseudoPhilip' or 'pseudoPerseus', made an attempt on the new province. He gathered an army said to number 16,000 men – described tendentiously as slaves – but was defeated by the quaestor Tremellius Scrofa, operating on the behalf of the praetor Licinius Nerva, who was hailed as *imperator*.[24] This was probably in 143 or 142. It was followed by the first attack made by a powerful Celtic kingdom, the Scordisci, which was based in the Belgrade region. The raid took place in

141 and resulted in a Roman defeat.[25] Not surprisingly, the Scordisci's raids continued.

Stability in Macedonia, and the effectiveness of the army's defence, was not helped by the extortion practised by at least one of the praetors, D. Iunius Silanus. The date of his period of office is not clear, but in 140 a delegation from Macedon went to Rome to complain of his conduct. It is characteristic of the self-centredness of Roman history at this time that we only know of this from the fact that Silanus' father, L. Manlius Torquatus, was so ashamed of his son's conduct, which had been demonstrated very clearly in a trial for extortion, that he forbade him his house. Silanus committed suicide.[26]

The effect on conditions in the province of this matter can only be conjectured, since the sources give no information. Provincials were no doubt habituated to a certain degree of extortion by Roman governors, but Macedon was perhaps different. It was under threat − four invasions in ten years − it was a new province, and it was doubtfully loyal. Silanus' career of extortion was also so blatant that the provincials were able to collect damning evidence as soon as he left. To so disturb and annoy such a sensitive population was indeed a criminal matter, and it was no doubt this aspect which annoyed Rome most.

It may have been the prospect of repeated bouts of warfare in the region which stimulated the Romans to the next act of imperialism in the Balkan region. Whenever a Roman army had been sent to fight a Macedonian king it had found itself blocked from a direct attack by the ease with which the route from the Adriatic ports eastwards could be blocked by a Macedonian force, most notoriously in the Third War, in 171–168. This had not happened with Andriskos, but his force had been pinned down in Thessaly by the Achaians and the survivors of Thalna's army when Metellus' army arrived, and Andriskos could probably not spare forces for duty elsewhere. (We do not know in fact just how Metellus' force reached Thessaly, though it was probably from the south by way of the Gulf of Corinth and the route through Phokis, but this also emphasized the difficulty of the direct route from the Adriatic ports.)

One of the methods developed by Rome to keep its grip on the Italian peninsula had been to construct roads which would permit its armies relatively easy and direct access to any trouble spot. Even in the recent past the consul A. Postumius Albinus in 151 had organized an east-west route in the Po Valley. Now, at some point in the late 140s or the 130s a new route was organized between the Adriatic ports of Epidamnos and Apollonia, across the Pindos Mountains, and through Macedonia as far as the Hebros River at Kypsela, which may have been the eastern boundary of the Macedonian province, and so of the Roman Empire.

These roads were not new-made, or 'constructed' in any physical sense. They followed old, sometimes age-old, tracks which had been pioneered and stamped out in the past, using the easiest and most convenient routes. Outside Italy the great roads were named and marked by the Romans but were still the roads which had existed before the Romans arrived. The road across the southern Balkans was organized by the praetor Cn. Egnatius, and so was called the Via Egnatia, though he worked on the instructions of the Senate. The exact date is not known, but it was certainly after 146, and probably after 141, since there is no room in the list of praetors for Egnatius in the 140s.[27] The 130s seems the most reasonable time, since it was in the following decade, the 120s, that two more imperial highways were organized, the Via Aquillia diagonally across Asia Minor, and the Via Domitia, extending the Italian network to the borders of Spain. These were clearly modelled on the Balkan road; indeed the Via Aquillia was, in effect, an extension of it. This new road was also clearly a response to the continuing military uncertainty in and around Macedon after Andriskos' invasion. In 141, in particular, the defeat of a Roman army by the Scordisci made it clear that the wars would continue. The road, a strategic highway, sometimes simply called the 'military road' (*via militaris*) was therefore as necessary as the Via Appia linking Rome and Campania.[28]

What Cn. Egnatius did, in fact, was to measure the road, set up the distance stones – two have been found, one at Salonica and another near Kavalla – and presumably engineer difficult sections.[29] There was no need to pave any of it, a task rather too great for a praetor in his two-year term of office (though he may have had an extension to finish the task). But the markers which were set up were inscribed in Latin and so were clearly designed for Roman rather than Greek use, and in particular for the information and guidance of Roman armies. They gave the information of distances to cities, and so allowed the commanders more easily to plan their journeys. They were not particularly easy routes, but then they necessarily followed the routes worked out over millennia, so they were in fact the easiest routes available.[30] Above all the roads were clear and visible marks of Roman authority, ropes binding the provinces to Italy and to Rome.

The terminus of the new road, at Kypsela in Thrace, is by no means certain, but the mileages do imply it. This was a town in Thrace, just across the Hebros River, and as the terminus of a major road it makes little sense. It appears that the Hebros was the provincial boundary, but the town is still an odd place to stop at. However, Kypsela was close to two Greek cities, Aenos and

Maroneia, which had suffered more than the normal vicissitudes of warfare and imperialism. They were on the eastern boundary of Macedon, and when Macedon was powerful they tended to become Macedonian, and when it was weak they reverted to independence, or were seized by some other empire. They were on the coast of Thrace, and when the Thracians were particularly aggressive, it was these cities they tended to raid. They had been subject to Athens, Philip II, Alexander, Antigonos I, Seleukos I and his successors, some of the Ptolemies, and by 146 had been under the control of the Attalids of Pergamon for some time. (Maroneia became a Roman ally sometime after 167, but the exact date is not known.)[31] The Attalids, in this case Attalos II, were Roman allies, and the king had sent his fleet to assist Metellus against Andriskos, and then part of his army to assist Mummius at Corinth. The terminus of the Via Egnatia therefore put Rome in direct contact by way of these two cities, with the Attalid kingdom by land.

The road also brought the Roman presence close to Thrace; one of the kings there, Diegylas, had been involved in the war in the 150s between Attalos and Prusias of Bithynia. In the course of these events, the Senate had sent no less than five sets of envoys to the region in attempts to mediate or control events. In a concentrated way this was the same procedure as had taken place in Greece in relations with Achaia and in its approach to the problem of Carthage. The result was much the same for in the end the Senate wearied of its repeated attempts to impose order on what it saw as a contumacious subject-ally, and Prusias' son was encouraged to rebel and murder his father. In the three problems – Bithynia, Carthage, Achaia – only the means of destruction were different. It was clearly quite unsafe to defy the Senate. And now the Via Egnatia, constituted during the reigns of Attalos II and the Nikomedes II, was a constant, Latin-marked reminder of the length of Rome's reach – and there was a Roman army camped within reach of Thrace, and not all that far from Bithynia and Asia. The effect of the new road was thus geopolitically very great.

One of the side results of the Roman concentration on Macedon and Greece and Carthage had been that events and developments in other parts of the Mediterranean were neglected. No governors in Spain, for example, proconsuls or praetors, are recorded between 149 and 146, and none from Hispania Citerior for 145, though presumably the usual praetorian appointments were made; the absence of records implies that none of them were able to engage in warfare; maybe the Senate ordered them to refrain, for perhaps part of their forces was taken away for the other, more urgent wars – or both, of course. One result was undoubtedly a revival of native Spanish confidence, particularly among the Lusitani.

Developments in the east had also been ignored, and this might also have repercussions. There was, for example, the close connection between Tyre and Carthage as founder and daughter cities. The civil war in Syria prevented any serious reaction, though no doubt Tyre will have received any Carthaginian refugees who got away. Matters in the east were confused and it behoved Rome to investigate. A powerful set of envoys, led by Scipio Aemilianus, went on a tour round the eastern Mediterranean from Greece and Macedon as far as Egypt in 144–143.[32]

So one effect of the sudden expansion of Roman power east and south was to compel a suddenly greater interest in the eastern states. Further, the Roman interest in Spain had only waned temporarily. The lack of action in the peninsula was no doubt due to the fact that the praetors will not have been given much in the way of troops, given that the other demands on Roman manpower were so great. In the past warfare in Spain usually subsided when Roman governors were denied adequate forces for aggression.

But the situation in Spain had changed from the quieter 160s. For one thing the bad conduct of the C. Sulpicius Galba in 151–150 had not just had its repercussions in Rome, where it presumably had some effect on the affair of Silanus and the Macedonians ten years later. In Spain one of Galba's victims, a young man called Viriathus, had not been killed in the massacres and had escaped, carrying within him a powerful hatred of Rome. He appears to have spent the next years – precisely those (150–145) when Rome's attention was elsewhere – developing his authority and recruiting an effective armed band, and in 146 or 145 he emerged to the attack, defeating a substantial army led by the praetor C. Vetilius.[33] For the next seven years he maintained the fight, repeatedly defeating Roman commanders, and at the same time stirring up trouble in other parts of the peninsula. These wars ranged over a large area, but he mainly fought in the Ulterior province, the homeland of his Lusitanian people, clearly mobile and difficult to catch. In the end, in 139, he was betrayed by a follower, and his assassination was arranged by a Roman commander.[34]

In the Citerior province the fighting resumed a little later than with Viriathus. He is given credit for stimulating it, but this was probably not necessary. It also took a rather different form. Viriathus was clearly a guerrilla leader, without any permanent base, which is why the Romans found it so difficult to catch him. The previous fighting in Citerior, on the other hand, had centred on the Celtiberian city of Segeda, which had developed by the synoecism of the two tribes of the Belli and the Titthi, who made it their *polis*. This place had been strong enough to resist some powerful Roman assaults, but in the end the people had abandoned their city and, joining with the Arevaci tribe, had founded a new one, at Numantia.

This became the centre of conflict for the next bout of warfare.[35] Again the war was a sequence of half-victories, defeats, aborted treaties, and from the Roman side, bad faith and humiliations (though it is likely similar behaviour happened on the Numantine side as well). It is curious that the war should have been pursued with such persistence by Rome, for it is evident that Numantia (and Segeda before it) could have been brought into subordinate alliance without much difficulty. It may be that it was felt necessary that consuls – the commanders in both provinces were almost all consuls or proconsuls between 145 and 133 – should be kept busy far from Rome. They might there gain renown, though most of them gained defeat instead. In the end, in 134, it was once more Scipio Aemilianus (holding an illegal second consulship) who secured Rome the victory with the capture and destruction of Numantia, and the sale into slavery of its surviving population.

It is also evident that the attitudes in Rome which dictated that Carthage and Corinth be destroyed and King Prusias be murdered had spread throughout the aristocracy. No competitor with Rome, however puny, was to be permitted to exist. Numantia repeatedly tried to give in, but wanted guarantees that it would survive – a reasonable request after the treatment of Carthage. No sort of bargaining in advance was to be permitted. Only destruction would suffice, since the city seemed to be a competitor with Rome for Spanish loyalties. Only abject submission would avert destruction – and not necessarily even then. If the defier was a man, not a city, assassination or murder would be his fate – so the death of King Prusias was paralleled by that of the guerilla Viriathus.

The sack, burning, and destruction of the two great cities of Carthage and Corinth therefore became symbols of the new, much harder, Roman attitude to both enemies and competitors. Further, these categories now clearly overlapped and may indeed have been identical in Roman minds. The sack of cities was, to Roman commanders, by way of pointing an example, so that other enemies would give in all the easier. The problem was that this did not work. Without a clear pathway of diplomacy and negotiation, the victim was just as likely to resist as not, since the uncertainty naturally produced suspicions that the Roman aim was destruction anyway.

In wider terms the destructions and assassinations also mark a decisive shift in the Roman imperial advance. Not since the conquest of the Carthaginian province in Spain in 206, and the reconquest of Cisalpine Gaul in the 190s had Rome expanded its direct rule. Now, in three years, Africa, Macedon, and Greece had all been taken, and the Roman Republic abruptly shifted from being one of the great powers among several to the status of the single superpower in the political system. In this Rome was aided, if inadvertently, by the withdrawal of Egypt from the great power competition after the death of Ptolemy VI, and by the dynastic collapse of the Seleukid kingdom in the 140s.

But Rome was not by any means confident of its strength. The brutality of the destructions of cities − Carthage, Corinth, Segeda, Numantia − and the officially-sanctioned assassinations of minor enemy figures, is surely a mark of the Romans' uneasiness with their power and their collective fear of any sort of opposition. It was, on the face of it, ridiculous to believe that the Roman Empire was in danger from Corinth, or even from Carthage, that the rule of Prusias, or the wars of Viriathus, was any sort of a threat. This nervous brutality is an advance signal that Rome itself was headed for the internal upheaval which came in 133.

The wars in Spain which followed the end of Carthage and Corinth made it clear that the city was still governed in a clumsy way; its army was skillful at the level of the infantryman, but hopelessly incompetent at the general officer level. Only two competent commanders, Marcellus and Scipio Aemilianus, can be discerned between 167 and the rise of Marius. Other victories were won largely by the hard fighting of the infantry legionaries. Its provincial system was inflexible and inefficient, for it consisted of sending out untrained and inexperienced men for a year or two into the region they were probably unfamiliar with, and where they were expected to recoup their expenses from the locals. And they were to be military commanders, judges, and administrators all in one. Misgovernment and extortion were the inevitable consequences.

Of course this was only a reflection of the generally awkward and inefficient system of government in Rome itself. The manipulation of the system by such men as Scipio Aemilianus might make it look as though it was flexible enough to withstand emergencies and shocks, and surmount new crises, but such conduct only reinforced the conservative attitude that the system needed to be made more rigorous, not less. And Scipio broke the rules again when he put himself forward, and was elected for a second consulship to fight the Numantines.

These strains were part of the reason the city resorted to the destruction of relatively minor enemies when the intelligent response would have been defeat and then assimilation. For the Western world's only superpower to have to spend over a decade in conquering a single city in Spain and eliminating a single enemy commander was an indication of deep inefficiency and incompetence.

All this was obviously evident to the Romans, but it proved extremely difficult to decide on the necessary changes. Thus the way was opened for the repeated bouts of civil warfare which began in the 130s and, once the resort had been made internal violence lasted for a century. But the decisive geopolitical shift had taken place in 146, and that change had been the result of the Senate's decisions in the previous four years to conquer its supposed enemies.

And while Rome was preoccupied with the problems of the western Mediterranean in Iran another revolution, stimulated by the internal collapse of the Seleukid kingdom, was under way.

Chapter 11

Parthia

The Parthian kingdom has featured marginally more than once so far in this book. It is time it took centre stage, but at the same time it must be set in its historical and geographical context. Until the accession of King Mithradates I in c.165 it had been only a peripheral power, though as a kingdom it had demonstrated a considerable ability to survive and recover after defeats and dismemberment. This toughness proved to be the foundation for its next historical adventure. Its kings found an ability to take advantage of their neighbours' difficulties, and although it was Iranian in personnel and ideology, the kingdom was capable of assimilating non-Iranians.

The Parthian kingdom had originated eighty years before Mithradates' accession when Arsakes, the leader of a nomad group in the Kara Kum desert east of the Caspian Sea, the Parni or Aparni, took advantage of the rebellion by the Seleukid governor in the province of Parthia to his south, and conquered that province. Henceforward they were 'Parthians'. The population of nomads from the steppe soon included mountaineers in the Elburz Mountains, farmers in eastern Hyrkania and the northern edge of the Kopet Dagh (the Elburz's extension eastwards), and former Seleukid subjects – that is, Greeks and Macedonians – in minor cities in Parthia and Hyrkania.[1] Such a mixture of peoples could only be given a geographical name.

The rebel Seleukid governor, Andragoras, did not last long, even though he had chosen a good moment for his *coup*. The legitimate Seleukid king, Seleukos II, was much preoccupied by a rebellion by his brother, Antiochos Hierax, and by the invasion of Syria by Ptolemy III. Andragoras and the new Parthians were not the only disaffected subjects of Seleukos to seize this moment; to their east the governor of Baktria, Diodotos (I) had shifted quietly into independence at the same time, behind, so to speak, the rebellion in Parthia, and had then managed to maintain that status not least because the new Parthian kingdom straddled the land route, the Royal Road, between Baktria and the Seleukid king's territories in the west.

Repeated expeditions were launched by Seleukid kings from the west to attempt to suppress the rebels and invaders and to recover control of the dissidents' lands, though they almost all failed. Seleukos II had to turn back because of his brother's rebellion in c.235. Antiochos III was largely successful in 210–205, when he re-took much of the old Parthian satrapy from the Parthian king, but left the kingship intact and the kingdom reduced but still in existence. His diplomatic reconstruction of the eastern lands had failed by 190, and he set out in 187 to restore it. He was killed before getting farther than Elymais in southern Iran. Antiochos IV had some success in 165–164 before succumbing to disease in 164, with his expedition incomplete.

Interspersed among these military adventures were diplomatic agreements which restricted the activities of both sides. The return of Antiochos III to the east in 187 was probably aimed at restoring the position he had organized twenty years before, which had fallen apart with the death of Euthydemos of Baktria. The expedition of Antiochos IV was probably stimulated by the almost simultaneous arrival of new kings onto the thrones of Parthia and Baktria – Mithradates and Eukratides – and the consequent need to arrange matters, hopefully to his own advantage.

The sudden death in mid-expedition of Antiochos IV should have provided Mithradates I with an opportunity to exploit the power vacuum which ensued – for Antiochos' successor was his child-son Antiochos V, and the Seleukid kingdom experienced much upheaval in the next years. However, Mithradates was probably preoccupied with the turmoil to his east in Baktria. The *coup* which brought Eukratides I to the Baktrian throne at the same time as Mithradates' own accession in Parthia was followed by a long period of civil war. In the process Mithradates acquired two border provinces from Baktria, either by conquest or as a bribe to keep him from intervening. The treaty by which he acquired Turiva and Aspionos, which were two provinces probably lying in the valley of the Atrek River in Areia, also established peace between the two kings.[2] In accordance with normal Hellenistic diplomatic practice this peace would last until one of the contributing parties died. Both kings could then turn away to confront other enemies – Baktrian rivals in Eukratides' case, and the prospects of further conquests in Iran for Mithradates.

In the meantime the Seleukid kingdom had been convulsed first by a rebellion by the commander of the field army which had been under Antiochos IV in Iran, Philippos. He marched it almost to Antioch before being defeated by the regent for Antiochos V, Lysias. Then Timarchos in 162–160, whose original office was as governor of Media and viceroy of the eastern provinces – that is, Iran – and so was one of Antiochos IV's appointments, rebelled against Demetrios I, who had killed Lysias and Antiochos V. We do not know when Mithradates and Eukratides made their peace, but it is unlikely that Timarchos could have risked his rebellion if Mithradates had been free to attack him from the east. So either Mithradates was fully occupied against Baktria, or he and Timarchos came to an agreement – the latter seems marginally the more likely. Timarchos' rebellion failed, thereby freeing Mithradates of any agreement he had made with him, but then the Seleukid state under Demetrios I was strong enough to deter any adventure by the Parthian King. Whatever forces had been removed by Timarchos were no doubt quickly returned to Iran.

Mithradates got his next chance ten years later, when, after the death of Demetrios I, his supplanter Alexander I Balas was necessarily on guard in Syria against an attack by Demetrios' son Demetrios II. It appears that there was some fighting in Iran, for the governor there, Kleomenes, secured a victory which is commemorated by a carving of Herakles Triumphant and an inscription at the Bisitun Pass, dated June 148.[3] The enemy he beat was probably the Parthians, though certainty on this is not possible, and there were other political elements in Iran he could have been fighting.

These other political authorities in Iran were in the mountainous areas of the north and south, the centre of the plateau being under Seleukid direct rule. In the north-east was Media Atropatene, under its own kings, who were apparently content to accept Seleukid suzerainty. Little is actually known of this kingdom, for it is mentioned in the surviving records only very occasionally, as when it collided with the Seleukids, or later with the Parthians or the Romans. It was confined to the mountainous area, now Iranian Azerbaijan, and was given the name Atropatene from its first king, Atropates, who had been a high aristocrat in the Akhaimenid Empire, and had joined Alexander. By retiring, in effect, into the mountains he had maintained his independence, but he and his descendents had to accept Seleukid suzerainty when it was enforced – as it was by Antiochos III in 209. It was a kingdom which, like those in the south, was deliberately and self-consciously Iranian.[4]

In the south were two kingdoms, one in Persis, the old homeland of the Akhaimenid kings, and the other in Elymais, occupying part of the old region of the ancient kingdom of Elam. These had to be coerced into accepting Seleukid suzerainty, and it was in attempting to raid the temple of Nanaia in Elymais that Antiochos III was killed in 187.[5] Of course the more the Seleukid kings were preoccupied in the west, the looser their supervision of these Iranian kingdoms.

Elymais, like Atropatene, was a mountain kingdom, surviving in the hills of southern Iran, north of the old Elamite capital of Susa. Like Atropatene it is barely known during the heyday of Seleukid power, but a local chieftain called Hyknapses had sufficient authority at some time in the 160s to be able to mint coins in his own name, a traditional mark of, and claim for, independence, though he seems to have been quickly suppressed.[6] (But the dating is indicative, for it was a time of the death of a king in Iran and of the rebellions of Philippos and Timarchos; Hyknapses was seizing the moment, and indeed others did so more successfully later.) The ancient Elamite kingdom was undoubtedly part of the inherited ideology of Elymais – for the ancient Elamites have been partners of the Persians and Medes in constructing the Akhaimenid Empire. It did not take much encouragement for them to emerge from their hills, and raiding in the area was probably endemic.

The saving of the temple which Antiochos III had been attacking, and the death of the Seleukid king during his attack, probably led to the emergence of a local ruler who could – thanks to the death of Antiochos, which he claimed to be responsible for – claim the royal title. This was a man called Kabneskir (Kamniskires in Greek sources), who is rather shadowy in the sources, but who seems to have claimed the epithet *Soter* ('saviour'). If he was the defender of the temple against Antiochos III this title was therefore fully justified. He claimed the title in Greek, so his claim was directed as much at the local Greek population in Susa and the other cities as at his own people.[7]

Southwest of Elymais was Persis. This was the original homeland of the Akhaimenid dynasty, and it was a good deal more remote from the centres of Seleukid power than even Elymais in its mountains. Indeed, there seem to have been local kings who coined in their own names by about 250 BC or perhaps even earlier, which means the kingdom was effectively independent – the date is about the time of the Baktrian and Parthian secessions. Antiochos III was successful in imposing his authority there for a time, but the region was self-consciously loyal to the memory of the Akhaimenid Empire. The old royal centre at Persepolis was, even though ruined, only slowly abandoned, and a new political centre at Istakhr developed not very far away, with an important fire temple. By the 170s the local ruler was once more coining in his own name, and by 160 or so Oborzos was the local ruler, followed by kings with such Akhaimenid names as Artaxerxes and Autophradates.[8]

The desire for independence of Seleukid authority in all these Iranian kingdoms is evident. They all depict their kings as Iranian rulers, and were devotees of the fire temples inherited from Akhaimenid times. It is just as clear that until the 140s none of them had the power to do more than operate as local rulers. Rebellions, as by Hyknapses, were quickly suppressed, and the arrival of a Seleukid king generally produced rapid submission. Into this group of self-consciously Iranian states the Parthians fitted quite neatly.

The great imperial road from Seleukeia-on-the-Tigris and Babylon through the Zagros Mountains at the Bisitun Pass – hence the bombastic victory inscriptions – and on east to Baktria, was the basis of Seleukid government in Iran. This, like the Via Egnatia, was an age-old route which had become a major Akhaimenid road, and had been strongly fortified by the Seleukids. They held the cities scattered along that road, patrolled the road itself, and a powerful viceroy, the governor of the 'Upper Satrapies', supervised all – this was Kleomenes' post. To the north were Atropatene and Parthia, to the south Elymais and Persis. These were, however, separated from each other, and continued to be dominated by the power of the Seleukids, which physically intervened between them, and controlled a good half of Iran, and the richest half at that, a long wide corridor along the road. So far the kings had held on to this central spine, but their control must have been weakened by Timarchos' rebellion, which implies a less than total loyalty of both the Iranians and the Greco-Macedonians. And again, the casualties suffered in the victory of the governor Kleomenes in 148 were not all replaced – indeed it is likely that one of the results of that victory would be the withdrawal of some of the Seleukid soldiers elsewhere, on the assumption that their victory will have deterred all local known enemies for the present. The pressure on Alexander I by 147 was great enough for him to get help from Ptolemy VI, and he will have collected as many of his own soldiers into Syria as possible before asking for help from outside the kingdom.

The route from Babylonia onto the Iranian plateau led through the Zagros Mountains at the Bisitun Pass to a string of cities, some of which had been deliberately founded by Seleukid kings. There was the old Median capital of Ekbatana (now Hamadan), which was still two centuries later called 'the metropolis of Media and its treasury', Concobar (Kangavar) and Demavar, both Median in origin but refounded as Greek *poleis*, and Laodikeia, a Seleukid city (now Nihavand). This cluster of populous, defended cities in a group about 200 miles across was the guard of the western end of the old Royal Road which crossed Iran to Baktria. The road, 400 or so miles further on, passed through Rhagai, just south of the modern Teheran. Rhagai is described later as 'the greatest of the cities in Media', though this was a development of the next centuries. Its position on the road was one cause of this distinction, but it also commanded a pass northwards through the Elburz. This mountain range is a formidable barrier which is pierced by few passes, so each is of particular strategic value. Rhagai was the last stop before the Caspian Gates, which is the natural geographical boundary of Media and Parthia, 'a long narrow valley'.[9]

The Caspian Gates is a pass through a mountain range which spreads out south-eastwards as far as the central Iranian desert. It was one of the key strategic posts of the ancient world, and was thus inevitably heavily guarded. At the western end of the Gates, about thirty miles beyond Rhagai, was a fortified place called Charax ('fortified'), no doubt a guard post controlling

the access to (and exit from) the gates. East of the gates, which are about
ten miles long, the road ran through two more Greco-Macedonian cities,
Apamea, which was the equivalent of Charax at the eastern end of the pass,
and, 200 or so miles further west, Hekatompylos ('Eight Gates', now Shahr-
i-Qumis), which is now in the desert.

These several cities were populated mainly by Iranians but ruled as Greek
cities by the Greek inhabitants; they also contained garrisons of Seleukid
soldiers, and other garrisons were distributed in strategic places – at Charax,
for example. To the north of the road was Atropatene, against which there
were garrisons, one of which at Karafto Caves has been found and examined.[10]
It was clearly sited to defend against, or threaten, Atropatene. North of the
Elburz, between the mountains and the Caspian Sea, was Hyrkania (the
modern Mazanderan), a fertile land, difficult to access from the south because
of the mountains, but relatively easily accessible from the east and west, and
so one of the earliest conquests of the Parthians. The mountains were also in
large part inhabited by independent tribal groups; Antiochos III had a major
battle in his eastern expedition to get through these mountains.[11]

A substantial portion of the Seleukid armed forces was therefore stationed
along this route-corridor – some in the cities, others in such border posts as
Karafto and Charax. This concentration of forces had been too much of a
temptation for two governors in the past – Molon and Timarchos – who used
them as the basis for their grasps at the throne. Despite the size of their forces,
therefore, the control of the Seleukid kings over this region was vulnerable.
The Parthians had been nibbling away at it.

There were other Seleukid cities in Iran, which were strategically placed
to exert influence and to emphasize dominance. Persis, for example, had a
city, Antioch-in-Persis, as its neighbour on the coast of the Persian Gulf.
This was a Greek city of the regular type, with a mint which produced coins
with the Seleukid king's image, partly as a means of emphasizing his political
presence in the region. It was visited by Antiochos III on his return from
his eastern conquests, in 206.[12] Elymais faced two major cities, Seleukeia-on-
the-Eulaios, and Susa, also called Seleukeia. The latter was a major power
centre with a substantial Greek garrison and population.[13] More crucially it
was the old Elamite city of Shustar, the seat of the succession of Elamite kings
and dynasties who ruled for 2,000 years before the Akhaimenid Empire. In
Seleukid hands it was a brutal demonstration of Elamite subordination, yet it
could hardly efface the long pre-Alexander traditions associated with the city.

From 148 onwards, King Alexander Balas fell into wars in Syria which
lasted until his death. This was followed by the troubles faced by his supplanter
Demetrios II. This long preoccupation with affairs in Syria changed the

situation in Iran drastically, and two kings took advantage of it: Kabneskir and Mithradates. Beyond Parthia, the Baktrians were by now fully occupied with their wars in India, and with the renewed menace of the nomads from the north; so long as Eukratides lived, he and Mithradates were at peace. Both Mithradates and Kabneskir saw the opportunity which the withdrawal of Seleukid forces presented, and seized their chance.

The Parthians' dynastic origin was in the steppes north of the Kopet Dagh in the Kara Kum. The city of Asaak is located at the place where the first king was proclaimed, and the dynasty claimed the royal title from the start, unlike those in Elymais and Persis. This was probably because their first king gained a victory over Andragoras, the rebel Seleukid governor, who also in all likelihood claimed a royal title – he certainly minted coins in his own name. That first Parthian king exercised a powerful influence over his successors. All of them took his name, Arsakes, as their throne names, though both ancient and modern historians tend to use their given names to reduce confusion. Thus Mithradates I was actually Arsakes to his subjects, the sixth king to use that name. They also counted their history by an era beginning in 247 BC, which is assumed to be the year the first Arsakes became king (though it may only be a back-counting from later). In this they were copying the Seleukids, who originated the continuous dynastic dating. Such a counting emphasizes the length of the dynasty's rule, and contributed strongly to the kings' sense of legitimacy, just as the continued use of the royal name Arsakes suggested a stern continuity of policy (even though chops and changes are quite obvious).[14]

When they moved into the Parthian satrapy, the city of Hekatompylos became their second capital, and brought them under serious Greek influence, and they had other Greek subjects, settlers in Hyrkania and at Apamea.[15] When Antiochos III attacked them in 209 he found that they had secured control over at least the eastern part of Hyrkania, where he had to capture two small Greek cities from them.[16] His victory and the subsequent peace pushed the Parthians back to the edge of the plateau for the next two decades, but the death of Antiochos in 187 permitted them to advance southwards again. King Phriapatios (185–170) was free of diplomatic obligations and was able to cautiously advance his boundaries. Phraates I (168–165) was able to reach the Caspian Gates, and this implies his control over all the old Parthian satrapy. It was an attempt to recover this territory which brought Antiochos IV to Iran in 164.

Small advances into the old Parthian satrapy and into Hyrkania were, however, only recovering lost ground. By the 160s Phraates I was in a position to establish his control over the Caspian Gates, which was a major strategic advance. He is recorded as having planted a colony of Mardians, recruited in the Elburz (whether forcibly transplanted or volunteers is not clear) into the place Charax which guarded the western end of the pass.[17] This means he had already gained control over the land to the east of the gates, including both Apamea and Hekatompylos, and much of Hyrkania, and, of course, the Gates themselves.

It was from this base that Mithradates began his career of conquest. He had been very cautious. He had first had to protect himself against the projected attack by Antiochos IV, which does not seem to have reached him, and then guard his eastern border by the treaty with Eukratides, and then to watch as Timarchos' insurgency failed. After this the Seleukids on the plateau were no doubt fully alert and well armed during the reign of Demetrios I. In 148 the governor Kleomenes won a victory, probably over Mithradates (though this is not certain) which implies that at this point the garrisons and field army of Seleukid Iran were up to strength. At least the commemoration of the victory is dated June 148; the battle probably took place earlier; the date may merely be that of the inscribed commemoration. And yet it is obvious that at that date the Seleukid King Alexander I remained in control of the Royal Road from the Bisitun Pass as far as Rhagai, while Mithradates ruled from Charax eastwards.

It cannot have been very long after that inscription was made that the whole Seleukid position came under another attack. And the proximate cause was surely the contemporary war in Syria. It was in 147 that Ptolemy VI began his march along the Palestinian and Lebanese coast road to come to the assistance of his son-in-law Alexander, beset by attacks from Demetrios II. In such circumstances it is highly likely (though we have no proof) that Alexander will already have called to Syria all the troops who could be spared – and more – from the provinces. This would inevitably mean extracting soldiers from Iran, which would leave that region even more vulnerable than normal.

There is perhaps another aspect also. The Parthian kings, as their use of the dynastic title and their particular era imply, were very conscious of their royal legitimacy. The only other dynasty they were in contact with which pretended to the same, or a superior, dynastic legitimacy was the Seleukid. (The Ptolemies and the Antigonids could do so as well, of course, but Parthian knowledge of these dynasties is not known.) Yet the advent of Alexander I Balas was a clear break in the legitimate succession. Even if one accepted that he was the son of Antiochos IV, he was still the son of a courtesan, not a royal wife. One might believe that the Arsakid dynasty would have a powerful respect for their formal overlords, second only to that felt by all Iranians for the extinct Akhaimenids, even if they saw them as enemies. (The Arsakids eventually claimed to be of Akhaimenid descent.) The arrival on the Seleukid throne of an illegitimate usurper could only be regarded with distaste, at least, by the legitimately-minded Arsakes/Mithradates I. With such a personal feeling of disdain, Mithradates could easily justify his invasion of Seleukid Iran. He could claim to be both sweeping away the rule of the usurping Seleukid, and reviving the old rule of the Akhaimenids.

The date of Mithradates' invasion of Iran is not known, though it was either late 148 (after Kleomenes' inscription) or early 147. Nor is the progress of the Parthian conquest known, except that it occurred. The obvious course would be for Mithradates to march along the Royal Road, capturing the cities as he advanced (though he may have used the route west through Hyrkania and invaded by way of Atropatene). Once Rhagai was taken he would have a clear road to the group of cities at the head of the Bisitun Pass, including Ekbatana, the satrapal capital of Media. The Parthian army, however, was largely a cavalry force, derived from the dynasty's nomad origins, so it would seem unlikely that Mithradates could spend much time besieging the cities. It is clear, however, that by 145 he had taken control of at least a substantial part of Media, for by then he had appointed his brother Bagasis as its satrap.[18] This does not necessarily mean that all of Media had been conquered, but it does imply that at least a large part of it had fallen. One clue is that the mint at Ekbatana does not seem to have produced much coinage for Alexander Balas. A hoard from Susa, a large proportion of which is composed of Alexander's coins, contains not one coin minted at Ekbatana. Only one coin from the city was recovered at Susa; no dated coin of the king is listed in the latest catalogue.[19] It would seem, therefore, that the city fell to Mithradates fairly soon during his campaign.

The Parthian invasion and conquest of Media, however, was not the only political change being produced in Iran at the time. Probably in 147 the city of Susa fell to Kabneskir, who had long been the chieftain of the Elamites. In one late source he is said to have lived to the age of ninety-six, and he is generally assumed to be the man who had led the defence of the Elamite temple against Antiochos III in 187.[20] It seems likely that, as with Mithradates, Kabneskir was taking advantage of the new military weakness of the Seleukids in the region. He does not seem to have lasted long after his capture of Susa, but was quickly succeeded, probably still in 147, by Kabneskir II, who was presumably his son. In fact the son might have been the actual victor in the fighting at Susa, for it seems unlikely that a 96-year-old would be an active warrior. As evidence for this is the fact that the son took the epithet *Nikephoros* ('victorious'), which appears on his coins.

As an indication of the old king's success there is an inscription found on an Elamite temple at Bard-e-Neshandeh. It is in the script used in the second century AD, but it is a record of tax exemption for the temple donated by 'Kabneskir, the great king'. On the coins of Kabneskir I he is referred to by that description, but in Greek ('*basileos megalou*') as well as *Soter*. So within the brief period of his victory he was exercising his royal powers in matters of tax and property just as his son was exercising his as a military commander.[21]

Whether there was any serious fighting over Susa in 147 is not known; the city may well have fallen quickly due to drastic thinning out of the Seleukid garrison. There are, apart from the conquests in Susa and Media, other signs of the weakness of the Seleukid hold in the region. In Babylonia in August 145 Arabs 'entered Babylon'.[22] Until then Babylonia had been free of raids from the desert, but such groups, like the Iranian kings, swiftly took advantage of military weaknesses.

145 seems to be the key year in fact throughout the east. It was the year of the deaths of Ptolemy VI and Alexander I in battle in Syria (Chapter 7), after which Demetrios II cleared out the Ptolemaic forces from Syria but then found himself reliant on his mercenary army, and was then challenged by Diodotos of Kasiana in the name of Antiochos VI (Chapter 12) – meaning that the Seleukid dynastic war continued. In Babylonia Arabs began raiding, and these raids continued intermittently for the next century or so, contributing seriously to the reduction in Babylonian prosperity over that period. In Media Mithradates I handed over the command to his brother Bagasis and retired to Hyrkania.[23] This means that Mithradates had spent two years and more campaigning in Media, assuming he began his campaign early in 147, and retired to Hyrkania sometime in 145. This suggests he had to fight hard to take the cities, for his cavalry forces would generally be able to dominate the open country fairly easily. The reason for his retirement eastwards is not known, but it is quite likely that it was connected with the death of Eukratides in that year in Baktria and the conquest of part of the Baktrian kingdom by the Yuezhi nomads from the north (Chapter 5). Suddenly the eastern Parthian border was once more vulnerable to attack, not only by the successor to Eukratides, who was not bound by the treaty with Mithradates, but also by the Yuezhi, only part of whom settled into Baktria; other groups outflanked it to both east (into India) and west, into Drangiana, which became Seistan ('Saka-stan'), mounting a long-standing threat to Parthia's eastern borders.

This is also the year when a serious attempt was made by the new Seleukid King Demetrios II to recover the eastern losses. It seems that Kabneskir had proceeded from the capture of Susa to an invasion of Babylonia. The Seleukid commander in Babylonia, named by the Babylonian diarist as Ardaya, which must be a local variant of a Greek name, perhaps Ardaios, mobilized to combat the invasion. A proclamation by Demetrios II had been read in Babylon and other cities the month before (that is, in September), and so it seems probable that he had acquired some control over the administration there. Thus it is likely that the king directed that the Elamite invasion be countered, though it must also be assumed that the Seleukid government in Seleukeia-on-the-Tigris would have reacted to that invasion, as in fact it did, even without royal instructions. The Babylonian chronicler reports that the 'King of Elam marched around victoriously against the cities and rivers of Babylonia; they plundered cities... and carried off their spoil'.[24]

The result of this fighting, whose details are largely lost, lay in Elam, where Demetrios II was able to have coins in his name issued at the Susa mint during 145. Ardaya was thus swiftly successful.[25] There are also a number of large hoards of coins buried about this time.[26] So one may assume that Ardaya was able to reply to Kabneskir's invasion of Babylonia by his own invasion of Elam. All this took place in the autumn of 145. The Babylonian source fails between October of that year and July of 144, but then it is recorded that there was still fighting in and around Susa, though the tablet has too many gaps in it for real precision. The troops were then described as those of 'Antiochos son of Alexander', who can only be Antiochos VI.[27] Maybe they had switched sides on the news of the proclamation of Alexander's son in the west, but they certainly continued to fight against Kabneskir. (Ardaya is not mentioned again.)

It seems probable that Kabneskir in fact was eventually victorious for he was in power in Susa later, to be attacked by Mithradates. Also Kabneskir II produced eight successive issues of bronze coins, interpreted as annual productions, which fits in with a reign from 147 (his father's conquest of Susa) to 140 (his defeat by Mithradates).[28] Therefore it would seem that he eventually defeated the invasion from Babylonia, aided no doubt by political reverberations out of Syria.

The Babylonian chronicler, and so even more certainly the Seleukid government in Babylonia, was well informed of events in Syria. He repeatedly reports what he had heard of events at 'Antioch which is on the Sea', by which he means Antioch-on-Orontes. The stress of the continuing and complicated conflicts in the west can only have weakened the authority of the Babylonian governor, whoever he was. The Arab raids indicate his local military weakness, for example, which was surely aggravated by the campaign against Kabneskir – and since that was a Seleukid defeat it will have further reduced his military forces.

By 144, therefore, the political situation in Iran had changed drastically from only four years before. The former Seleukid satrapy of Media, which until 148 was being successfully defended by its governor, had fallen to Mithradates I, but just how far to the west he had penetrated is not clear. It is probable that the cities clustered at the eastern side of the Bisitun Pass had fallen, given that Mithradates seems to have had almost three years to do the job. The mint at Ekbatana issued no coins for Demetrios II, who became king in 145, though it had produced at least one issue for Alexander I and did so for Mithradates; it therefore seems that Demetrios never controlled the city, and that it had fallen to Mithradates by 145, or probably before. It was the only mint in Media, and coins would be needed particularly badly if there was fighting, both to pay the troops and to purchase supplies, and to advertise who ruled in the city.

In the south, however, the independence of Kabneskir II of Elam was not yet achieved. He had certainly gained control of Susa for a couple of years (147–145), but by invading Babylonia he had provoked a powerful reply which led to a Seleukid army retaking the city, after fighting in the region which compelled several people to hide their money. All the more convincing of trouble is the fact that they failed to recover these hoards, even though Kabneskir himself succeeded in recovering full control of the city and its region in 144 or 143.

This war was no doubt one of the factors in Mithradates' decision to abandon further advances in the west and to retire to Hyrkania. In 145 a Seleukid army was briefly victorious in Susa, and Media may have been its next target. Presumably considerable numbers of the Seleukid troops who had been stationed in Media had removed themselves to Babylonia in the face of Mithradates' victory, and this reinforcement of the Babylonian garrison was probably sufficient to allow general Ardaya to campaign against Kabneskir. This conflict made it clear that no immediate Seleukid attempt to retake Media was mounted, but, since ambition grows by what it feeds on, that army might go on from Susa to Ekbatana.

Ardaya's exact position in the Seleukid government is not clear. He is described, the first time he appeared in the Babylonian chronicle, as 'the general in Borsippa'; this is somewhat ambiguous, since it may mean that he was the governor of all Babylonia (who is usually referred to in Babylonia as 'the general who is over the four generals'), or that he was a subordinate commander whose headquarters were in Borsippa.[29] After several years of civil war (152–145) it is very likely that the command structure in Babylonia had been thoroughly disrupted. There had been the conflict between Demetrios I and Alexander, then between Alexander and Demetrios II, and from 144 between Demetrios II and Antiochos VI. The reference to the army in Elymais being that of Antiochos son of Alexander is a clear sign that allegiances shifted in the east, but did so perhaps to a different rhythm than in the west. And as they shifted the most obvious casualties would have been the senior men, such as Ardaya, who had been all too obviously loyal or obedient to the previous king.

As an illustration of the other possibility, of a politic shifting of allegiance, there is in the south of Babylonia, the province of Mesene, or the 'province by the Erythraean Sea'. This was governed by a man called Hyspaosines, who had been in office since about 165. His origin has been suggested to be Baktrian; if so, the date is perhaps significant; he could be a refugee of high social standing, escaping from the *coup* of Eukratides, who was welcomed by Antiochos IV (again this is perhaps a clue as to Antiochos' own ultimate aims in his Iranian campaign).

Hyspaosines had clearly survived the various changes of king – in 164, 162, 160, 150, and now 145 and 144 – but his province had been in part the object of Kabneskir's invasion from Elymais, as well as Babylonia, so loyalty to the Seleukid could pay off. On the other hand, Hyspaosines' political agility may well not have been replicated among the Babylonian governors, and the confusion was obviously a source of weakness. It is reasonable to assume that Hyspaosines' continued occupation of the governor's palace at Charax Spasinou (formerly Antioch-by-the-Erythraean Sea), his capital, was a source of local stability – and the longer he stayed in office, the more appreciative his subjects would become, surrounded as they were by confusion and warfare. The progress of the crisis of the Seleukid collapse shows that the kingdom was in effect collapsing from the east, just as it was in the west, and as the Baktrian kingdom was as well. It would take an uncommon political ability to survive. Hyspaosines seems to have been able to do so (he continued in power until the 120s, and founded a dynasty); it remained to be seen if Mithradates and Kabneskir would be able to do the same. But the key to the future for all these regions and men lay in the issue of the fighting in Syria.

Chapter 12

The Burning of Antioch

For a brief moment, at the end of 145 and early in 144, the changes which had altered the geopolitical organization of the world halted. Pataliputra was recovering from the sack; Ai Khanum was in ruins and would stay that way; Mithradates of Parthia, having conquered Media, had gone back to Hyrkania, and the Seleukid General Ardaya had not yet attacked independent Elymais; Demetrios II was king from the Mediterranean to the Zagros Mountains; there was a new king in Egypt, Ptolemy VII, settling onto his turbulent throne; Rome had crushed Andriskos, destroyed Carthage and Corinth, and had suddenly emerged as the greatest power in the west. The only possible contender for equal power with Rome was the Seleukid kingdom, but only if it could recover its recently lost eastern lands. With Rome pausing for breath and looking again to Spain, it was the policy and deeds of the teenage Demetrios II in Syria which were crucial to the future. And he had major problems on his hands.

After the deaths of Kings Ptolemy VI and Alexander I Balas in the battle by the Oenaparos River in mid-145 Demetrios II became the sole king. He and his mercenary commander Lasthenes became fully occupied with the immediate problems of expelling Ptolemaic troops from the Phoenician and Palestinian cities, and of finding money to pay Lasthenes' soldiers. The escape of Hierax and Diodotos, the officials of Alexander, was probably regarded as of minor importance, though annoying, for they were prominent parts of the former regime. But, as is the way of matters of minor importance, this issue grew to threaten the whole monarchy.

Diodotos came from Kasiana, a town near Apamea, the great Seleukid military centre, where the troops trained and the elephants were stabled and trained.[1] He probably – we do not know much about him – had military experience, if not a full-fledged military career. He emerged in the 140s as Alexander's minister alongside Hierax, which suggests that he had joined Alexander early on. He is referred to as '*strategos*', which could mean either general or governor.[2] He was loyal to Alexander only until Ptolemy VI broke with him, then, with Hierax, engineered the unsuccessful offer of the Seleukid kingship to the Egyptian king. After the Oenoparos battle, with Alexander

and Ptolemy both dead, he left Antioch and went home. By this time his main
motivation was apparently a strong antipathy to Demetrios II and the whole
Seleukid dynasty.

He clearly knew where Alexander's son Antiochos had been secreted. This
had happened when Demetrios II attacked, in repetition of Demetrios I's
action back in 152 or 151, when he sent two of his sons to safety. Alexander
now also left a similarly primed mine for Demetrios II. (It is noticeable that
he did not entrust the child to his wife, the boy's mother, Kleopatra Thea;
her marriage to Demetrios II would obviously have put the boy in danger;
Alexander's claimed father, Antiochos IV, had been guardian to his nephew,
and had had him killed, even though Antiochos himself was married to the
boy's mother; Alexander clearly apprehended the same fate for his son.)

Diodotos does not seem to have had a specific plan in mind at the time he
left Antioch. His refuge was somewhere in the region of Apamea, quite likely
at his home town, Kasiana. As an eminent man at the head of the previous
government no doubt he had been able to hand out favours to people in his
home region, and will have had supporters there. His contacts and his circle
of friends and clients who had benefitted from his patronage while he was in
power would provide shelter as well as support.

It was, however, not an initiative of Diodotos' which brought him into
action once again, but a series of political mistakes by Demetrios. The king was
persuaded, or compelled, by Lasthenes to deliver to him and his mercenaries
effective authority to collect taxes. Lasthenes was, of course, under pressure
to pay the men he had recruited, but the land was obviously much damaged
by the civil war, and the most productive region, Babylonia, had to direct its
resources to the war in the east. In effect Lasthenes was made minister of
finance, and his primary object was to deliver the wealth of the kingdom to
the soldiers. How far his authority reached is unclear, but the trouble which
followed was concentrated in Antioch, so perhaps it was from the people of
that city that Lasthenes aimed to secure his wealth.

The principal targets in the first phase were, not surprisingly, the more
prominent supporters of Alexander's regime. (It may well be that it was at
this point that Diodotos left Antioch.) They were targeted for punishment
and despoliation, but the purpose of the confiscations was the payment of
the mercenaries. In normal circumstances, such confiscations were often later
revoked or reduced, and lost property could be reclaimed. If the goods and
property had been liquidated, however, this was no longer possible – and
the soldiers were obviously hoping to take their pay and leave the kingdom.
Further, it seems that the process was haphazard, which is what is presumably
meant by the 'outlandish punishments' said to have been imposed.

Of course, the soldiers went about the collection of the fines and confiscations with a will, and, of course, being soldiers, they resorted to force very early in the process, and were opposed. At Lasthenes' demand, Demetrios discharged the garrison of Antioch, and perhaps of other cities, and reduced the pay of the militia. All this was in the name of directing that pay to the mercenaries. In the circumstances Demetrios came even more under Lasthenes' control, and so became steadily more unpopular. The Antiochenes, who seem to have been the principal victims of this reign of terror, objected. Clashes in the city developed into something close to rebellion. The attackers were prevented from entering the palace by the mercenaries, who were reinforced by a contingent of Jewish soldiers sent by Jonathan Maccabee from Judaea, in exchange for a vague promise of future concessions. The original purpose of these men may have been to act as a royal force to balance or replace Lasthenes' mercenaries, but in the event the two forces joined in defending the palace against the attacks by the Antiochenes. The citizens were largely unarmed and the soldiers, taking up positions on the roofs and firing missiles, cut them down without difficulty. A fire started, or was started, and spread throughout much of the city, whose buildings were largely of wood. The soldiers discontinued killing and then turned to looting.[3]

This was followed by more punishments, which became increasingly arbitrary, and included executions. The soldiers had clearly been frightened by the citizens' reaction, and so had, no doubt, the king. Demetrios had no control over the men acting in his name, however, and the royal palace had been the main target of the city riots. Refugees fled the city, carrying the news of the events in the main city of the kingdom to the other Syrian cities.[4]

Not all the Antiochenes left, of course, and there were undoubtedly some who took the king's side. The Jewish soldiers were apparently quickly dismissed and sent back to Judaea as soon as possible; Jonathan's hopes of concessions were never realized, and it seems that the mercenaries vanished just as quickly — they are not mentioned again.[5] Both groups took their loot away. The result was a devastated and impoverished city, and a great deal of work had to be done to rebuild. Since the whole crisis seems to have been concentrated mainly in Antioch, and the culmination of the riots and the burning had probably lasted only a few days, Demetrios would be able to bring in troops from elsewhere to form his personal guard and to restore and maintain order in the city. But to the angry citizens this must have seemed like an occupation force — and the imported troops may well have been sympathetic to the citizens in their troubles. We know, of course, that there was a substantial army in Babylonia the year before, under the general Ardaya. The cities of Syria and Palestine were garrisoned, and these contingents could be thinned out to provide a force for Antioch and Demetrios. In the west there was at this time no international threat − Ptolemy VII had plenty of problems in Egypt, starting with the serious problem of his own personal unpopularity.

It was at this point, sometime in 144, that Diodotos bestirred himself. It is evident that Demetrios was in serious political difficulties. For Diodotos these events were confirmation that Demetrios was incompetent and a tyrant, and details of the sufferings of the refugees probably grew with the telling. Further, from his refuge in or about Apamea Diodotos could note that the garrison had been reduced, and, no doubt, it was the most loyal troops who had gone to Antioch. He was an experienced soldier and administrator, now with a particular political agenda, and it seemed that he was being proved right in his dislike of the new king.

Diodotos could also recall the original popularity of his patron Alexander, and he could argue, probably convincingly, that in a straight fight Alexander would probably have beaten Demetrios and Lasthenes. The victory of Demetrios in the Oenoparos battle was due to Ptolemy's forces. These forces had now withdrawn, Ptolemy was dead, and the Ptolemaic troops were most unlikely to return. Demetrios, apart from the detestation he had brought upon himself, was militarily and politically vulnerable.

In other words, Diodotos could see an opportunity to reverse the judgment of the battle. He had considerable assets on which he could capitalize, though apart from his own ability, they were largely negative, in the general dislike for Demetrios. It was quite possible that he could overthrow the king, but to do this he required a figurehead, just as Herakleides and Attalos and Ptolemy VI had required a figurehead in the person of Alexander for their campaign against Demetrios I. Diodotos was apparently not yet confident enough to do without one, but he had one to hand in Alexander's son Antiochos.

The sequence of events in Diodotos' insurrection is not certain. He may have begun his rebellion first, having recruited a force from his Apamean friends and from the Antiochene refugees, fuelled at first by anger at the events in Antioch; only when he had gained some success did he bring Antiochos forward as a figurehead. This is the sequence in the only historical account we have, that of Diodoros. Once the initial anger had subsided − which may not have been so intense in other cities − Diodotos needed to proclaim the child Antiochos as a rival king. This gave the forces Diodotos had recruited a renewed focus.

The fact that it was not until sometime in 144 that the new king was proclaimed, sometime after Diodotos' rebellion began, suggests that this sequence is correct. Diodotos would need to make an estimate of his chances, and of the strength of support he might find away from Antioch and Apamea, and seek out allies. It seems, in fact, that he recruited as his first allies the regiment of cavalry which was based at Larissa, a town on the Orontes halfway between Antioch and Apamea. He was also allied with the Arab sheikh, variously called Iamblichos, Diokles, and Malchos, who had been acting as guardian for Antiochos and was able to recruit Arab forces. Then he established himself at Chalkis, a town in the north of Syria not far east of Antioch. It was, like Larissa, a well-chosen position, close to the disaffected city, and in touch with the Arabs of the desert. From there he commanded a communications-node and so could send out his anti-Demetrios propaganda to all the cities in northern Syria.

The evidence for the subsequent war is partly the occasional anecdote preserved in the written sources, and partly the monetary history of the city mints. The war was largely confined to Syria, with some excursions into Palestine and Kilikia. In addition, of course, there were the changes of the allegiance of the army in the east, but this had no real effect on the central fight, except to reduce the possibility of either side bringing up reinforcements from the east. The main contest was for control of the great cities in northern Syria.

These cities were the four founded by Seleukos I in 300 BC, and named after himself, his wife, and his parents – Seleukeia-in-Pieria, Antioch, Laodikeia-ad-Mare, and Apamea. All were major cities, though Antioch had outstripped the others by becoming the royal government centre (a role probably originally intended for Seleukeia). Seleukeia and Laodikeia were major ports, and Apamea was the site of the main military base for the kingdom. Between them the four cities divided up the whole area between the Eleutheros River (the old Seleukid-Ptolemaic boundary) and the Amanus Mountains. As a result this region had become known as the Seleukis. Given control of the four cities, a king or a pretender could dominate the rest of Syria with ease and use their wealth and manpower to gain control over the rest of the kingdom. It was in part because Alexander and Demetrios had been in competition for control of these cities between 148 and 145 that Mithradates of Parthia had been able to campaign for three years in Iran without interruption. (There were also half a dozen smaller cities in the region, between Antioch and the Euphrates, but we have no information about their role in this war, except that of Chalkis.)

Diodotos' earliest moves, at Larissa and Chalkis, did not alarm Demetrios in Antioch. He presumably felt safe enough there, having collected what was intended to be a sufficient force around him from other regions. He referred to Diodotos as a brigand, which was probably the result of his having recruited Arabs into his force, 'and ordered his soldiers to arrest him'. Their failure to do this was an initial victory for Diodotos. It would convince some indecisive supporters to join him, and he recruited, as Diodoros says, 'an army of unexpected size'. But it would only be when the child Antiochos VI was proclaimed at Apamea that the threat posed by this insurrection became clear.[6]

The coins of the new king were produced at Apamea beginning in 144, but the monograms of the moneyers were those which had been originally used at Antioch in the first year of Demetrios II. There were eight of these marks in use at Antioch in that year, and seven of them appear on Apamean coins of Antiochos VI in 144. One does not appear, but did reappear after a gap of a couple of years. Two of the marks ceased to be used during 144 at Apamea, and a new one appears – one may assume that this marks the death or retirement of two of the original moneyers and the promotion or recruitment of a replacement. Perhaps the one which was not used had been that of a man captured, or who went into hiding.[7]

In other words this shows that the refugees from the violence in Antioch included the greater part of the staff of the mint in the city. They fled to Apamea, not necessarily because Diodotos was there, but to get away from the violence in the city, and, since they were willing to work for Antiochos, they were also escaping from Demetrios. They were therefore present in Apamea and willing to work for him when Diodotos' insurrection reached the stage of proclaiming Antiochos VI.

The written sources are vague on the progress and development of this rebellion, but to some extent it is possible to see what was happening by looking at the coins issued by the mints of the various cities. In each case the issuing ruler was presumably in control of the city itself, and if that control changed so would the name on the coinage. The difficulty in relying on numismatic evidence to trace political events is that there are large areas which did not produce coins, but did use the coins produced elsewhere. In the east there seems to have been one mint in each province, which means that all Media was provided with coinage by the single mint at Ekbatana. In the west the number of mints was much greater, but still there were substantial cities without one, while others produced only intermittently. In these cities we cannot therefore know which of the competing kings exercised control.

In the case of the early development of the rebellion we can see that Diodotos gained control first of Apamea in 144, and then of Antioch during 143, because the moneyers from Apamea returned home and continued minting coins there in the name of Antiochos VI. Demetrios, on the other hand, retained control of the mint and city of Seleukeia-in-Pieria, Antioch's near neighbour, and produced other coins at an unlocated mint somewhere in North Syria. It was normal for a king on campaign to take with him a mobile mint, to produce coins which would be used for paying soldiers and purchasing supplies, the main purposes of Hellenistic coinage.

Demetrios' control of other cities, however, slipped. The two mints in Kilikia, at Tarsos and Mallos, switched to producing coins for Antiochos VI in 143, about the same time as Antioch changed. Similarly in Palestine the major city of Ptolemais-Ake switched to Antiochos in that same year. Given that this had been a favourite residence of Alexander this suggests that Diodotos was playing on nostalgia for Alexander's reign. But this would not necessarily work everywhere. Tyre and Sidon, for example, continued to produce coins for Demetrios II throughout these wars.[8]

It appears, from the isolated reference in the Babylonian Diaries to the army in Elymais being that of 'Antiochos son of Alexander', that at least for a time Antiochos was accepted as king also in Babylonia.[9] How extensive this recognition was is not clear. Many mints in the east appear to have ceased production, which itself suggests that the administration was less than active, or was preoccupied and short of cash. The allegiance of Babylonia, however, was important, since it was the richest and economically the most productive region of the kingdom. Seleukid kings had usually been assiduous in paying attention to and honouring the Babylonian gods, so marking by this means their appreciation of the region's importance. It would seem that there was a struggle for control in the region, one which was probably won by Demetrios. However, this was a conflict which had no effect for several years on that in the west, since whoever was in control in Babylonia had to pay more immediate attention to events in Media (Mithradates had seized this by 145) and Elymais, where the fighting against Kabneskir was at first initiated by an army recognizing Demetrios, then by one of 'Antiochos son of Alexander' – but this was the same army. Having been driven out of Elymais it seems that the higher command in Babylonia became divided.

In Syria and its neighbouring areas, the struggle was indecisive. That is, so far as the coinage suggests, neither of the kings gained a clear advantage. Demetrios held on to the Phoenician port cities, and to Seleukeia-in-Pieria, where his wife stayed; he is also recorded at Laodikeia where he is said to have been active only in his pleasures. But he is also said to have continued the reign of erratic terror which had made him so disliked in Antioch. This would suggest that he faced opposition in the city, and that clamping down and picking off the most prominent opponents was the only way to maintain control.[10] There can be little doubt that Diodotos/Antiochos VI faced the same problem in the cities they controlled. The fact that we have information about Laodikeia rather suggests active anti-Demetrios propaganda picked up by the later historians. Diodotos therefore held the great cities of Antioch, Apamea, and Ptolemais-Ake but made little progress elsewhere. By late 143, after a year of Diodotos' insurrection, it seems clear that the struggle had produced a stalemate.

Into this confusion there arrived a group of Roman envoys. It was composed of three men, and collectively their names would have sent shivers down the spines of any Greek. The leader, fresh from the destruction of Carthage, was P. Cornelius Scipio Aemilianus, now sporting the extra cognomen Africanus in recognition of his military achievement. He was accompanied by L. Caecilius Metellus Calvus, the brother of the Metellus who had reconquered Macedon, and Sp. Mummius, the brother of the destroyer of Corinth and dismantler of the Achaian League. This was a set of men responsible in themselves and their families for the deaths of two great cities and three states.[11]

The purpose of the embassy was not to do anything, but to investigate the new conditions in the eastern Mediterranean states. Rome's own preoccupations in the past five years had precluded much interest in affairs in the east (just as it temporarily reduced interest in Spain). But in that period great changes had taken place. The last Roman embassy of a comparable weight had been that led by Ti. Sempronius Gracchus to Asia and Syria, and that of T. Manlius Torquatus to Egypt, both in 162. These travelled east just after the *coup* of Demetrios I in the Seleukid kingdom, and the definitive division of the Ptolemaic kingdom between Ptolemy VI and his brother. There had been others in the years since, but usually they were sent to attend to specific issues, such as the several embassies sent to attempt to sort out the war between Attalos II and Prusias II. The Gracchan and Scipionic embassies were much grander and wider-ranging. Their purpose was evidently to find out what was going on after major political changes, to make contact with the major political players – and presumably to decide if any of them posed a threat to Rome.

It is not quite certain in which order the embassy visited the several countries, but Diodoros implies that after Egypt they went on to Cyprus and then to Syria. Probably they therefore visited Greece and Macedon first; Cicero, however, lists their visits as 'Egypt, Syria, Asia, Greece', though this is not necessarily the sequence, since Cicero was not dealing with what the embassy did, only that it went to all these places.[12] But it does seem that other regions were visited before Syria, and that therefore we may assume that the embassy reached Syria in 143.

There was plenty to investigate. Egypt's new king, Ptolemy VII, was known at Rome as a constant agitator in the past against his recently deceased brother, Ptolemy VI. He had recently abandoned the last Ptolemaic posts in the Aegean at Methana, Thera, and Itanos, presumably in order to keep clear of any possible collision – even contact – with Rome, whose presence was now constant in Macedon and overshadowed all Greece.[13] The envoys also went to Cyprus, also part of Ptolemy's lands. The wealth of Egypt, still under relatively good governance only a year after the death of Ptolemy VI, impressed Scipio; the new king was also capable, but he already had dynastic troubles, which limited his effectiveness, and he never showed much interest in foreign affairs.[14] The envoys visited Rhodes, whose commerce was being adversely affected by the free port Rome had set up at Delos, and so could be assumed to be disgruntled over it; their visit could best be interpreted as a warning. The condition of Greece in the year or so after the imposition of peace and of Macedon after yet another pretender was driven out was no doubt still unsettled. The loyalty of Attalos II had recently been demonstrated in most practical ways. There was not much in Greece and the Aegean to concern the Roman embassy so soon after the major victories. In all cases the envoys were estimating the political condition of the lands they were visiting, in order to assess their threat, or otherwise, to Rome. According to Polybios they were to try to reconcile opponents, but, if so, they comprehensively failed – in Egypt Ptolemy VII followed their visit by a busy purge of his opponents; in Syria the civil war continued without interruption.

When the envoys arrived in Syria is not known, but it was obviously during the war between Demetrios and Diodotos. Of the two dates suggested for the tour, the later (140–139) would put the visit in the time of Demetrios II's fight in Babylonia against the Parthians. This has produced the criticism that they ignored the advances of the Parthian power.[15] However, not only do we know nothing of what they reported on their return to Rome, but a concern for the Parthian advance was only something which developed at Rome fifty years later. The earlier date for the embassy (144–143), of course, would make their ignoring of the Parthians – if they did ignore it – much more comprehensible. As it is, if they spent any time in Syria, and talked to any of the principal figures, they would have been told of the problems, not only of the dynastic dispute, but of the consequences of the earlier fighting for the Seleukid kingdom in the east. They probably did not see that it concerned Rome. The divided and weakened condition of the Seleukid kingdom probably reassured them – for their perspective was a Roman one.

None of what they saw or did had any effect on the spot in any of the places they visited. The embassy was not sent for the purpose of affecting events or effecting change, but to review the local conditions. Its purpose was to see if Rome needed to be concerned at what was happening, a concern developed by the recent events in Greece and Africa. It is evident that Rome was safe – the continuing civil war in Syria, the crumbling of the Seleukid kingdom in the east, the weakening of Rhodes, the Attalid alliance and quiescence, the new king in Egypt and his total lack of interest in anything outside Egypt, were all presumably reassuring.

In the circumstances of the stalemated war semi-independent lands like Jonathan Maccabee's Judaea gained an enhanced significance. Jonathan took sides with Diodotos, and was rewarded by another vague promise, the appointment of his brother Simon as governor of the land 'from the Ladder of Tyre to the borders of Egypt'.[16] This meant a good deal less than it seemed, and there is little sign that Simon ever exercised much power or influence in the area, except once at the head of an army. It was no more than a hope, for it is evident that most of the Palestinian area held to Demetrios; even cities, such as Ptolemais-Ake which were on Diodotos' side ignored Simon's pretensions.

Jonathan, of course, aimed to exploit the Seleukid crisis to his own advantage. He was not the only one. The city of Gaza had originally taken Demetrios' side, but had deserted him, though it had not declared for his opponents; evidently the Gazans were interested in achieving an increased degree of independence. Jonathan moved into the region with his army. The city of Ashkelon, just north of Gaza, submitted to him, as it had earlier when he had attacked Ashdod, and he moved on to Gaza. Here he met resistance, instituted a blockade, and ravaged the city's lands. In the end the Gazans, who had come to favour Demetrios once more when Jonathan menaced them in the name of Antiochos VI, gave in, accepted an alliance, and gave hostages – the demand for hostages making it clear that the city was not really to be trusted.[17]

Quite possibly it was in relation to this episode that Demetrios sent an expedition south to challenge Jonathan. Demetrios was apparently by no means rendered immobile by his situation, and was able to send an army into Palestine, though it cannot have been a very powerful one. Jonathan meanwhile had laid siege to the fort at Beth Zur, at the southern end of Judaea, which was held by a Seleukid garrison, and had become a refuge for the Maccabees' Jewish opponents. Here Simon was in command. The approach of Demetrios' army was thus dangerous, with the Judaean forces being divided, and Judaea menaced from both south and north.

Jonathan, with his part of the Judaean army, met the Demetrian army north of the Sea of Galilee at Tell Hazor. He fell into a fairly basic and simple military trap, being engaged in the fight only to be surprised by the sudden appearance of a hidden part of the enemy army. The Judaean army fled and was rallied some way south, but the Demetrian generals did not pursue very actively. (If their purpose was to relieve pressure on Gaza, it was too late.) The Judaean army was gathered together again at a narrow part of the road along the western coast of the Sea of Galilee. Jonathan was able to dash back to Jerusalem, presumably to make sure that no coup was mounted as a result of his defeat, then returned to the army, perhaps with some reinforcements. The army had taken up a defensive position at Hammath Tiberias, just south of the modern town, where the hills approach the lake, leaving only a narrow route.[18] There it faced the approach of the enemy.

But the Demetrian army did not advance. Instead, leaving their watch-fires burning, the soldiers retired during the night. Presumably this was because the army had been recalled by Demetrios. Certainly it was not due to any military activity by the Judaeans, though it could be that the strong Thermopylai-like position they had taken up was a sufficient deterrent. Of course, Jonathan claimed credit for seeing off the attack, despite being defeated. Meanwhile Simon had succeeded in forcing the surrender of Beth Zur.[19]

The wavering loyalty of the Palestinian coastal cities, as at Gaza, was again shown at Joppa. Apparently at first taking Diodotos' side, it was perceived as being liable to shift over to Demetrios. Simon marched his army along the coastal plain and put a garrison into the town, no doubt in the name of Antiochos VI, but they were actually Maccabean troops.[20] In the midst of the civil war, therefore, the Maccabees had extended their power down to the coast and into the south.

About the middle of 142, King Antiochos VI died. There were conflicting accounts of this, either that he died under the surgeon's knife or was murdered by Diodotos.[21] The first is obviously the story put out by Diodotos, the second equally obviously came from his enemies. There is also no obvious reason to disbelieve either, but death-by-surgeon is hardly unlikely, and is a reason which is certainly unlikely to be invented – plenty of people must have known the child was ill and was subject to medical attention. Of course, politically it mattered little how the boy died, but it seems clear that his death dealt more damage to Diodotos than his enemies, and for that reason his version is perhaps to be preferred. Diodotos' enemies, of course, benefited both in accusing him of killing the child, and in the elimination of the child as a potential competitor; Antiochos was a more potent symbol of enmity to Demetrios than was Diodotos.

One reason people and historians were prepared to believe that Diodotos had murdered his ward was that he quickly developed a new and self-magnifying policy. He proclaimed himself king, taking the throne-name Tryphon ('Magnificent'). It was, of course, assumed that he had killed the boy in order to seize the throne himself; it is, however, equally likely that he seized the throne because the king died and he had lost the figurehead of his anti-Demetrios movement. Suspicions might also be aroused because Tryphon launched a new propaganda scheme, in which he emphasized certain elements in the old Seleukid ideology in a new way, or which had not been highlighted before. Noticeably he put on his coins a picture of the Macedonian shield, to emphasize the Macedonian origin of the state, and to appeal to the Macedonian-descended element in the population.[22] In fact this had always been an element in Seleukid claims; the kings, for instance, were always described as 'the Macedonian' in their titulature. The Macedonian connection had been reinforced by several marriages with the Antigonids of Macedon, including the marriage of Demetrios I's sister (and wife) to King Perseus; Demetrios' own name, and that of two of his sons (Antigonos and Demetrios) were actually names used in the Antigonid dynasty and not earlier in the Seleukid. So Tryphon's Macedonian emphasis was something already in train among his opponents. But Tryphon went further. He began a new political era with the seizure of the kingship, so that the Seleukid year 171 (142/141 BC) became Tryphon's 'Year I'.[23] He was now claiming that he was making a new beginning for the kingdom.

The purpose of this was partly to appeal to the Macedonian heritage which was present among the governing elite and to the descendents of the original Macedonian settlers from the army of Alexander the Great, but also to imply the revitalization of the kingdom in the face of recent Seleukid decadence. No doubt Demetrios I's drunkenness and Demetrios II's incompetence and civic violence were heavily emphasized, but the reputation of Alexander I for indolence and illegitimacy was probably largely ignored.

How far this new policy was successful is not known. The coins of Tryphon were produced by the same mints as those which had worked for Antiochos, though two cities, Byblos and Ashkelon, now began coining for Tryphon. Ashkelon, of course, had befriended Jonathan Maccabee in his anti-Demetrios campaign against Gaza, so this was no real change. Byblos was going against the Phoenician grain in coining for Tryphon (and briefly for Antiochos in 142 before his death); perhaps the city had fallen to Diodotos. Otherwise there seems to have been little change in the overall political situation as a result of Tryphon's self-proclamation. Demetrios II was still the same enemy, and his generals controlled the cities loyal to him – though perhaps they were loyal because they were under the generals' control. Diodoros, in noting Tryphon's self-enthronement, detailed four of these generals: Dionysios the Mede in Mesopotamia, the land between the rivers Euphrates and Tigris, the land the Arabs later called al-Jazeira; two men were in Koile Syria, Sarpedon and

Palamedes, and this effectively diminished Simon's authority there; Aischrion was in Seleukeia-in-Pieria, where Kleopatra Thea was also living.[24]

Tryphon's ideas, however, do smack of some desperation, and the fact that he made no real progress beyond the position he had already reached when Antiochos VI was alive is a clear sign of this. No usurper had ever succeeded in the Seleukid kingdom. The only possible exception was Alexander I Balas, and he claimed to be, and perhaps was, a Seleukid — and even he only lasted five years. It was the same in both the Egyptian and Macedonian kingdoms; they were dynastic states and people, and the citizens at least, clung to the dynasties as the one element which made political sense. No usurper ever gained power in any of these kingdoms. In Macedon in the absence of a legitimate heir to Philip V, an illegitimate son, Perseus, was accepted — just as Alexander I was in Syria — and even twenty years later the kingdom was resurrected out of four independent republics at the appearance of a transparently fake Antigonid pretender, simply because he claimed to be a member of the dynasty. (And at least two more men tried the same thing in the next years after Andriskos was suppressed.)

So Tryphon really did not have much hope of succeeding; his use of Antiochos VI as a figurehead rather suggests he knew this. His support was negative, in that it was based on a widespread, but by no means universal, dislike of Demetrios II. The bases of that support were the three cities of Antioch, Apamea, and Ptolemais-Ake, all with particular and personal reasons for dislike of Demetrios. But suppose Demetrios was replaced by another, more acceptable, Seleukid; then Tryphon would fade.

Meanwhile Tryphon had to shore up his support wherever it flagged. It seems that he had suspicions of the loyalty of Jonathan Maccabee, not unreasonably, for he must have understood his motives. He came to Ake-Ptolemais and was met there by Jonathan, who arrived outside the city with an army, and went into the meeting with a guard of a thousand men – so the suspicion was mutual. It did no good; the citizens attacked and defeated his guard, and Jonathan was made a prisoner.[25] This may in fact have been an initiative of the citizens, who had no liking for the Judaeans, who had attacked the city before. Tryphon, however, made the best of it, and paraded Jonathan in front of Judaea demanding concessions.

This ploy failed and Tryphon eventually killed his prisoner.[26] The whole episode shows that Tryphon had no real strategy other than opportunistic gestures. The one aim which both Demetrios and Alexander had pursued with respect to Judaea was to maintain a grip on that land, however slight. There was still a garrison in the Jerusalem Akra, but it was apparently loyal to Demetrios, and as he marched away northwards, his Judaean enemy,

Simon, angered at Tryphon's murder of his brother, tendered his allegiance to Demetrios, who responded by confirming him as high priest.[27]

The apparent emptiness of Tryphon's policy indicated clearly that he was not going to win. (At some point also he lost a considerable force when a *tsunami* swept part of his army into the sea as they marched along the Palestinian coast.[28]) That the result of Tryphon's southern expedition was so poor may well have suggested to Demetrios the next step he took, which seemed rather surprising, but was almost successful. He was only able to make territorial progress in Syria by means of Tryphon's mistakes, as in Judaea. But Tryphon was not making progress either. Neither he nor Demetrios was likely to recover the major cities held by the other, for all were now well-garrisoned by their forces, and the citizens were loyal even if by default, as those in Ptolemais–Ake had shown. So if there was a Syrian stalemate, and his generals were loyal to him, the best move Demetrios could make would be to leave the region. The areas he did not control were antipathetic to him personally and so were out of his reach, but by removing himself he might expect that support for Tryphon would weaken.

Demetrios took part of his forces and marched to Babylonia where he became involved in yet another war (Chapter 14). If his calculation really had been that his presence in Syria was not conducive to reducing the power of Tryphon then that calculation seems to have been correct. After he had spent a year or so in Babylonia, and was still fighting, his brother Antiochos arrived in Syria. He had been sent into exile by his father, just as had Demetrios, but the two boys had been kept separate. It seems that Antiochos spent most of his exile in the city of Side in Pamphylia – whence his nickname 'Sidetes' – and from there he could keep a close eye on what was going on in Syria. (Side had also contributed ships to Scipio Aemilianus' forces in the fighting at Carthage; events in the western Mediterranean were clearly well known in the east.[29])

At Side Antiochos was very close to another city, Korakesion. This became notorious later as a pirate city, which is to say it was a city from which pirates sailed to practice their profession. (Side also gained a similar reputation, but as a flourishing market at which pirates sold their thefts.[30]) The blame for the origin of this piracy is sometimes laid at Tryphon's door.[31] This may well be yet another of the calumnies heaped on him by his enemies, and yet it is so curious an accusation that there may well be some truth in it. Tryphon presumably hired pirates to interfere with the trade of the cities held by Demetrios, many of which were ports. He also destroyed Berytos, one of Demetrios' ports.[32] No doubt one of the main sources of finance for Demetrios' war effort was the customs duties collected at the ports of Seleukeia, Tyre, Sidon, and others, including Berytos, and so interfering with the trade of those cities would be a reasonable war aim for Tryphon. Equally, only Demetrios will have had any maritime sea power, since he controlled the main naval bases. Hiring pirates in this way was in fact a normal wartime practice – during his war with Rome, Antiochos III had hired bands in the Aegean to supplement his own navy. It seems likely that the pirates became highly practised at their trade during their work with Tryphon, and they did not give up their work once peace had returned.

Antiochos arrived at Seleukeia-in-Pieria during 139. Almost at once he married Kleopatra Thea, who was actually the wife of his brother Demetrios (and the widow of Alexander I and the mother of Antiochos VI).[33] She appears to have stayed in Seleukeia ever since the uprising against Demetrios began. The marriage, of course, was bigamous, but public opinion by this time was well inured to the peculiar marriage practices of royalty. (Ptolemy VII was now married to both his sister and his niece, and he had murdered his nephew.) The situation in Syria was, of course, essentially a dynastic emergency. Further, Antiochos developed into a most effective ruler. Within the next year he had besieged Tryphon in Dor in Palestine, and then pursued him when he escaped. Tryphon finally died not far from his home, near Apamea in 138.[34] At about the same time, as it turned out, Demetrios was finally defeated and captured by Mithradates. Antiochos VII therefore became the sole ruler of the Seleukid kingdom, though it had been reduced to little more than an enlarged Syria by that time.

Syria had undergone civil warfare for the past fifteen years, since Alexander Balas landed at Ptolemais-Ake in 152. The fighting had been intermittent, even sporadic, but had never really ceased, and had resulted in considerable destruction, notably in Antioch and in Berytos, though no doubt elsewhere as well. One of the effects of ancient warfare was that captured prisoners, military and civilian, were more often than not sold as slaves (as at both Carthage and Corinth in 146). Captured mercenary soldiers could well be recruited into the victorious army; civilians, if they survived, were usually sold. There were good – or at least comprehensible – economic reasons for this, for armies always needed money, and the income generated from the sale of slaves could be used to pay the soldiers, or to hire more. Individual soldiers' captures were regarded as personal booty.

The effect of this practice of Syria can only be imagined. We have no direct information on the subject, but the wandering armies could easily capture slaves as they moved about, largely among the rural population, and no questions as to origins or loyalties would be asked. The enslaved prisoners were usually exported, and the main market became situated on the island of

Delos in the Aegean. From there most of the slaves seem to have been sold on into the Roman dominions, notably southern Italy and Sicily.

In this connection, one of the mysteries of Syrian history in the next twenty years is the slowness by which the kings attempted to recover the lost eastern territories. Antiochos VII was an accomplished commander and a first-rate administrator, yet it took him seven years to gather the forces for an attempt to recover the east. The reason is never stated, but it would seem that the devastation produced by the wars was one reason, but also the loss of population, both in direct casualties and in the export of the enslaved people, must have been the main reasons for it.

The effect of these wars extended to the form of the kingdom itself as well. Demetrios II fought a long and difficult battle in Babylonia to recover the lands lost in the east, while in the Syrian region cracks appeared, and widened, in the structure of the kingdom. The two brothers staved off the end for a time, but their difficulties eventually overwhelmed them; their remaining territories meanwhile were disintegrating under their feet.

Chapter 13

Fragmentation

The Seleukid kingdom had long been liable to disintegrate. It had originally been put together in separate pieces by the founder, Seleukos I, and these sections had never been fully integrated into a properly unified whole. He began with Babylonia, added Iran, and then defended what he had in a war lasting several years, in the process acquiring much of Mesopotamia. An expedition to the east secured Baktria, but forced him to surrender any claim to India and to several of the eastern regions. He acquired North Syria by joining a new coalition against Antigonos Monophthalamos. All this took twelve years and after another twenty years he gained most of Asia Minor after he defeated Lysimachos. He was murdered as he was about to move on to establish his rule in his homeland Macedon, which had also been ruled by Lysimachos. The whole sequence took him over thirty years.

This was the kingdom's widest extent, and from that point on, it lost sections fairly regularly, either by defeat or by secession – Baktria and Parthia in the 240s, Asia Minor finally in 190, though it had broken away for a generation earlier, and now Media and Elymais in the 140s. The only compensation had been the acquisition of Phoenicia and Palestine, secured from the Ptolemies in 200. By 145 the kingdom, about to face the rebellion of Diodotos and Antiochos VI, had been reduced to Syria and Palestine, with Kilikia, in the west, and Babylonia and Mesopotamia to the east. But this was a territory in which there were also movements for independence by various ethnic groups. In many cases these movements came to a head during the war between Demetrios II and Tryphon or soon after. And Mithradates of Parthia had not yet finished his career of conquest.

This chapter will be devoted to the internal disintegration of the kingdom; the next will look at the final fight with Mithradates, which confirmed the decisive weakening of the kingdom, though it had one final fight left in it. As it happens these divisive developments did in fact occur in that order (breaking, then Parthian invasions), and Mithradates clearly had an easier fight on his hands than if the kingdom had been united; even so, it will be seen that he had a hard time. It is clear, taking a long-term view, that the main agent for the destruction of the Seleukid kingdom was Tryphon, and behind him Alexander I Balas and his co-conspirators. They were not the only agents, of course, and the Parthian invasions were equally responsible, but the civil wars of the 140s did administer a fatal blow. The kingdom whose lands stretched from the Sinai Peninsula to Central Asia in 150 was reduced to little more than Syria and Palestine a dozen years later. None of the participants in the civil/dynastic wars intended or expected this, but their activities certainly made it possible.

And yet the kingdom actually broke up on pre-existing lines of weakness, social, political, or geographical. As an example there is the case of Hyspaosines, the satrap of Mesene/Charakene. He ruled the area at the head to the Persian Gulf, or it may be better described as the land around the estuary of the Tigris-Euphrates. It was a relatively small area but awkward for outsiders to dominate because of the marshes in the estuary area. This would be especially difficult terrain for an army like the Parthian, which was composed largely of lightly armed cavalry archers and barely trained infantry. The region thus had considerable natural defences. He ruled from a fortified city, a Macedonian colony called Antioch-on-the-Erythraean Sea, which became called Charax Spasinu ('Hyspaosines' fort').

How it came about that Hyspaosines became governor of Mesene is not actually known, but the fact is that he ruled the area from about 165 until the 120s. This longevity in office is one of the clues to the wider problem of the disintegration of the kingdom. In the end Hyspaosines was able to establish himself as an independent king and then hand on his position to his son. He certainly fought the Parthians and the Elymaeans, and he was allied with Demetrios II in his Babylonian expedition. This all suggests that he had strong support in Mesene but also that he was a particularly wily and skillful political operator. No doubt he carefully proffered his loyalty to whatever new king showed up on his horizon. It may even be that the central Seleukid administration did not think he was important enough to remove when the king changed – or even that he was forgotten in the pressure of changing events. But his longevity in office and his achievement of independence and kingship are clear symptoms of the decay of the Seleukid state.[1] It was clearly unhealthy for the kingdom as a whole that one man should rule a province for so long.

In fact, so far as can be seen, he was actually a Seleukid loyalist, and may not have taken the royal title until the 120s when, after the catastrophe of the expedition of Antiochos VII in Media, it became clear that there was no longer any likelihood of another revival of Seleukid power in his region. He even campaigned north into Babylonia and held the city of Babylon for a time in the 120s. Eventually he was driven back into his kingdom by the Parthians and accepted Parthian suzerainty. It was perhaps a tribute to his local authority that the Parthians accepted him as a subordinate king. By then his land was being called Charakene, from the name now given to his city.

Hyspaosines is an example of a local governor left high and dry by the recession of Seleukid power. Babylonia had other examples, notably Adiabene to the north, since the Parthians seem to have held directly only the central region around the fading city of Babylon and the thriving Greco-Macedonian city of Seleukeia-on-the-Tigris. They established a supervising garrison at Ctesiphon, across the Tigris from Seleukeia, and this developed into an even greater city than either of its predecessors. In the same way Seleukeia had been designed to overawe Babylon, and much of the population of the old city had drifted to the new one during the Hellenistic period; the process of moving further, across to Ctesiphon began as soon as that city had been founded.

The Maccabees in Judaea are an example of another means of reaching independence, a successful rebellion. These leaders successfully exploited the several Seleukid dynastic conflicts in their own interests. Several examples of this, notably the exploits of Jonathan during the 140s have been noted already (Chapter 12), but it is worth looking back over the previous generation to see just how they did so, to examine the process, and put those references into context. It has frequently been argued, or assumed, that the Maccabean rebellion was the conflict which broke the Seleukid kingdom. It will be seen that this was not so.

The Jewish soldiers who had helped to wreck the great city of Antioch had been sent by Jonathan, who was the second of the Maccabee brothers to rule in Judaea. There had been six of these brothers, sons of Mattathias, a priest of Modiin in northwest Judaea. In 166, when an official of Antiochos IV had arrived at Modiin to conduct a sacrifice on behalf of the Greek god Zeus Olympios, Mattathias had refused to take part, despite well-chosen and persuasive words from the official. Then, while the sacrifice was taking place, and his neighbours were participating in the rite, Mattathias suddenly seized a knife or a sword and killed both the Greek official and the man of Modiin who was at that moment at the altar.[2]

This is generally reckoned to be the moment when the Maccabean rebellion began, though it was only one incident of this type among several, and was actually only one further stage in a crisis in Judaea which by then had been under way for several years. The original problem had been concentrated on the person of the high priest, who was an appointee of the king, but who, until the crisis developed, had always been a member of a particular family.

Antiochos IV had been persuaded that there was strong support in Jerusalem for a high priest who would favour the Hellenization of the city. And so there was, though this support was largely concentrated in the city itself; in the countryside — at Modiin, for example — support was much less.

A misunderstanding about a riot in Jerusalem which took place while Antiochos was involved in his war in Egypt led him to make a raid on the city, and this naturally produced an anti-Seleukid reaction. The king decided that the hellenization of the Judaean community on its plateau had not gone far enough, and when it was suggested to him that the Jewish god Yahweh was really Zeus Olympios in a different guise, he sanctioned the re-consecration of the temple in Jerusalem to the Greek god. In order to ensure that everyone knew and understood what was happening, altars were set up in various places — such as Modiin — where the Jews could be informed of the new system and could participate in the worship of Zeus.[3]

Mattathias' violent reaction was probably not the only example of this type of rejection. He died soon after the murders at the altar, and his six sons took to the Gophna Hills nearby, less to act as guerrilla fighters than to hide. After the killings Mattathias had marched through Modiin proclaiming what he had done; no one supported him, hence the fleeing of the brothers into the hills.[4]

Other Jews had done the same in other parts of the country. These dissidents, including the Maccabees, were few in number, for the majority of the Jewish population had accepted the new system without serious demur, and, like Mattathias' neighbours, willingly participated in the new sacrifices. Furthermore, the dissidents were divided amongst themselves. Some clung to the absolute and unchanging letter of the Jewish law, including the refusal to do any work on the Sabbath (which included fighting or defending themselves), and this left them vulnerable. Another group, the Hasidim, appear to have been prepared to meet the Seleukid attacks and to discuss the means of accommodation — though being in the middle this group was soon crushed between the more intransigent extremes. The third group, which included the six Maccabee brothers, accepted that the law would need to be adjusted to the new circumstances — and so they were prepared to fight on the Sabbath if necessary — but rejected totally the new religious dispensation.

After Mattathias' death the leader of the group was his eldest son Judas, given the name Maccabee ('the Hammer'), apparently from the shape of his head, and this became the name for the insurrection. He had two main tasks: to persuade the rest of the Jewish population to accept his ideas and his leadership, and to drive out the king's officials and forces. In the first he largely succeeded, using terrorist methods such as murder, extortion, and forced circumcision where it had been neglected; in the second aim he failed, for this necessitated raising an army out of a population with no recent military tradition. Ambushes produced some successes, and enabled the rebels to equip themselves from captured weapons, but after several years of fighting, Judas was finally killed in battle in 161 against a well-lead and professional army sent by Demetrios I.[5]

The subsequent occupation of Judaea by Demetrios' garrisons, in a dozen or so forts, including the Akra in Jerusalem, was accompanied by the continuing terrorization of the country population under the leadership of Judas' brother Jonathan. He and the youngest brother Simon were the last of the six, and were allowed to live in a supposedly out-of-the-way corner of northeast Judaea, but they were still able to go on with their internal campaign, though clandestinely. Eventually, of course, when Alexander Balas landed at Ake-Ptolemais, just to the north of Judaea, Jonathan's time came. During the Seleukid civil war which followed, the garrisons in the Judaean forts were reduced or withdrawn. Jonathan emerged, courtesy of Alexander, as Jewish high priest, and so in effect as the head of the autonomous Jewish region of Judaea, though a Seleukid presence remained, primarily in Jerusalem, where a garrison still held the Akra.

The achievement of this limited version of autonomy was not enough for Jonathan and his party; independence was their aim. On the other hand, autonomy was the most they could expect for the moment, and to convert autonomy into full independence would require an effective army. Until then Jonathan could only operate as an ally of the insurgent Alexander. Jonathan took the opportunity of the war between the kings to build up that army, and to fortify Jerusalem, where he was able to block off the Akra fort from the rest of the city. The eventual victory of Alexander did not alter Jonathan's ambition; he remained high priest and effective governor of Judaea. But he had achieved these positions as a participant in the civil war between the kings, so when a new war erupted in 148 he had to take part, if only to defend the position he had achieved. He was therefore willing to intervene again — and this time he had a much more effective army at his command.

The attack on Alexander I by Demetrios II's forces brought a rebellion in Demetrios' favour by Alexander's governor in Palestine, Apollonios Taos. Jonathan fought him, but with the aim, as would be expected, of enhancing his own political position rather than only supporting Alexander. During the fighting Jonathan took the seaport of Joppa, and defeated Apollonios' forces in battle. He captured and sacked the city of Ashdod, but made no attempt to hold onto it. Most of its people survived to complain later. Nor does he seem to have held on to Joppa, though it is probable that he would have wished to do so, since it was the only worthwhile port on the Palestinian coast south of Ptolemais and the Bay of Haifa; eventually it did become the main port of Judaea. Any possibility of holding any town on the coast was ended by the march of Ptolemy VI's army along the coast of Palestine and Lebanon in 147. This made it clear that Jonathan's power was still confined to the hills.

The sack of Ashdod involved in particular the destruction of the temple of Dagon, the city's god.[6] This was another case of Maccabean intolerance. Having developed out of the rejection of the hellenization of Judaea, and of the conversion of the Jerusalem temple to one of Zeus Olympios – 'the abomination of desolation' – this intransigent attitude was first vented on the Jews who had accepted the religious change, and now it was directed against non-Jews as well.[7]

The Maccabees in fact were promoting a double ambition. First there was the purging of the Jewish population. This involved an insistence on the 'correct' worship, the veneration for the Torah, the holy book, driving out, or killing, those Jews who would not conform, and the concentration of worship in the temple at Jerusalem, so that competing temples, at Mount Gerizim and across the Jordan at Iraq el-Amir, were destroyed. This part of the programme was virtually completed by Jonathan. The second part of Maccabean ambition was directed against any competing gods. Hence the destruction of the Dagon temple in Ashdod, and in the future an intermittent campaign was waged to destroy nearby Greek cities. This part may be described as imperialism, but of a particular, even peculiar, sort. Greek, Macedonian, and Roman imperialism had normally involved merely conquering a region and then requiring the surviving population to pay taxes and to behave. This could be brutal enough, as the Carthaginians discovered, but, as at Corinth, those who escaped were not usually pursued. Maccabean imperialism was directed at the people, and required their conversion to Judaism, which was an incomprehensible requirement for Greeks and Romans. It did, of course, follow on quite automatically from the purging of the Jews and from the Jewish hostility to other gods and temples.

This imperialistic programme had not yet developed very far, in part because it was not yet possible for Jonathan to command a sufficiently powerful armed force. It was certainly possible to raid neighbouring lands, to destroy temples, and even to defeat small Greek armies such as that commanded by Apollonios Taos, but the Judaean region was not populous or powerful enough to allow him to hold on to conquered territory outside Judaea. This was demonstrated very clearly by the march of the Ptolemaic army along the Palestinian coast. Of course Ptolemy VI and Jonathan, as supporters of Alexander Balas, were technically on the same side but Jonathan could not have been pleased to find Alexander's uncertain grip being replaced by a restored Ptolemaic administration under the very capable Ptolemy VI.

Ptolemy, who was no doubt aware of the nuances of the political situation in Palestine, ensured Jonathan's compliance by taking him along on the march as far as the Eleutheros River, the Judaean army enclosed, as it were, within the Ptolemaic.[8] By then sending him back from that point, Ptolemy emphasized that his own programme of imperialism was aimed at restoring the old Ptolemaic empire in Palestine and Lebanon, whose original boundary had been along that river, and therefore that Judaea would be in the Ptolemaic suzerainty in the future.

Over the next two years Jonathan was sidelined, and eventually faced a profound difficulty. The final battle of the kings at the Oenoparos River left his allies dead and his enemy Demetrios II alive and in control. Worse, Demetrios rapidly recovered control of all the coastal cities Ptolemy had seized, while Jonathan's only possible saviour, Ptolemy VII, was fully occupied in establishing himself in power in Egypt, and afterwards consistently showed total indifference towards expanding his control outside Egypt.

The reward which Alexander had given to Jonathan for his battles against Apollonios Taos was three towns and their territories, Lydda, Ramathain and Apharaima, which expanded his territory north from Judaea into the plain, but which therefore also rendered him more vulnerable – for the Judaean plateau had proved to be very defensible in the past and these acquisitions were in the lower land – though richer and more productive of tax revenues than the rather barren plateau.[9] No doubt this was in Demetrios' mind when he came south. Jonathan negotiated with Lasthenes, Demetrios' Cretan commander. Lasthenes had no wish to repeat his predecessors' difficult campaigns in Judaea, and Jonathan had no wish to confront the new king in a war he might well lose and which would certainly cause considerable damage to his lands. A compromise resulted by which Jonathan recognized Demetrios as king and no doubt promised to pay tribute; Demetrios, in a formal letter quoting another from himself to Lasthenes, his 'father', in return accepted Jonathan's autonomy, and recognized the expansion of the territory provided by Alexander. But the Seleukid garrisons in the Akra and other forts which Jonathan had been attacking were not removed.[10]

The two men were thus in effect now allies, a restoration of the position Jonathan had been in as an ally of Alexander. So far Jonathan had showed himself an intelligent opportunist, willing to negotiate with whoever was king, and capable of extracting useful concessions. But to expand further Jonathan required continual Seleukid troubles, and now he made a mistake. It seems unlikely that the teenage Demetrios was cunning enough to lead Jonathan into the trap he now entered; perhaps we may assign the credit to Lasthenes. Jonathan agreed to send a contingent of his army to defend Demetrios in Antioch.[11]

The participation of Jewish soldiers in the suppression of the Antioch riots and in the sack to the city had little direct effect in Judaea in itself, other than to increase the worldly goods in the hands of the returned soldiers. The apparent alliance between Jonathan and Demetrios did not survive the rebellion of Diodotos and Antiochos VI. Ostensibly he changed sides to support the insurrection because Demetrios did not reward him for Antioch, though Demetrios' promise had been highly ambiguous; Jonathan had read into it what he hoped for. Jonathan, though now supposedly on the side of Diodotos, actually, as before was using the new Seleukid civil war for his own advantage. He attacked Gaza, though he was unable to capture the city, and then had to fend off an invasion from the north.[12] There he was defeated at Tell Hazor, though his brother Simon did succeed in capturing the fort at Beth Zur in the south, and in expelling the Jewish dissidents who had taken refuge there.

Jonathan was thus clearly on the side of Diodotos, and continued to be so once he had made himself king as Tryphon. But he was not really trusted, and in 142 fell into Tryphon's hands at Ptolemais-Ake. The reaction to his capture in Judaea was instructive. In Jerusalem Jonathan's brother Simon in effect carried through a *coup d'état* which placed him in Jonathan's place as governor and commander of the army, though Jonathan retained his position as high priest even in captivity.[13] Tryphon's attempt to use his possession of Jonathan was therefore blocked at the start, since no concessions Jonathan made, forced or voluntary, would be accepted by Simon and the Judaeans. Tryphon offered to return the high priest in exchange for a ransom and to accept Jonathan's children as hostages, but found a means of evading compliance when the ransom was paid, clearly understanding that returning Jonathan to power would simply place Judaea even more decisively amongst his opponents. He marched his army along the coast road, presumably aiming to invade the plateau, but was blocked by Simon, who moved the Judean army to block the successive routes from the plain which Tryphon might have used to invade the hills. All this reinforced Simon's authority, for Tryphon's capture of Jonathan, followed by his failure to keep his word to release him, and by his attempts to invade, solidified Judaean hostility to him.

Tryphon made an attack on Beth Zur, the fort which blocked access to Judaea from the south, but it was successfully defended. He attempted to send supplies to the Jerusalem Akra by a cavalry raid, but this was stopped by a surprise snowstorm – and the garrison in the Akra was composed of men who supported Demetrios, so his purpose was probably as much to gain control as to send in supplies. He took his army back northwards, then east and across the Jordan. At a place north of the Sea of Galilee, Bacsama, Jonathan was murdered, an action which had been all but certain ever since Tryphon had refused to release him when the ransom was paid.[14] The result for Tryphon was, of course, a political defeat. Simon, who had at some point in all this succeeded in installing a garrison into Joppa, now succeeded to the high priesthood, both by election by the people, and by hereditary right. He communicated with Demetrios, who, with nothing to lose now, confirmed his succession – but Simon had already taken the post, and would have exercised its powers whatever Demetrios said.[15] It was in effect a declaration of Judaean independence.

Two exploits confirmed and extended that new status for Simon and for Judaea. The non-Jewish population of Joppa was expelled.[16] The methods of Maccabean imperialism were thus demonstrated to all: expulsion and forcible conversion. In 142–141 also two military campaigns succeeded. The town of Gezer, a fortified place on a hill linked to the plateau but also commanding the coastal plain, was taken by siege and assault. This ensured a better access to Joppa and a better defence for Judaea. And at last, after an intermittent blockade lasting well over twenty years, the Jerusalem Akra was forced to capitulate. These campaigns set the seal on Simon's authority, and on Judaean independence.[17]

These two examples of regions of the Seleukid kingdom shifting into independence, Charakene and Judaea, show that routes towards independence varied for different sections of the kingdom. Hyspaosines ended as an independent king by way of a consistent policy of loyalty to the Seleukid king, whoever he was. Judaea became independent as a result of a consistent policy of antagonism towards every Seleukid king, and a deliberate exploitation of the Seleukid dynastic disputes. In both cases the new rulers found it necessary to fight frequently to attain their aims, one against foes of the Seleukids, the other against all Seleukids. In neither case was the condition of independence eventually attained really complete. Hyspaosines was constrained to submit to Parthian supremacy; Judaea faced an attack by Antiochos VII in 134 which resulted in the state once again submitting to Seleukid suzerainty for a time. Judaea was also unstable internally, and this was to be a difficulty for the next century. It was the assassination of Simon in an attempted *coup d'état* by his son-in-law which brought Antiochos in. Simon's own *coup*, of course, had shown the way, but any state which originates in a rebellion will be unstable for some time, even when independence has been attained – indeed independence, and the consequent relief from external pressures, is often the moment when suppressed internal tensions become intolerable.

In the course of the Seleukid wars of the 140s, it also became clear that some of the cities of the kingdom were restless under Seleukid control. This restlessness was primarily due to the failure of the Seleukid state to provide the security which had been the norm since the kingdom had generally been founded. In the main cities in North Syria the rival kings' garrisons and generals – Aischrion, Sarpedon, Palamedes, and no doubt others – maintained their control, probably by force and in a dictatorial way. These were some of the great and necessary prizes in the fighting, and the rival kings felt fully justified in this policy of forcible control. In other areas, however, the citizens could express their disenchantment more openly.

In Palestine political conditions were even more complicated than elsewhere: frequent changes in royal personnel, wars with the Judaeans, the Ptolemaic invasion, all caused serious damage to the loyalty of the cities to the dynasty. This loyalty, of course, may only have been skin-deep to start with, since the region's history of being part of the Ptolemaic kingdom was still remembered. There were, for example, few cities founded by Seleukid kings in the region, which was the bedrock of loyalty among cities in, for example, northern Syria. So it is hardly surprising that several cities took to acting independently, even if they did not actually achieve full political independence. In Ptolemais-Ake the citizens took matters into their own hands when Jonathan Maccabee came to meet King Tryphon. Jonathan's guard of a thousand men – so claimed by the book of Maccabees – was overwhelmed by the citizens, and Jonathan was captured and handed over to Tryphon.[18]

This action is assumed to have taken place without Tryphon's agreement. Certainly it presented him with an awkward problem. He could not release Jonathan without annoying the citizens; by keeping him he annoyed the Judaeans, whom he wished to keep on his side. And, of course, he made a mess of the opportunity the capture might have seemed to give him. The action of the citizens was the result of the enmity which already existed between Jews and Greeks in the Palestinian region. Several Greek towns and cities had been attacked or destroyed by Jewish armed bands, or by the Judaean army, including Ptolemais-Ake itself. So Jonathan's capture was a revenge action by the Ptolemaians. It is a mark of the capacity of even the most apparently docile city (and one at the time hosting Tryphon's army) for independent action, though in this case the aim was not independence.

To the south, however, two other cities did act independently and probably with the aim of achieving some sort of independence of their own. Twice the city of Ashkelon made agreements with the Judaean army under Jonathan, first when it attacked and sacked Ashdod, a few miles to the north, and second when Gaza was attacked. To be sure, at some point the city mint produced coins for Tryphon, but not until both of those events were in the past. In other words, for a time in the 140s the city appears to have been making its own decisions, though it also submitted to Ptolemy VI's army when he came through, and presumably to that of Demetrios II after Ptolemy's death. Tryphon's coins were produced in the city in his Years 1, 3 and 4, which is 142/141–138/137.[19] Gaza was also involved in these events, attacked by Jonathan because it was acting as though it was going to defect from Tryphon's cause. By failing to take the city, Jonathan in fact ensured that it shifted decisively towards Demetrios. In both of these cities therefore the citizens acted as if they were in independent states, though the arrival of a major army outside their gates was usually sufficient to induce a submission – Jonathan's army was clearly not menacing enough.

These reactions by individual cities might be dismissed as the sort of political confusion which a period of civil war can produce, in which the citizens pursued a healthy policy of appeasing whoever came close with an army. The citizens of the city of Arados, however, were purposeful and determined and had inherited a long-lasting civic aim of gaining complete independence. Situated on an island about a mile from the Syrian coast, Arados had been the only Phoenician city to fall into the Seleukid share of Syria when the land was partitioned in 300 BC. It was very close to the boundary between the Seleukid and the Ptolemaic parts, and so was able from the start to use its strategic situation to acquire some measure of autonomy, pursuing a similar policy as the Jews in exploiting periods of Seleukid weakness or confusion. This political autonomy waxed and waned over the next century and a half, but whenever it had the opportunity, Arados attempted to gain independence. In 145, or a year or two earlier, the city made an attempt to secure control over its *peraia*, the mainland opposite the island, by bribing Ammonios, the minister of Alexander Balas.[20]

For this was the second part of Arados' ambition, to eliminate the competition which came from a series of small ports strung along the adjacent coast – Gabala, Balanaea, Marathos, Simyra. These had been at times part of Arados' own territory, and at others they were separated. This was the situation in the 140s which the bribe to Ammonios was designed to change. It did not work, because an Aradian was so disgusted by the plot that he swam to the mainland and alerted the Marathians there, whose city, Marathos, was the immediate object of Arados' ire.

This attempt failed, though Arados' own autonomy continued. Both Judaea and Arados therefore aimed at their own independence and also aimed to deprive their neighbours of any independence and often of their lives and property as well. And both used periods of Seleukid weakness and division to try to achieve their aims. Arados had been attempting this ever since the origins of the Seleukid state, and Judaea since the 160s, but in the end both achieved their aims at the same time, in 129, when the great army led by Antiochos VII into Iran was destroyed. Then the Judaeans reasserted the independence they had lost a few years before to Antiochos, and the Aradians launched a vicious attack on Marathos. That community was destroyed in the same way that Carthage and Corinth had suffered, its people were sold, and its lands were distributed among the Aradian rulers. This, it will be seen, is not only the same action the Romans took at Carthage and Corinth, but is very similar to that by the Judaeans in Joppa, and later in Idumaea and other places.

There were therefore three ways by which countries broke away from the Seleukid kingdom: by a frontier loyalty which left Charakene alone and surrounded by enemies; by insurrection, such as that which Judaea and Arados had repeatedly attempted; and by a minimum assertion of neutrality in the civil wars by which cities such as Ashkelon and Gaza insensibly drifted towards independence; this last tactic, however, invariably failed, since it was based on weakness, which was not a condition conquerors respected.

On the other hand, there was another action, by small provinces which, like Charakene, were ruled by the same governor for long periods, and which in the end were left, like Gaza and Ashkelon, in a condition of effective independence. These provinces were also weak, but not so obviously defenceless as the single cities, though like both Judaea and Charakene they were peripheral in terms of power and geography. Kommagene was a frontier province in the north of Syria which faced the independent kingdoms in Asia Minor. It was largely a section of the valley of the Euphrates where the river flows through the Taurus Mountains, enclosed by mountains and partly isolated. From about 163 onwards it was governed by a man called Ptolemaios.[21] He occupied that position until about 130, but did little or nothing towards making himself independent other than stay in office; presumably he succeeded in avoiding the enmity of any of the competing kings over that period. When he died his son, Samos, took over his position. This was at the time when Antiochos VII was busy in Iran, and the destruction of his army in the next year left Samos in command in Kommagene. No doubt the success of his father in keeping civil warfare at bay had generated a local loyalty to the family. The direct inheritance of the governorship was a mark of, at least, autonomy for the region; it led a generation later to the assumption of the royal title and independence.

There are other regions which may well have gone through the same process – Adiabene, for instance, in the valley of the Tigris but north of the region which was taken control of by the Parthians, was a Seleukid sub-province like Kommagene, and became a kingdom, though direct evidence only appears some time later. Just across the Euphrates from Kommagene was the province of Oshroene which had a king by 132 BC; it was centred on the city of Edessa, and was ruled by an Arab dynasty, another example of the encroachment of the desert Arabs into the settled lands, as in Babylon and Syria in the 140s. The exact dates for the independence of these regions cannot now be determined, but the coincidence in the time of the death of Antiochos VII and the destruction of his army, with the completion of the independence movements of Judaea and Arados is clearly significant. But this coincidence only occurred because of the drastic weakening of Seleukid power, and of the authority of the dynasty, which was brought about by the dynastic wars of 152–138.

There is thus considerable evidence by 140, not only of the conquest of parts of the kingdom by outsiders, but of the beginning of disintegration in that part of the kingdom still under the rule of the king. None of this was definitive, and the emergence of a powerful and determined king could still reverse all these developments. For a time it was to seem that Antiochos VII was that king, though in the end he found the task too great. But before he made his attempt to recover the kingdom's lost parts, his elder brother also made a valiant effort to anticipate him. Again he failed, but perhaps only by the skin of his teeth: Demetrios II made an even greater fight for the future of his inheritance than his brother.

Chapter 14

The Kingdom's Last Chance

While Demetrios II had been fighting first Antiochos VI and then Tryphon during 144–141 the east had remained relatively quiet. Mithradates of Parthia was apparently in Hyrkania, or more likely further east, perhaps preoccupied with the situation in Baktria, which may have threatened to spill over into Parthia, and Kabneskir of Elymais had also, so far as we know, been confined to the kingdom he had seized. But during 141 Mithradates came west again, descended with his army through the Zagros passes (observing no doubt the statue of the fat reclining Herakles on Kleomenes' boastful inscription at Bisitun which commemorated, probably, a defeat inflicted on Mithradates and the Parthians). He had then captured Seleukeia-on-the-Tigris and Babylon. The Babylonian Diarist's account of these events is fairly fragmentary, but it is clear enough that the capture took place in June, and that by next month 'Arsakes' was accepted as king.

The governing centre of Babylonia was Seleukeia-on-the-Tigris, a totemic city of the Seleukid dynasty. It had been the first city founded by Seleukos I, in the first province he had secured, and it was probably the largest city between Antioch and Pataliputra. Further it was one of a group of four, the other three, Babylon, Borsippa, and Opis, were original Babylonian cities. Their combined population probably rivalled that of North Syria, or even of all Greece. They were rich, populous, and politically quiescent, though there was occasional trouble from the royal forces at times of dynastic disturbance. Mithradates' aim in securing these cities was clearly to establish full control over the economic powerhouse which was Babylonia. Its loss was a crucial blow to the Seleukid kingdom.

The Babylon Diarist recorded Mithradates' approach march, and he may well have sent a warning message on ahead that he was coming, for the Diarist indicates that a message of some sort was received in advance and published, though it could also have come from a victim of Mithradates' advance. Either way it is clear that Babylonia was not surprised by the Parthian arrival.

Mithradates arrived from Hyrkania, and had therefore marched through Media. His approach was hardly secret at any point, yet there is no indication that any fighting was involved. It would seem therefore that either the

Babylonians had been left effectively defenceless, or Mithradates had by preliminary intrigues arranged the surrender in advance. (There is no sign of the army which Ardaya had commanded in 145, and which had fought in the name of Antiochos VI next year and Ardaya himself had apparently vanished already.) The fighting in Elymais had ended in 144 in a Seleukid defeat, which had presumably reduced the army's numbers. Having switched its allegiance to Antiochos VI, it then had had to cope with Antiochos' death (and the rumours around it), Tryphon's usurpation, and the fight being put up in Syria by Demetrios II. We have no indication of the size or the political complexion of the surviving Seleukid army in Babylonia by the time Mithradates arrived, but it is very likely to have been confused, perhaps even paralyzed. Some of the troops, once it was clear in 144 that Mithradates was not campaigning in Media or Babylonia, may have been withdrawn to fight in Syria.

When he arrived at Seleukeia Mithradates appointed as his new viceroy (the 'general above the four generals') a man called 'Antiochos son of King Ar'abuzana'. This king is not otherwise known; he may have been the king of Atropatene, or of some other sub-kingdom of the Parthian kingdom – there is a reference to 'Assyria' in this section of the tablet, but there is a break before it – 'Assyria' was the Babylonian name for what was later the kingdom of Adiabene. A few days later a general called Nikanor was appointed as governor (*strategos*) of Babylon, one of the 'four generals', whose superior was Antiochos.[1] Nikanor later carried out a sacrifice in the temple at Babylon for the life of the king.

The names of the two generals, being Greek, rather imply that Mithradates' arrival was not unwelcome. Nikanor was, it may be presumed, a man of the local Macedonian elite, though his appointment as governor implies that he had a military background, presumably in the Seleukid forces. Antiochos, son of a king, was probably from one of the Parthian sub-kingdoms, and Atropatene is the most likely. The Greek name of the son of an Iranian king is a good indication of the interpenetration of cultures which had taken place in the previous couple of centuries.

The complete lack of reaction to Mithradates' conquest is, to say the least, surprising. This, for once, is not simply a lack of sources, for it is clear from the Diaries that there was no resistance in Babylonia. Mithradates had had to fight for two or three years to conquer Media, yet he was able to take over central Babylonia with no more effort than that involved in travelling to it. The whole campaign, according to the dates noted by the Diarist, lasted less than a month. The preliminary message sent on parchment to the governor of Babylon was received on the 22nd day of the third month of 171 (which was

June/July 141 BC), and by the 28th day, somebody – there is a break in the tablet, but it was surely the king – 'entered Seleukeia, the royal city'.[2]

The lack of opposition must be accounted for. It has been noted that Mithradates' arrival was not a surprise; indeed it was assumed in advance. So the explanation must lie in Babylonia. It is possible that none of the commanders in the region had a sufficient force with which to mount a defensive battle. The best place would have been at the Bisitun Pass, but Mithradates clearly got through without difficulty. Two considerations seem relevant. The regime could have been militarily weak, as a result in part of the defeat and reduction of the local army in the campaign into Elymais in 144, or the probable transfer of troops to Syria to be used in the civil war there. Neither of these is more than a conjecture, but the general situation must make them probable. The other explanation for the lack of resistance is that there was a general lack of will in Babylonia to fight on behalf of either Demetrios II or Tryphon, and that the rule of the Parthian king was preferable to being a battlefield for the two kings fighting in Syria. The last time the army is mentioned in the Diarist's account it was referred to as that of 'Antiochos son of Alexander', so it had changed sides once already. We do not know what its, or the province's, allegiance was by 141. The collective decision, possibly reinforced by news of a benevolent Parthian government in Media, may well have been that both kings were not worth supporting.

There is also the possibility of treason and intrigue. This is easy to suppose, but difficult to prove. The fact that a local Greek – Nikanor – was quickly emplaced as viceroy might imply that he was a former official who had defected. There were plenty of examples in the Hellenistic world for this type of action. More convincing is the fact that this acceptance of Parthian rule did not last, and there were soon rebellions, and that when Demetrios II arrived he was welcomed. Perhaps a combination of political confusion, treason, and general exhaustion would best explain the ease of the Parthian conquest.

Whatever the precise reasons for the Babylonian collapse and the ease of the Parthian conquest, it was a situation which Demetrios II had to address. The longer he stayed fighting in Syria, the smaller the kingdom he would have at the end (if he won, of course). Unable to prevail against Tryphon in Syria (Chapter 12), he now decided to attempt to recover Babylonia first, and then presumably return with a victorious army to polish off Tryphon. It was a decision he could portray as putting personal ambition aside in favour of rescuing his subjects from the attentions of the nomad barbarians. And if Babylonia had fallen easily because it was lightly defended, it could be that it would fall back into the hands of the legitimate Seleukid king when the

Greco-Macedonian population was appealed to, especially if that king arrived at the head of an army to resolve any confusion.

Demetrios therefore collected an army and supplies in Syria, and marched east. This process will have taken some time. Mithradates' conquest took place in June/July, and the news probably took a month or so to reach Syria. Demetrios then had to consider and decide what to do, probably consulting with his commanders, then he had to collect an army and supplies. The march east, a distance of at least 700 kilometres, will have taken up to two months. He can hardly have reached Babylonia much before the end of 141, and probably not until the spring of 140.

The gathering of the army and the preliminary consultations and planning also gave Demetrios time for diplomacy. Mithradates' authority in Babylonia was scarcely very firm as yet. His ease of occupation required his acceptance of the local powers continuing in office, and it is clear that he depended on locals to govern in his name. There was plenty of material around for diplomats to operate on. The likely disenchantment of the Greco-Macedonian and Babylonian population at being conquered was one aspect, especially if a large Parthian army of occupation arrived, or if internal security failed. Raids by Arabs, for example, continued. If they were to be combated, a considerable army would be needed — both of these might well fuel local resentment.

Then there were the neighbours. A clay tablet from Uruk in the far south of Babylonia, dated by Mithradates' reign, indicates that he was acknowledged there, but in the southern extremity of Babylonia, where the Seleukid governor Hyspaosines — 'Aspasine' to the Diarist — was still in office, it is unclear what the reaction was.[3] Hyspaosines had been in office since about 165 BC, Antiochos IV's reign, and his seat of power was Antioch-on-the-Erythraean-Sea, which Hyspaosines had extended by building a large and wider enclosure, so that it then became called Spasinou Charax.[4] It seems unlikely that he would have easily acknowledged the authority of Mithradates.

On the other hand, he was presumably to some extent under the authority of whoever had been governor in Babylonia. The failure of the Diarist to do more than refer to the pre-Parthian 'general who is above the four generals' by his title, and not to name him, prevents us from seeing to what extent the Seleukid administration still functioned. The four generals were all, so far as we can see, located in the central Babylonian cities. Hyspaosines was therefore at a distance from the centre of power, but the Babylonian viceroy was clearly superior to him. If there was a viceroy in office when Mithradates arrived, either he submitted or he fled — Nikanor took his place. In either case Hyspaosines could feel he was released to make his own decisions, since if the viceroy did either of those things he could be regarded as a traitor or a deserter.

The rapid expansion of Parthian power was undoubtedly unwelcome to Hyspaosines, whose whole career implies a loyalty to the Seleukid king, and it is reasonable to believe that he came out in opposition to Mithradates at once. Similarly it was also unwelcome to Kabneskir in Elymais, who now found himself surrounded on north and west, and perhaps on the east, by Mithradates' power. Here then was the raw material for a set of alliances, but it may be assumed that neither Kabneskir nor Hyspaosines, neighbours and on opposite sides in regard to the Seleukid kingdom, were keen on joining with each other. Kabneskir after all had defeated the Seleukid army only three or four years before.

Nevertheless there is nothing like a common enemy to bring about a quick friendship. Mithradates' new success brought a response from all his neighbours. Justin records that an alliance was formed between Demetrios II, the Elymaians, the Persians, and the Baktrians.[5] The Elymaians, of course, meant Kabneskir, whose own ambitions to seize control of Babylonia for himself had been made clear enough in the past few years, and who will have quickly seen the threat posed to him by Parthian control of both Media and Babylonia. The 'Persians' in this case probably means the ruler of Persis, the land east of Susiana and Elymais. Who this was is not known, but the area had been virtually independent for several decades; it is possible that Mithradates or Kabneskir had already reduced Persis to vassalage, but it would be obvious that the expansion of Parthia posed a threat to Persis as well as the rest. To gain the alliance of these two Demetrios can only have promised them independence; they would have accepted nothing less. Whatever the result of the war Demetrios was beginning, his kingdom would be smaller at the end of it.

Which Baktrian king was involved is not known either. It may have been Heliokles I, the son of Eukratides I. Heliokles was the last Greek king in Baktria with any significant territory or power, so far as we know. Alternatively, Demetrios may have contacted some of the new nomad conquerors. Both of these are likely to have been enemies of Mithradates, with as much to fear from an increase in Mithradates' power as anyone else. Hyspaosines is not mentioned in the list in Justin, but he was a subject of Demetrios' already, and of course took his side.

This alliance must have taken some time to form, since Demetrios' envoys would need to traverse Parthian territory to make their contacts, but a man alone could move much more quickly than armies. This was true enough, for at least six months elapsed between the Parthian conquest of Babylonia and Demetrios' march eastwards. Mithradates himself stayed in Babylonia from the time of his conquest in June 141 until January 140, and it was during this time that his enemies evidently became organized.[6] The problem was that none of the allies alone had the necessary power or the ability to concentrate sufficient force so as to provide a real threat to the Parthians. Mithradates, though surrounded by these enemies, now had the advantages of a large territory, a central position, and the prestige and confidence of past victories. Not only that, but his enemies tended to be distracted by other threats, including from each other.

Heliokles (or some other Baktrian king) was beset by local enmities, which had already deprived his kingdom of much of its territory north of the Oxus River and parts of the lands south of it, and he was at enmity with the Greek king of the Punjab, who was probably Menander, the captor of Pataliputra, and who ruled the Punjab and much of the Indus Valley. No Baktrian king could rely on these enemies to remain neutral if he devoted his power to fighting the Parthians.

Kabneskir, after several years' fighting to gain independence, and defeating the invasion of the Seleukid army in Babylonia, was surely weakened, and probably not in the mood to be very trusting of Demetrios II as an ally (for it was in Demetrios' name that Ardaya had attacked him). He was not distracted by an enemy in his rear for the present, but even allied with Persis he was scarcely a major threat to Parthia proper. It seems unlikely that Persis could contribute much to the common cause, other than not distracting Kabneskir. Hyspaosines may have had a good defensive position amid the marshes of the south, but he was hardly a powerful ruler. And Demetrios II, of course, was already involved in his longstanding civil war with Tryphon, now king. As a set of allies, this was not very convincing.

The Diarist records that Mithradates and his army left for Media in December 141 or January 140. At more or less the same time he recorded that 'the Elamite and his troops' had invaded southern Babylonia, and were attacking the city of Apamea on the Silhu River (close to the modern city of Kut el-Amarna). Apamea was said to be burned, though the population had apparently left to take refuge at a place called Bit-Karkudi.

This invasion was presumably part of an attack to be co-ordinated with the arrival of Demetrios in the north, though it is evident that it was launched too early. Mithradates' departure, in winter, with his army may well have been in response to trouble on his eastern frontier, possibly generated by a Baktrian attack. The problem was that an invasion of Babylonia by 'the Elamite' was bound to produce a vigorous response from the Babylonians, who saw these invaders in particular as hereditary enemies. Antiochos the viceroy, 'representing King Arsaces', marched out to confront these invaders.

The Diarist's entry for December 141/January 140 is confusing and fragmentary, and it was perhaps confused originally. He records the General Antiochos leaving the city of Seleukeia to fight the Elymaean invasion, but then in a later entry of the same month he appears to be recording that fighting had reached Babylon. 'The people, their children, their possessions, and their wives', follows a reference to the Elamite war. Then he notes, in the same passage, that 'the nobles of the king who had entered Babylonia and the few people they had gone to the sea', which cannot be a reference to Babylon, but may be a description of an evacuation of anti-Parthian refugees, either south to join Hyspaosines, or north west to the Syrian cities (the Diarist always refers to the Syrian Antioch as 'Antioch-by-the-Sea'). This section ends (still in the same month) with a reference to damage caused to the Marduk Gate (in Babylon), and to brickwork being damaged by an enemy on the Euphrates side, presumably referring to the city walls. The enemy is not named, and it seems unlikely that Demetrios had reached Babylon yet, so it is possibly an Elamite attack, or perhaps a local rising against the Parthians, or even an attack by Arabs from the desert. Either way it is obvious that all Babylonia was convulsed by this fighting.

Demetrios is not mentioned by the Diarist. Western written sources, however, credit him with victories. Justin claims he defeated the Parthians several times.[7] Josephus claims that he had support among the Greco-Macedonian population, who had appealed to him to rescue them from Parthian rule.[8]

It was thus into a complex local situation that Demetrios moved in the spring of 140, apparently welcomed by his former subjects — though since at least the local elite had taken the Parthian side, this welcome cannot have been unanimous. By then the Elamite invasion of the south had been defeated by Antiochos the viceroy. Whatever attacks by the Baktrians had taken place did not seriously affect matters, for Mithradates was soon able to invade Elymais: that is, while Antiochos the viceroy fought the Elamite army at Apamaea, a Parthian army from Media attacked Elymais from the north. The coinage produced at Susa in the name of Kabneskir implies that he ceased to reign in 140. An inscription on the relief carving of Mithradates and Kabneskir (III) shows the latter being installed as governor of Elymais — satrap not king — and therefore as a subordinate of Mithradates. Therefore Mithradates invaded Elymais in 140, presumably out of Media and clearly successfully.[9]

To this extent therefore the concentric alliance against Mithradates had been successful. Mithradates had marched out of Babylonia at a time

(December/January) when travel through the Zagros Mountains was very difficult; this implies an emergency in Media or on his eastern boundary, hence probably the Baktrian attack, or at least a threat. Kabneskir's invasion of Babylonia happened as soon as Mithradates had left, and his forces may well have reached as far north as Babylon itself; he certainly preoccupied the viceroy Antiochos and his army. Mithradates no doubt ensured that the Baktrian attack was stopped, perhaps by his Median viceroy Bagasis, his brother, then turned to attack Kabneskir's homeland, and Kabneskir found himself attacked by Mithradates out of Media and by Antiochos from Babylonia. (There is no sign of any activity by Hyspaosines, but he may well not have had time to react.) While Mithradates and Antiochos were busy with Elymais – a war which surely took up much of 140 – Demetrios arrived from the north.

The sources for the fighting which took place between spring 140 and spring 138 are either poor or totally absent. The western sources are no more than the sentence. The Diarist's account is missing. The coins from the Susa mint, and the inscriptions, indicate that Mithradates conquered Elymais by 140. But he did lose his grip on central Babylonia at about the same time, for the Seleukeian mint issued coins in the name of Demetrios in 140/139, though Mithradates recovered the city in 139, when it was minting in his name.[10] The main conflict was always between Mithradates and Demetrios, and once Kabneskir had been suppressed the fighting continued in Babylonia. Again, no details are known other than the eventual Parthian victory, though a much later source suggests that Demetrios attacked twice, and Justin says he won several battles.[11] Demetrios coined extensively at Nisibis in Mesopotamia, which would thus seem to be one of his rearward military bases.[12] Certainly the war between the kings lasted over two years, beginning in spring 140, or even longer if the earlier Elamite attack at Apamea is included. It did not end until July 138, when Demetrios was captured.

The Diarist says that 'King Arsakes' – that is, Mithradates – came from Media to Babylonia and 'brought about the defeat of his [Demetrios'] troops and seized him and his nobles'.[13] The story in the Greek sources was that he was tricked into being captured by an offer of peace, though this may be no more than the assumption of Oriental duplicity which Greek and Roman historians implicitly accepted.[14]

Fighting went on into and beyond the next year, even after Demetrios' capture. The Diarist's account survives for much of 137, though with gaps. It is clear that the war in Elymais had resumed and that Hyspaosines was now fighting. There was apparently trouble in the Parthian ranks, for Mithradates gave orders for a general (his name is missing) to be killed. Some force entered

Seleukeia but was driven out by Mithradates' army. An Elamite invasion caused panic — coins from Susa bear the name of Tigraios between 138 and 133, so presumably the satrap Kabneskir (III) did not last long. Hyspaosines is recorded fighting against the Elamites, and so presumably in defence of his own lands.[15]

The record is confused, and probably reflects a general confusion at the time. The fighting evidently ranged over all Babylonia, from Hyspaosines' lands to the north — one of Demetrios' victories is located at Arbela. The great city of Seleukeia was fought over by at least two armies, and will have suffered damage in the process, just as Babylon suffered from Arab and Elyemaean attacks. The speed and ease of the original Parthian conquest was thus repaid in full, with several cities wrecked or at least badly damaged.

Back in Syria Tryphon does not seem to have been able to use Demetrios' absence in the east between 140 and 138 to any good effect. At first little seems to have changed in Syria. Those western mints which coined for the rivals before Demetrios went eastwards continued to coin for the same men all through the next two years. It would seem that Tryphon had achieved his greatest success before Demetrios left for the east — and that this was presumably one of the considerations in Demetrios' decision to go. He had left his wife Kleopatra Thea and their children (two boys and a girl) in Seleukeia-in-Pieria, along with the General Aischrion.[16] He and she competently held on to his position in Syria, though she was as unable to make any advances as her opponent. She was soon helped by the arrival of Demetrios' younger brother Antiochos.

He had lived at Side in Pamphylia for a time while Demetrios fought Tryphon and campaigned against Mithradates, but later moved to Rhodes.[17] He returned to Syria during 139. And here, at once, we have a problem. According to the Babylonian Diarist, Demetrios II was captured by Mithradates in June 138. The coins issued by the mints at Antioch and Seleukeia-in-Pieria were minted in 139 in the name of Antiochos as king, and others were minted at Tyre.[18] Therefore, it appears that Antiochos had made himself king several months, perhaps a year, before Demetrios was captured.

Josephus' account of Antiochos' arrival in Syria, while somewhat confused in parts, is quite clear that he was invited to come by Demetrios' wife Kleopatra Thea. She was living in Seleukeia-in-Pieria with her children and apparently feared an attempt by a group in the city to admit Tryphon's forces. This, of course, fits with other indications, as earlier at Laodikeia, that most cities were divided in their allegiances — she may also have feared a change of heart by the garrison commander, in which case she and her children would surely be the first victims. According to Josephus she proposed that Antiochos marry her, a marriage which would also give him the kingship.[19]

Josephus therefore puts the sequence of events as: (1) Demetrios' capture, (2) Kleopatra's message, (3) Antiochos' arrival. Appian's account is so brief as to be misleading, though he does say that Antiochos came to Syria from Rhodes.[20] In literary terms, it was obviously easier to follow the story of Demetrios II through to his capture by Mithradates in Babylonia, then go back to Syria, bring in Antiochos VII, and follow the war which was fought between Antiochos and Tryphon. None of the ancient literary sources are concerned about the comparative chronology of the careers of the two brothers, and all see the events in Syria and Babylonia as separate. The Babylonian Diarist never mentions Antiochos VII until he got to Babylonia several years later; coins of Antioch and Seleukeia are, of course, silent on events in Babylonia. Nevertheless the interlinking of events make it clear that Antiochos was operating as king in Syria before Demetrios was captured. The overlap between them is partly confirmed by the fact that dated coins of Demetrios were produced in two mints in 174, though neither mint can be located, which might suggest that they were both somewhere in the east, perhaps mobile mints with the army or temporarily located in places he had captured, and so under Demetrios' control.[21]

It seems unlikely that Kleopatra would so deliberately and publicly betray her husband. She had, of course, had a brutal lesson in royal marriage from her father, who had abruptly taken her from Alexander Balas and given her to Demetrios. Her mother was now forcibly married to her uncle, who had also married her sister (both women also called Kleopatra). Presumably Kleopatra Thea reckoned she could transfer herself as her father had. And the process had shown that whoever her husband was, he would have direct access to the kingship – this has been the purpose both of her marriage to Alexander and of her transfer to Demetrios. Josephus' explanation – that she feared she would be captured by Tryphon if Seleukeia fell – is very plausible. Further, if Seleukeia fell its capture would be a major triumph for Tryphon. This was the name city of the founder, and Tryphon already held the great cities of Antioch and Apamea and Ptolemais-Ake, while those remaining to Demetrios were generally of the second rank. Capturing Seleukeia and Kleopatra and her children might well persuade the rest of Syria that he was the winner, and produce a domino-fall of the rest in his favour. So, however unlikely it seems that Kleopatra would so publicly ditch Demetrios while he was still fighting desperately in the east, there were comprehensible reasons for it. Above all, it does suggest that her situation in Seleukeia was very serious.

The question arises, of course: did Demetrios know of Kleopatra's problem and of her solution to it? Also, if he knew, did he approve of it? Did he even suggest it, possibly before he left for the east? No ancient historian even hints at this aspect of the issue, but it would surely not be surprising if some collusion had taken place between the various parties involved. The Seleukid family had a history of such doings; Seleukos I had handed on his second wife to his son; Antiochos II had left one wife for another, and had later apparently returned to the first; the mother of Demetrios II and Antiochos was her husband's sister; their grandmother had been married to three brothers in succession. The transfer, by her own decision, of Kleopatra Thea from one brother to another was only marginally different from these examples. Royal families made their own marriage rules, and these were principally designed for political purposes.

Josephus' account, that Kleopatra invited Antiochos into Seleukeia, must certainly omit a process of negotiation between the two before his arrival. Antiochos by that time was living at Rhodes, so messages would take several days each way. Antiochos, clearly the man in demand, could lay down conditions, one of which presumably was that he become king, if only as a means of ensuring his command over the Seleukid armed forces. No doubt Kleopatra was not averse to marriage to a virile 20-year-old (they had five children in the next eight years).

It is highly unlikely that either of these people would put themselves into the hands of the other without precautions and guarantees. Some time must therefore have passed between Kleopatra's invitation and Antiochos' arrival. The negotiations probably took several months, beginning almost as soon as Demetrios left for Babylonia, in which case they may well have had his blessing. Further, if Seleukeia-in-Pieria was in danger of falling to Tryphon, Antiochos would need to bring more than his person to the city. Rhodes, of course, would be a useful place to gather ships and mercenaries for such an expedition – it had been Demetrios II's base after his father's death.

It is clear therefore that Kleopatra Thea took her new husband in marriage while her first still lived, and before he was captured. Antiochos took his brother's position both in his bed and on his throne as King Antiochos VII while Demetrios was fighting in Babylonia. It was perhaps lucky for the kingdom that Demetrios was then captured by the Parthians. He was paraded through the cities to demonstrate that his cause was finished, and then sent to Hyrkania to a comfortable prison. In Hyrkania he was consoled by a marriage with a daughter of Mithradates, Rhodogune, with whom he had two children.[22] This was obviously a Parthian response – and perhaps one by Demetrios as well – to the marriage of Antiochos and Kleopatra, and it also gave Mithradates' grandchildren by Rhodogune as good a claim to the Seleukid kingship as the children of Kleopatra by Antiochos VII, or Demetrios, and a better one than that of Tryphon. There was now a confusing number of children who had more or less equal claims to the kingship: twenty years before, Demetrios I had been the only representative of the dynasty left alive.

Antiochos was not tainted by Demetrios' past mistakes, and he was also very largely clear of the unpopularity which had developed around his father. He was several years older at his accession than his brother had been, but above all, he was capable, a fresh face, and not Demetrios, all of which qualities Tryphon had also possessed – but he was of the royal family, and so represented stability and continuity, as opposed to Tryphon's attempt at radical change. With little delay all Syria fell to him. Kleopatra Thea's city of Seleukeia-in-Pieria was his first base. During the rest of 139 – he cannot have arrived before May or June – coins in his name were issued at Seleukeia, in Kilikia, at Antioch and, in succession to Demetrios, at Sidon and Tyre. Tryphon, whose coins carried a new era dating from his own accession to the throne, produced 'Year 4' coins (174 SE = 138/137 BC) only at Byblos, Ptolemais–Ake and Ashkelon.[23] The only 'Year 5' indication is on a sling bullet found at Dor, where Tryphon's forces were besieged near the end of his career, and this suggests his end came not long after the beginning of that year.[24] All this meant that Tryphon had lost most of the most important area, North Syria, fairly quickly. Late in 138 he was confined to Dor in Palestine. He escaped early in 137, and Antiochos caught up with him finally near Apamea, and defeated and killed him.[25]

Tryphon's death proved to be the end of the fighting in Syria, where Antiochos VII and Kleopatra Thea ruled for the next several years, though Demetrios' capture did not bring an immediate end to the war in the east. Demetrios was paraded through the cities which Mithradates had conquered, to show that their former king was now a prisoner; no doubt this largely stilled the fighting. Mithradates then kept him in captivity, for use later if necessary or possible, or perhaps because killing him might have provoked a new rebellion.[26] Mithradates suffered a stroke some time in 138 to 137, but lived on for some years, according to the latest interpretation of the difficult chronology, dying in about 132. He had several brothers, and more sons. No doubt a regency government was organized for his final years, but the situation will have also weakened Parthia.

The Diarist records at the end of his account of the capture of King Demetrios that there was 'plenty, happiness, and good peace in the cities of Media'. This was almost immediately contradicted, for he goes on to record fighting throughout Babylonia for the next fifteen years. But for the next several years there was no possibility that Antiochos VII could campaign in the east until he had secured control in Syria. He did make a valiant attempt in 131–129, but, like Antiochos III and Antiochos IV, died in the attempt; Demetrios escaped from his comfortable Parthian prison, but died in a desperate attempt to recover enough power in the west to try again. That is, by 138, the kingdom's last real chance to recover the east had failed, and the repeated attempts to do so over the next decade and more only debilitated both Syria and Babylonia still more. By 138 the Seleukid kingdom was shrunken, reduced to a fragmentary Syrian region, where Judaea, Arados, Osrhoene, Kommagene and then the major cities struck out for independence in the next years. The final blow was the continuing quarrels between the children of Kleopatra Thea, in which she meddled with selfish intent.

Conclusion – The World in 140 BC

It is worth pointing out, first of all, that elements of chance in this complex story are present in all the decisions made by the participants. Under no circumstances can we see that any planning was involved other than on the very short term. No king or councillor or senator or general in 150 had any idea that the world ten years later would appear as it did. The Roman expansion to the east and south can be attributed in large part to the Romans' reaction to events in Africa and Greece and Macedonia. Indeed one might with some plausibility claim that if the Macedonian pretender Andriskos had not made his attempt to revive that kingdom, or had been stopped right at the start – any number of people, including the Roman Senate, might have done so – the Romans would not have embarked on that expansion.

In 150 the Senate as a whole showed no real interest in, and certainly no enthusiasm for, the annexation of Carthage, despite Cato's rhetoric – which in fact was not aimed at annexation, but at destruction. If the Carthaginians had complied with the Roman demands, and moved inland, their state would probably have continued in existence in some form or another, and no doubt their city-site would have been gradually reoccupied. But the collapse of the Roman dispensation in Macedonia, and the defeat of a Roman army did require that a new system be instituted there, and so annexation became the vogue at Rome and remained the Roman preference from then on. In the half century between 200 and 150, only Cisalpine Gaul (a special case) and parts of Spain were acquired; in the half century after the annexation of Macedon, Asia, Africa, more parts of Spain, Narbonnese Gaul, Cyrenaica, and various other bits and pieces were annexed.

In the same way it was the nomad invasion of the Baktrian kingdom which released the Parthians from concern for their eastern frontier, at least for a short time, so that they could campaign into Iran. They might have begun earlier, but until the destruction of Ai-Khanum and the decisive reduction of the Baktrian state, the Parthian king must have always been conscious of the threat it posed to his eastern frontier – something it is evident that Demetrios II understood. A powerful Baktrian king might well take advantage of the Parthian move to the west to recover the provinces earlier taken by the Parthians, or even more. Now that concern was lifted. It was, of course, replaced by concern over what the nomad conquerors would do, and in the 120s the Parthians had to campaign hard to hold back another nomad invasion of their own territory, and in the process they had to surrender territory to those invaders. The Parthian expansion into Iran and Babylonia, therefore, took place during a brief period when their eastern frontier was not actually under threat. Had that threat existed in 145, rather than 130, Mithradates would not have been able to campaign in Media – and it would only have taken a slight change of direction to bring the Yuezhi into Parthia rather than Baktria.

The destruction of the Baktrian state also had its effect on the Greek position in India. Despite the antagonism between the dynasties which ruled in the two countries, they did in effect support each other in indirect ways. The Greek raid on Pataliputra drew attention away from wrecked Baktria as decisively as the destruction of Ai-Khanum aided the Parthians; and success in India provided some compensation for the destruction of the Baktrian kingdom, so that Greek rule in northwest India lasted another century and a half.

These developments in the east and west were clearly, as we can see in hindsight, the signs of the future, but the central event, geographically and politically, was the prolonged crisis in the Seleukid state, and here the elements of chance are less institutional than personal. It is in the events in Syria – the death of Demetrios I, the invasion by his son, the rebellion of Diodotos –- that we can discern some more individual choices which had disproportionate effects on the whole situation.

It must, however, first be emphasized that the events in the Seleukid kingdom affected all the rest of the Hellenistic world. It was in Antioch that Andriskos developed his ambition to make himself king in Macedon, and his success there stimulated the Roman response which drove the Italian city to the decisive annexations in 146, which in turn fuelled the career of Scipio Aemilianus and eventually more conquests in Spain. And it was the collapse of Seleukid authority in Syria which permitted Mithradates to turn west and conquer Media and Babylonia. His alternative strategy might well have been to render assistance to the Baktrian kingdom against the nomad power, which clearly threatened both of them – a mutual enemy was always a stimulus to joint action. The survival of a strong Greek Baktria would obviously have an effect in India.

The most obvious of the individual enterprises which had increasing effects as time went on was the activity of Herakleides of Miletos in his efforts to promote the cause of Alexander Balas. Why he had not been eliminated by Demetrios I when Timarchos was defeated and killed is not known, but his campaign was a powerful signal that the Hellenistic political world was riddled with personal loyalties and enmities which could easily cut across what later historians have too easily assumed to be inevitable developments.

But Demetrios I himself was also the author of decisions which were relatively minor but had major consequences. His attempt to steal Cyprus from Ptolemy was part of the old Seleukid aims. The island had been claimed by Seleukos I and direct attempts to seize it had been made by Antiochos III and Antiochos IV, but Demetrios' intrigue needlessly antagonized Ptolemy VI, who until then was friendly towards him. By driving Ptolemy to support Herakleides' plot Demetrios brought on himself the war in which both of them died. And note that Demetrios also spared Andriskos, who could only have been inspired to invade Macedon by the success of Alexander in Syria.

The actions of Diodotos/Tryphon were even more disruptive. His political enmity toward the Seleukid family, and his loyalty to the memory of Alexander, made him an enlarged version of Herakleides, and his career produced a thoroughgoing disruption of the whole Seleukid state. It was never to recover from this uprising. Demetrios II's determined defence of his inheritance was never to be enough, though quite possibly his expedition to recover Babylonia delayed further Parthian expansion westwards; his brother died in a similar expedition later, by which time the Parthians were about to be beset by the nomads out of Central Asia, and made no further advance to the west for another generation.

So it may be that without these personal decisions by Herakleides, Demetrios I, and Diodotos/Tryphon, the Seleukid state could well have survived intact through the 140s. And without Alexander Balas' example to follow him it is unlikely that Andriskos would have attempted to capitalize on his resemblance to an Antigonid, which in turn might have not stimulated Rome to a new bout of expansion.

Counter-factual history is fun, but it is also a means of isolating the decisive events in real history. By 140, after ten years of upheaval from Spain to India, events which were obviously interconnected, Rome was clearly the dominant power in the Mediterranean and Parthia the dominant power in the Middle East. For the next century these two nibbled away at the fragmented political region between them, until they bumped into each other in the Euphrates Valley. Their advances were slow because each had its own problems, internal and frontier. The collapse of the Seleukid kingdom between 150 and 140 meant that neither needed to bother much about the lands between them. It was therefore the collapse of that state, not the Roman advance, not even the

Parthian conquests, which was the crucial geopolitical development of the decade.

Nevertheless the events of the 140s did emphasize the contrast between the three state types – the Roman Republic, Hellenistic monarchy, Parthian semi-nomad kingship. Of the three the Seleukid collapse brought out the fragility of the dynastic state, depending as it did all too much on the activity, ability, and vigour of the king. The Parthian kingship, superficially modelled on the prevailing Hellenistic type, was somehow tougher, in part because it was underpinned by the cavalry aristocracy. These men might be only doubtfully loyal, but in military terms, as the Seleukids, the nomads, and the Romans (eventually) discovered, they were effective; also the Parthian acceptance of local monarchic authority produced a loosely organized state which was very much to the taste of the local kings – and they could translate that into loyalty, of a sort.

The Roman Republic came out of the crises of the 140s superficially in good shape, though its constitutional organization was creaking badly, and began to break within a decade. But underneath it all was a state method, for all its brutality, corruption, and the arrogance of its aristocracy, which was better liked than any other. It is striking how relatively easy it always was for Rome to acquire allies during its wars: that is, it was understood to be a more acceptable overlord than any of the others. This made it tougher and stronger, with a greater potential for stability than any other. This was the foundation of the empire which lasted for the next eight centuries.

To come back to the issue this study has addressed, in the two decades which followed 140, Parthia finally secured its grip on Babylon, and fended off the nomadic attacks in the east; Rome found itself fighting the first of a series of slave wars (against slaves who had been sold out of the Greek lands and whose leaders called themselves 'King Antiochos' and 'King Tryphon'), and then had to cope with the breaking of the ramshackle constitution it had held onto for far too long. Suppose the Seleukid kingdom of Syria and Babylonia had existed, under a longer-lived Antiochos VII (who actually died in 129 at the age of only thirty), the binary world of the centuries to come would have been very different.

Notes and References

Chapter 2

1. Josephos, *Antiquitates Judaicae* 12.389–390; Appian, *Syrian Wars* 47; Livy, *Epitome* 46.
2. Appian, *Syrian Wars* 45; Diodoros 30.7.2.
3. Justin 35.2.1.
4. II Maccabees 4.20.
5. The case for Alexander's royal parentage has most recently and convincingly been put by D. Ogden, *Polygamy, Prostitutes and Death*, London 1999, 143–144; yet certainty is impossible.
6. Polybios 31.11.1–15.12; Justin 34.3.8.
7. Appian, *Syrian Wars* 47; Diodoros 31.27a.
8. Polybios 28.1.1–9. 20.1–2; Appian, *Syrian Wars* 45, 47.
9. Diodoros, 31.32a.
10. Polybios 33.5.
11. See J.D. Grainger, *Wars of the Maccabees*, Barnsley 2012, 51.
12. J.D. Grainger, *The Cities of Pamphylia*, Oxford 2009, 129–133.
13. I Maccabees 10.1; Josephos, *Antiquitates Judaicae* 13.35.
14. I Maccabees 10.2.
15. I Maccabees 10.4–10.
16. Polybios 33.8; Josephos, *Antiquitates Judaicae* 13.36; Justin 35.1.5.
17. I Maccabees 10.15–21.
18. A. Houghton *et al.*, *Seleukid Coins: a Comprehensive Catalogue*, Lancaster PA, 2002–2006.
19. Justin 35.1.10; Josephos,, *Antiquitates Judaicae* 1.53–61; I Maccabees 10.48–50.
20. Livy, *Epitome* 49.
21. I Maccabees 10.54–56; Josephos, *Antiquitates Judaicae* 13.80–82.
22. Justin 35.2.2.

Chapter 3

1. Polybios 24.15.5 and 27.7.5–6; Livy 42.14.8.
2. For Macedon see, conveniently, R.M. Errington, *A History of Macedonia*, California 1990; for more detail, N.G.L. Hammond *et al*, *A History of Macedonia*, 3 vols, Oxford 1972–1988; for the terms imposed on the country in 167, Livy 45.17–18; Plutarch *Aemilius Paullus* 34.
3. Diodoros 31.8.7–9.
4. Livy 45.18.
5. Polybios 36.17.13.
6. Livy 45.39.11.
7. Polybios 34.4.10–12.

8. Sources for Andriskos are: Livy 45.18 and *Epitome* 48–50; Diodoros 31.40a, and 32.15, 9a and 9b; Zonaras 9.28; Polybios 36.10 and 12.
9. C.B. Welles, *Royal Correspondence in the Hellenistic Period*, New Haven, 1934, nos 65 and 67; R.C. Allen, *The Attalid Kingdom*, Oxford 1983, 130–131 and 174–175.
10. J.M. Helliesen, 'Andriscus and the Revolt of the Macedonians 149–148 BC', *Ancient Macedonia* IV, Thessaloniki 1986, 307–314, mentioning settlers from Macedon at half a dozen places.
11. Zonaras 9.28.3–4.
12. Livy, *Epitome* 50.
13. Livy, *Epitome* 50; Zonaras 9.28.
14. Ibid.

Chapter 4
1. A clear and sensible account of all this is R.M. Errington, *The Dawn of Empire, Rome's Rise to World Power*, London 1971.
2. J.S. Richardson, *Hispaniae, Spain and the Development of Roman Imperialism, 218–82 BC*, Cambridge 1986, 112–114.
3. P.A. Brunt, *Italian Manpower 225 BC–AD 14*, Oxford 1971, Appendix 23, 'Legions in Spain, 200–90 BC'.
4. Appian, *Spanish Wars* 56.
5. Appian, *Spanish Wars* 44–45.
6. Appian, *Spanish Wars* 56–57.
7. Appian, *Spanish Wars* 48–49.
8. Appian, *Spanish Wars* 49; Polybios 35.4; Livy, *Epitome* 48.
9. Appian, *Spanish Wars* 50.
10. Appian, *Spanish Wars* 51–52.
11. Appian, *Spanish Wars* 53–55.
12. Appian, *Spanish Wars* 58.
13. Appian, *Spanish Wars* 55, 58–60.
14. Livy, 32.27.6.
15. A.E. Astin, *Scipio Aemilianus*, Oxford 1967, 37–40.
16. H.H. Scullard, *Roman Politics, 220–150 BC*, Oxford 1951, 234.
17. Appian, *Spanish Wars* 60.
18. Livy 43.2.1–11; *Richardson, Hispaniae*, 114–118.
19. Livy, *Epitome*. 49; Cicero, *Brutus* 80, 89–90; Valerius Maximus 8.1; Astin, *Scipio Aemilianus* 58–60; Richardson, *Hispaniae*, 138–140.
20. W. Kunkel, *An Introduction to Roman Legal and Constitutional History*, trans. J. M. Kelly, 2nd ed., Oxford 1973, 64–66.
21. Polybios 36.10.
22. Pausanias 7.10.11; Polybios 30.7.5–7; Livy 45.31.9; Zonaras 9.31.1.
23. Polybios 33.12–3; Appian, *Mithradatic Wars*. 3.
24. Appian, *Mithradatic Wars*. 4–7; Polybios 33.14; Strabo 13.4.2.
25. Livy 42.6.7.
26. Appian, *Libyan Wars* 68.
27. Appian, *Libyan Wars* 69; A. E. Astin, *Cato the Censor*, Oxford 1978, 126–127.
28. Appian, *Libyan Wars* 70–73; Astin, *Scipio Aemilianus*, 47, 270–272.

29. Appian, *Libyan Wars* 74.
30. Appian, *Libyan Wars* 75.

Chapter 5
1. For the Diodotid kingdom, F.L. Holt, *Thundering Zeus*, California 1999.
2. On the recent conditions see F.M. Holt, *Lost World of the Golden King, in Search of Ancient Afghanistan*, California 2012.
3. See R.N. Frye, *The Heritage of Central Asia*, Princeton NJ, 1996, ch. 1.
4. M. Mitchiner, *The Early Coinage of Central Asia*, London 1973, 26–29.
5. Polybios 11.39.5–5.
6. Mitchiner, *Early Coinage*, 19–25.
7. Polybios 5.79.3 and 7.
8. Strabo 15.1.3; Justin 4.1.8, both based on Apollodotos of Artemita.
9. P. Leriche, 'Baktria, land of a Thousand Cities', in Cribb and Herrmann (eds), *After Alexander*, 121–154.
10. P. Bernard et al. *Fouilles d'Ai Khanoum.*
11. J.-C. Gardin and P. Gentelle, 'Irrigation et peuplement dans la plaine d'Ai Khanoum de l'epoque achemenide a la époque musulemane', *Bulletin de l'Ecole Francais d'Extreme-Orient* 61, 1976, 59–99.
12. C. Rapin, 'Nomads and the shaping of Central Asia', in Cribb and Herrmann, *After Alexander*.
13. A.K. Narain, 'The Greeks of Baktria and India', *Cambridge Ancient History*, VIII, 2nd ed, 1989, 399–400.
14. Strabo 11.11.1 ad 15.1.3; K. Kartunen, *India and the Hellenistic World*, Helsinki 1997, 274, though he identifies the great conqueror as Demetrios I.
15. Justin 41.6.
16. G.F. Assar, 'Genealogy and Coinage of the Early Parthian Rulers', *Parthica* 7, 2005.
17. Justin 41.6.4–5.
18. The latest, and convincing, examination of these matters is by C.G.R. Benjamin, *The Yuezhi, Origin, Migration, and the Conquest of Northern Baktria*, Turnhout, Belgium 2007.
19. Justin 41.6.5.
20. Benjamin, *Yuezhi*, 181–188.
21. R. Andouin and P. Bernard, 'Tresor de Monnaies grecques et greco-bactriennes trouvées a Ai Khanoum (Afghanistan)', *Revue Numismatique* 1975, 23–57, translated as 'The Ai Khanoum Coins: the 1973 Hoard (I) and (II)' in O. Guillaume (ed), *Greco-Baktrian and Indian coins from Afghanistan*, New Delhi 1991, 117–164.
22. Benjamin, *Yuezhi*, 180, note 41, quoting D. MacDowall.
23. Summarized by Holt, *Lost World*, 103–104.
24. Justin 41.6.5.
25. Assar, 'Genealogy and Coinage'.
26. P. Bernard et al., *Fouilles d'Ai Khanoum*, IV, Paris 1985, 98–105.
27. P. Bernard, 'Ai Khanum on the Oxus: a Hellenistic city in Central Asia', *Proceedings of the British Academy* 53, 73–95, at 77–79.
28. Benjamin, *Yuezhi*, 147–156.
29. Ibid, 97–111.

30. P. Bernard, 'The Greek kingdom of Central Asia', in J. Harmatta *et al.* (eds), *History of Civilizations of Central Asia*, vol. II, Delhi 1999, 99–130, at 104–114.
31. Benjamin, *Yuezhi*, 189–90, 204–208.

Chapter 6

1. Appian, *Syrian Wars* 55.
2. Listed by K. Karttunen, *India and the Hellenistic World*, Helsinki 1997, 306–307.
3. As shown by the names of clerks at Ai Khanum; cf Karttunen, 308.
4. Karttunen, ch. 3.
5. Polybios 11.39.1–12.
6. Accepted by Indian historians, e.g. A.K. Narain, *The Indo-Greeks*, Oxford 1957 and 1980, 9, and H. Raychaudhuri, *Political History of Ancient India*, 8th ed., with a commentary by R.N. Mukherjee, Delhi 1996, 311.
7. Raychaudhuri, *Political History*, 313; R. Thapar, *Asoka and the Decline of the Mauryas*, rev. ed., Delhi 1997, 201.
8. Thapar, *Asoka*, 260–261.
9. Polybios 11.39.9.
10. Narain, *Indo-Greeks*, 23–24.
11. Diodoros 28.3.1; Strabo 16.1.18.
12. Raychaudhuri, *Political History*, 329–330.
13. Ibid, 330–332.
14. Ibid, 322–324.
15. Narain's successive ideas are in the two editions of *Indo-Greeks,* and in his chapter in *CAH* VIII, 420–421; others are in *Fouilles d'Ai Khanoum*, vol. VIII, appendix IV (by O. Bopearachchi), though he has changed some items since.
16. Narain has a grid, *Cambridge Ancient History*, VIII, 421; an alternative is in *Fouilles d'Ai Khanoum*, VIII, app. IV; they differ, of course.
17. F.L. Holt, *Lost World of the Golden King*, California 2012, 144.
18. Narain, *CAH*, VIII, 399–400.
19. Strabo 11.11.1.
20. Narain, *CAH*, VIII, 400–401.
21. Strabo 11.11.1; Karttunen, 274.
22. Justin, 41.6.4–5.
23. Strabo 11.11.2.
24. Justin 41.6.5.
25. G.F. Assar, 'The Genealogy and Coinage of the Early Parthian Rulers, 2', *Parthica* 7, 2005.
26. Narain, *Indo-Greeks*, 97–99; Raychaudhuri, *Political History*, 338–339 and 655.
27. Raychaudhuri, *Political History,* 345–346 and 645.
28. Karttunen 316.
29. Raychaudhuri, *Political History*, 349; Narain, *Indo-Greeks*, 82.
30. Narain, *Indo-Greeks*, 82–83.
31. G. Erdosy, 'Early historic Cities of Northern India', *South Asian Studies* 3, 1987, 1–24.
32. Arrian, *Indica* 10.5 (from Megasthenes); Karttunen 88–89; Erdosy (previous note) 18.

Chapter 7

1. Diodoros 33.5.1.
2. John Malalas, 207.

3. Justin, 35.2.1.

4. Josephos, *Antiquitates Judaicae* 13.86, I Maccabees 10.67.

5. Josephos, *Antiquitates Judaicae* 13.88, I Maccabees 10.69.

6. Josephos, *Antiquitates Judaicae* 13.91–92, I Maccabees 10.74–77.

7. Josephos, *Antiquitates Judaicae* 13.92–98; I Maccabees 10.77–83.

8. Josephos, *Antiquitates Judaicae* 13.102–98; I Maccabees 10.77–83.

9. L. Robert, *Gnomon* 35, 1963, 76; S.M. Sherwin-White and A. Kuhrt, *From Samarkhand to Sardis*, London 993, 223.

10. A.J. Sachs and H. Hunger, *Astronomical Diaries and Related Texts from Babylon*, vol. 3, Vienna 2002, '-161'.

11. Ibid, '-145'.

12. Josephos, *Antiquitates Judaicae* 13.103–105; I Maccabees 11.1–7.

13. I Maccabees 11.3.

14. E.T. Newell, 'Late Seleukid mints in Ptolemais-Ake and Damascus', *Numismatic Notes and Monographs* 84, 1939, and 'The First Seleukid Coinage of Tyre', *Numismatic Notes and Monographs* 10, 1921.

15. Josephos, *Antiquitates Judaicae* 13.112; I Maccabees 11.86.

16. Josephos, *Antiquitates Judaicae* 13.106.

17. I Maccabees 11.9–10l; Diodoros 32.9d.

18. Diodoros 32.10.2.

19. Josephos, *Antiquitates Judaicae* 13.108, 113; I Maccabees 11.13; Diodoros 32.9c.

20. Diodoros 32.9c.

21. Ibid.

22. Josephos, *Antiquitates Judaicae* 13.116–118; I Maccabees 11.17; Diod. 32.9; Livy, *Epitome* 52.

23. Josephos, *Antiquitates Judaicae* 13.135–142; I Maccabees 11.44–48; Diodoros 33.4.1–3.

24. Josephos, *Antiquitates Judaicae* 13.120.

25. G. Holbl, *A History of the Ptolemaic Empire*, London 2001, 195.

Chapter 8

1. Appian, *Libyan Wars* 74.

2. Appian, *Libyan Wars* 75.

3. Appian, *Libyan Wars* 76; Polybios 36.3–5.

4. Appian, *Libyan Wars* 78–80.

5. Appian, *Libyan Wars* 80.

6. Appian, *Libyan Wars* 81–90; Polybios 36.7.1–2.

7. Appian, *Libyan Wars* 91–92; Polybios 36.7.3–5.

8. Appian, *Libyan Wars* 94.

9. Ibid.

10. Appian, *Libyan Wars* 94–98.

11. Pol. 36.11.

12. Appian, *Libyan Wars* 99–100.

13. A.E. Astin, *Scipio Aemilianus*, Oxford 1974, 56–60.

14. Appian, *Libyan Wars* 102–104.

15. Appian, *Libyan Wars* 105–107; Livy, *Epitome* 50.

16. Appian, *Libyan Wars* 107–109.

17. Appian, *Libyan Wars* 109.

18. Appian, *Libyan Wars* 93, 111.

19. Appian, *Libyan Wars* 110.

20. Appian, *Libyan Wars* 111.

21. Side: Appian, *Libyan Wars* 123; mercenaries: e.g. Appian, *Libyan Wars* 126 (Diogenes).

22. Appian, *Libyan Wars* 111.

23. Appian, *Libyan Wars* 112; Livy, *Epitome* 49, 50; Astin, *Scipio Aemilianus* 61–67.

24. Appian, *Libyan Wars* 113–114.

25. Appian, *Libyan Wars* 115–117.

26. Astin, *Scipio Aemilianus*, 70, note 1.

27. Appian, *Libyan Wars* 117, 119.

28. Appian, *Libyan Wars* 119.

29. Appian, *Libyan Wars* 118, 120.

30. Appian, *Libyan Wars* 121–126.

31. Appian, *Libyan Wars* 126.

32. Polybios 38.7.6–8.15; Diodoros. 32.22.

33. Appian, *Libyan Wars* 127–130.

34. Appian, *Libyan Wars* 130–131.

Chapter 9

1. Polybios 30.13.1–5 and 11; Livy 45.31.5–9.

2. Livy 45.28.6–8, 31.15 and 31.1–2.

3. Livy 45.31.15.

4. Livy 45.3.14.

5. Polybios 30.20.1–9 and 31.9–12.

6. Polybios 30.13.6–11; Livy 45.31.9–11; Pausanias 7.10.7–8.

7. Livy 45.34.2–7.

8. P. Cartledge and A. Spawforth, *Hellenistic and Roman Sparta*, London 1989, 80–88.

9. J.A.O. Larsen, *Greek Federal States*, Oxford 1968, 484–485.

10. Polybios 35.6.1–4.

11. Polybios 36.11.1–4.

12. Pausanias 7.12.1 and 10.2.

13. Pausanias 7.12.2–7.

14. Pausanias 7.13.1–5; Pol. 3.5.6.

15. Summarized by A.J. Toynbee, *Some Problems of Greek History*, Oxford 1969, 408–411.

16. Pausanias 7.14.1.

17. Pausanias 7.13.1–4; Pol. 36.14.1–3.

18. Pausanias 7.13.7.

19. Polybios 38.9; Livy, *Epitome* 51; Pausanias 7.14.1–3; Cassius Dio 21, frag 72; Justin 34.1

20. Pausanias 7.14.2.

21. Polybios 38.9–11; Pausanias 7.14.3–4; Diodoros 32.26.3–4.

22. These measures have been enlisted to argue for social revolution in Achaia; the notion is refuted by A. Fuks, 'The *Bellum Achaicum* in its Social Aspect', *Journal of Hellenic Studies* 90, 1970, 78–89.

23. Polybios 38.12–13; Diodoros 32.26.5; Pausanias 7.14.4.

24. Polybios 38.13.6.

25. Polybios 38.12. 1–4; Pausanias 7.15.1.

26. A.E. Astin, *Scipio Aemilianus*, Oxford 1967, 73–74.

27. Pausanias 7.15.1.

28. Pausanias 7.14.1.

29. Polybios 38.13.9; this C. Fannius is probably not the one with Scipio in Africa.

30. Pausanias 7.15.2–6.

31. Pausanias 7.15.4.

32. Polybios 38.16.4 and 39.1.11.

33. Pausanias 7.16.1.

34. Ibid.

35. Zonaras 9.28.8.

36. Pausanias 7.15.5.

37. Polybios 38.17.1–10; Pausanias 7.15.11.

38. Pausanias 7.16.2–5.

Chapter 10

1. A.E. Astin, *Scipio Aemilianus*, Oxford 1974, 74, note 1.

2. Appian, *Libyan Wars*. 135.

3. Ibid.

4. Ibid.

5. Ibid; Pliny, *Natural History* 33.141.

6. Polybios 39.5.1.

7. Zonaras 9.31.6.

8. Pausanias 7.16.6–7.

9. Died: Livy, *Epitome* 52; Polybios 38.5.1; perhaps drowned: Pausanias 7.15.3.

10. Argued by R. Kallet-Marx, *Hegemony to Empire*, California 1984, 77.

11. Pausanias 7.11.9–10.

12. Ibid.

13. Kallet-Marx, *Hegemony to Empire*, 77–80.

14. *Palatine Anthology* 7.297 and 493, 9.151 and 284.

15. Olympia and Elis: *Inschriften von Olympia* 319; Argos: *Sylloge Epigraphicum Graecarum (SEG)* XXX, 365; Eretria: *SEG* XXVI, 1034.

16. Polybios 39.6.1.

17. *SEG* XXIII, 196.

18. Suggested by L. Pietila-Custren, 'Some Aspects of the Life of Lucius Mummius Achaicus', *Arctos* 12, 1978, 115–123.

19. Pausanias 5.10.5 and 24.6; Polybios 39.6.1; *Incriptiones Graecae* I, 306; Kallet-Marx, *Hegemony to Empire*, 89, note 141.

20. Plutarch, *Philopoimen* 21; this passage is curiously omitted in S.L. Ager, *Interstate Arbitration in the Greek World, 337–90 B.C.*, California 1996.

21. Pausanias 7.15.1.

22. Kallet-Marx, *Hegemony to Empire*, 12–16.

23. Zonaras 9.28.8.

24. Livy, *Epitome* 53.

25. Livy, *Epitome* 54; G. Morgan. '"Cornelius and the Pannonians", Appian, Illyrica 14.41 and Roman History, 143–138 B.C.', *Historia* 23, 1974, 183–216.

26. Livy, *Epitome* 54; Cicero, *De Finibus* 24; Valerius Maximus 5.8.3.

27. Kallet-Marx, *Hegemony to Empire*, appendix C, 347–349.
28. Cicero, *De Provinciis Consularibus* 4.
29. *Corpus Inscriptionem Latinarum* I, 2977; *SEG* XL 543.
30. N.G.L. Hammond, 'The Western Part of the Via Egnatia', *JRS* 64, 1974, 185–194, is clear that the route was a long-travelled one.
31. Kallet-Marx, *Hegemony to Empire*, 187–188, with references.
32. The date of the embassy is disputed, H. Mattingly, 'Scipio Aemilianus' Eastern Embassy', *Classical Quarterly* 36, 491–495, argues strongly for 144–143; the date accepted earlier, as by Astin, *Scipio Aemilianus*, was 140–139; the earlier date seems more likely in the international context.
33. Appian, *Spanish Wars* 61.
34. Appian, *Spanish Wars* 61–75; the assassination is in 75.
35. The Numantine war is in Appian, *Spanish Wars* 76–98.

Chapter 11

1. Strabo 11.9.2; Justin 41.4; A.H.D. Bivar in *Cambridge History of Iran*, vol 3 (1), Cambridge 1984, 28–30.
2. Strabo 11.11.2.
3. Bivar, *CHI* 3(1), 33, and other places, with slightly varying translations.
4. Polybios 5.55.1, is a reference to Antiochos III's reign; the kingdom is almost entirely ignored in *CHI*.
5. Diodoros 28.3; Strabo 16.1.18.
6. G. Le Rider, *Suse sous les Seleukides et les Parthes*, Paris 1965, 347.
7. J. Harmatta, 'Parthia and Elymais in the second century B.C.', *Acta Antiqua Academiae Scientiarm Hungaricae* 29, 1981, 189–217.
8. D. Sellwood in *CHI* (3(1), 299–306.
9. These descriptions are from Isidoros of Charax, *Parthian Stations*, ed. W.H. Schoff, London 1914, reprinted Chicago 1976, 6–7.
10. P. Bernard, 'Heracles, les Grottes de Karafto, et le sanctuaire de mont Sambalos en Iran', *Studia Iranica* 9, 1980, 301–324.
11. Polybios 10.29.2–31.4.
12. C. B. Welles, *Royal Correspondent of the Hellenistic Period*, New Haven RI, 1934, nos 31–32 and Austin 184, 190; Sherwin-White and Kurht, *Samarkhand to Sardis*, 162–166.
13. Le Rider, *Suse*.
14. M.A.R. Colledge, *The Parthians*, London 1967, 25.
15. J. Hansman, 'The Problem of Qumis', *JRAS* 1968, 111–139, and 'The Measure of Hekatompylos', *JRAS* 1981, 3–9.
16. Polybios 10.31.5–13.
17. Isidoros of Charax, *Parthian Stations* 7.
18. Justin 41.6; Bagasis is shown to be Mithradates' brother by Assar's study of the Nisa Ostraka.
19. O. Morkholm, 'A Greek Coin Hoard from Susiana', *Acta Archaeologica* 36, 1965, 127–156; Le Rider, *Suse*, hoard 5; H. Houghton *et al.*, *Seleukid Coins: a Comprehensive Catalogue*, vol 2, Lancaster PA, 2006 under Alexander I.
20. Lucian, *Macrobios*; 'Kabeskir' is the transcription of the Elamite name; in Greek he was 'Kamniskires', which appears on his coins.

21. J. Harmatta, 'The Second Elamaean Inscription from Bard-e-Neshandeh', *Acta Antiqua Academiae Scientiarm Hungaricae* 32, 1989, 161–167.
22. A.J. Sachs and H. Hunger, *Astronomical Diaries and Related Texts from Babylonia*, vol. III, Vienna 2002. These were clay tablets on which a succession of Babylonian scribes recorded their observations of the planets. They also had the habit of adding meteorological records and records of political events. The diaries were compiled, judging by their wording, every month; they are as close to contemporary records as can be found in the Hellenistic world.
23. Justin 41.7.
24. Sachs and Hunger, III, '-144'.
25. Ibid.
26. Notably that marked as 'Suse 5' by Le Rider, *Suse*, and that discussed by O. Morkholm, 'A Greek Coin Hoard'.
27. Sachs and Hunger, III, '-144'.
28. Harmatta, 'Parthia and Elymais'.
29. Ibid.

Chapter 12
1. Strabo 16.2.10.
2. Diodoros 33.3; Josephos, *Antiquitates Judaicae* 13.131.
3. I Maccabees 11.38 and44–50; Josephos, *Antiquitates Judaicae* 13.129–130 and 135–141.
4. Diodoros 33.4a and 28–28a.
5. Diodoros 33.4a.
6. Ibid.
7. A. Houghton, 'The Revolt of Tryphon and the Accession of Antiochos VI at Apamea', *Schweizer Numismatische Rundschau* 71, 1992, 119–141.
8. A. Houghton, et al, *Seleukid Coins: a Comprehensive Catalogue*, vol 2, Lancaster PA 2006, under Demetrios II (first reign).
9. A.J. Sachs and H. Hunger, *Astronomical Diaries and Relate Texts from Babylon*, vol. 3, Vienna 2002, '-144'.
10. Diodoros 33.9.
11. Diodoros 33.28b; Justin 38.8.8; the earlier date of 144–143 (rather than 140–139) is argued by H.B. Mattingly 'Scipio Aemilianus' Eastern Embassy', *Classical Quarterly* 36, 1986, 491–495; given the political conditions in the east, this seems the more likely.
12. Cicero, *de Republica* 6.11; Cicero, *Dream of Scipio*.
13. G. Holbl, *A History of the Ptolemaic Empire*, London 2001, 195.
14. Diodoros 33.28b.
15. A.N. Sherwin-White, *Roman Foreign Policy in the East, 168 BC to AD 1*, Norman OK 1984, 57–58 and 82–83.
16. I Maccabees 11.59–60; Josephos, *Antiquitates Judaicae* 13.156–157.
17. Josesphos, *Bellum Judaicum* 1.4.2.
18. This position is discussed in detail in my *Wars of the Maccabees*, Barnsley 2012.
19. I Maccabees 11.63–67 and 12.24–30; Josephos, *Antiquitates Judaicae* 154–162.
20. Josephos, *Antiquitates Judaicae* 13.125; I Maccabees 12.33–34.
21. Josephos, *Antiquitates Judaicae* 13.187 and 218–219; Justin 36.1.7; Livy, *Epitome.* 55; I Maccabees 13.31; Appian, *Syrian Wars* 68; Diodoros 33.28.

22. K. Liampi, 'Der Makedonische schild als propagandisches mittel in der Hellenistischen Zeit', *Meletemata* 10, 1990, 157–171.

23. Houghton *et al.* (note 8) under 'Revolt of Tryphon'.

24. Diodoros 33.28.

25. I Maccabees 12.41–53; Josephos, *Antiquitates Judaicae* 13.188–192.

26. I Maccabees 13.11–24; Josephos, *Antiquitates Judaicae* 13.196–212.

27. I Maccabees 13.31–42.

28. Strabo 16.2.26; Athenaios 333c.

29. Appian, *Libyan Wars* 123.

30. Korakesion: Plutarch, *Pompeius* 28.1; Side: Strabo 14.3.2.

31. Strabo 14.5.2; E. Maroti, 'Diodotos Tryphon et la Piraterie', *Acta Antiqua* 10, 1962, 187–194.

32. Strabo 6.2.19.

33. Josephos, *Antiquitates Judaicae* 13.222–223.

34. Strabo 16.2.10; Josephos, *Antiquitates Judaicae* 13.223–225; D. Gera, 'Tryphon's Sling Bullet from Dor', *Israel Exploration Journal* 35, 1985, 153–163.

Chapter 13

1. For his career see A.R. Bellinger, 'Hyspaosines of Charax', *Yale Classical Studies* 7, 1942, 53–67; for his kingdom see S.A. Nodelman, 'A Preliminary History of Charakene', *Berytus* 13, 1931, 91–121.

2. I Maccabees 2.1–28, 39–41, 45–49, 65–70; Josephos, *Antiquitates Judaicae* 12.265–278.

3. I have discussed this dispute in *The Wars of the Maccabees*, Barnsley 2012, chapter 1; the literature on the subject is enormous.

4. I Maccabees. 2.27–28.

5. Judas' methods: I Maccabees 2.39–41; II Maccabees 6.10–11, 18–31, 7.1–42; his defeat: I Maccabees 9.2–18.

6. I Maccabees 10.83–87; Josephos, *Antiquitates Judaicae* 13.102.

7. I Mac. 1.54.

8. I Maccabees 11.1–8; Josephos, *Antiquitates Judaicae* 13.102–105.

9. I Maccabees 11.34; Josephos, *Antiquitates Judaicae* 13.127.

10. I Maccabees 11.20–31; Josephos, *Antiquitates Judaicae* 13.121–128.

11. I Maccabees 11.43–51; Josephos, *Antiquitates Judaicae* 13.134–142.

12. I Maccabees 11.60–62; Josephos, *Antiquitates Judaicae* 13.149–153.

13. I Maccabees 13.1–10; Josephos, *Antiquitates Judaicae* 13.197–200.

14. I Maccabees 13.12–24; Josephos, *Antiquitates Judaicae* 13.201 -212.

15. I Maccabees 13.33–42; Josephos, *Antiquitates Judaicae* 13.213.

16. I Maccabees 13.11; Josephos, *Antiquitates Judaicae* 13.202.

17. I Maccabees 13.43–53; Josephos, *Antiquitates Judaicae* 13.215.

18. I Maccabees 12.47–48, repeated by Josephos, *Antiquitates Judaicae* 13.192–193; it is, however, a thoroughly misleading account.

19. I Maccabees 10.66 and 11.60; Josephos, *Antiquitates Judaicae* 13.101, 149, 180; A.B. Brett, 'The Mint of Ascalon under the Seleukids', *American Numismatic Society Museum Notes* 4, 1950, 43–54.

20. Diodoros 33.5.1.

21. Diodoros 31.19a.

Chapter 14

1. A.J. Sachs and H. Hunger, *Astronomical Diaries and Related Texts from Babylon*, vol. 3. Vienna 2002, '-140' (May/June 141: Mithradates' arrival and the appointment of Antiochos; June/July 141: mention of Nikanor: October 141 BC).
2. Ibid.
3. Note in N.C. Debevoise, *A Political History of Parthia*, Chicago 1938, 23 note 101.
4. Pliny, *Natural History* 6.139; Le Rider, *Suse sous les Seleukides Paris 1965,* 309–311; J. Hansman, 'Charax and the Karkheh', *Iranica Antiqua* 7, 1967, 21–35.
5. Justin 36.1.4.
6. Sachs and Hunger -140 (January/February 140 BC).
7. Justin 36.1.2–4 and 38.9.2.
8. Josephos, *Aniquitates Judaicae* 13.184–186.
9. Le Rider, *Suse* 355–361; for the interpretation of an inscription on a bas-relief at Hong e-Nourazi in Khuzistan with the wording 'Kabniskes, governor of Susa', see J. Harmatta, 'Parthia and Elymais in the 2nd century BC', *Acta Antiqua Academiae Scientiarum Hungaricae* 29, 1981, 189–217.
10. A. Houghton *et al.*, *Seleukid Coins: a Comprehensive Catalogue,* vol. 2, Lancaster PA 2006, 311–312.
11. Justin 36.1.4.
12. W. Moore, 'The Divine Couple of Demetrius II Nicator, and his coinage at Nisibis', *American Numismatic Society Museum Notes* 31, 1986, 125–143.
13. Sachs and Hunger -138 (July 138 BC).
14. Justin 36.1.5.
15. Sachs and Hunger, -138 (December 138).
16. Diodoros 23.28; Josephos, *Aniquitates Judaicae* 13.222–223.
17. Appian, *Syrian Wars*, 68.
18. Houghton, *Deleucid Coins,* 380–382 (of 174 SE).
19. Josephos, *Aniquitates Judaicae* 13.222.
20. Appian, *Syrian Wars*, 68.
21. Houghton, *Seleukid Coins*, 311–312.
22. Justin, 38.9.3; Appian, *Syrian Wars*, 67.
23. Houghton, *Seleukid Coins,* 345–347.
24. D. Gera, 'Tryphon's Sling Bullet from Dor', *Israel Exploration Journal* 35, 1985, 153–163.
25. Strabo 16.2.10; Josephos, *Aniquitates Judaicae* 13.223–225.
26. Justin 36.1.6.

Appendix

The Seleukid Royal Family

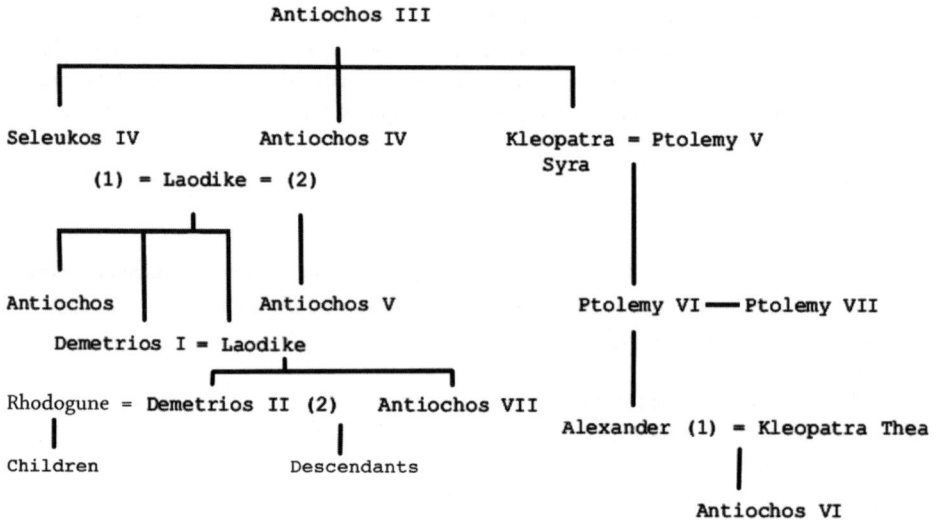

Antiochos III
```
        ┌───────────────────────┼───────────────────────────┐
   Seleukos IV          Antiochos IV          Kleopatra = Ptolemy V
                                                  Syra
        (1) = Laodike = (2)                         │
         ┌────────┬──────────┐                      │
   Antiochos   │   Antiochos V      Ptolemy VI ── Ptolemy VII
          Demetrios I = Laodike                     │
         ┌──────────────────────┐                   │
Rhodogune = Demetrios II (2)  Antiochos VII   Alexander (1) = Kleopatra Thea
     │                    │                          │
 Children           Descendants                 Antiochos VI
```

Bibliography

S. L. Ager, *Interstate Arbitration in the Greek World, 337–90 B.C.*, California 1996

R.C. Allen, *The Attalid Kingdom*, Oxford 1983

R. Andouin and P. Bernard, 'Tresor de Monnaies grecques et greco-bactriennes trouvées a Ai Khanoum (Afghanistan)', *Revue Numismatique* 1975, 23–57, translated as 'The Ai Khanoum Coins: the 1973 Hoard (I) and (II)' in O. Guillaume (ed), *Greco-Baktrian and Indian coins from Afghanistan*, New Delhi 1991, 117–164

G.F. Assar, 'The Genealogy and Coinage of the Early Parthian Rulers, 2', *Parthica* 7, 2005

A.E. Astin, *Scipio Aemilianus*, Oxford 1967

A.R. Bellinger, 'Hyspaosines of Charax', *Yale Classical Studies* 7, 1942, 53–67

C.G.R. Benjamin, *The Yuezhi, Origin, Migration, and the Conquest of Northern Baktria*, Turnhout, Belgium 2007

P. Bernard et al., *Fouilles d'Ai Khanoum*, IV, Paris 1985

P. Bernard, 'Ai Khanum on the Oxus: a Hellenistic city in Central Asia', *Proceedings of the British Academy* 53, 1964, 73–95

P. Bernard, 'The Greek kingdom of Central Asia', in J. Harmatta *et al.* (eds), *History of Civilizations of Central Asia*, vol. II, Delhi 1999, 99–130

P. Bernard, 'Heracles, les Grottes de Karafto, et le sanctuaire de mont Sambalos en Iran', *Studia Iranica* 9, 1980, 301–324

A.H.D. Bivar in *Cambridge History of Iran*, vol 3 (1), Cambridge 1984

A.B. Brett, 'The Mint of Ascalon under the Seleukids', *American Numismatic Society Museum Notes* 4, 1950, 43–54.

P.A. Brunt, *Italian Manpower 225 BC–AD 14*, Oxford 1971

P. Cartledge and A. Spawforth, *Hellenistic and Roman Sparta*, London 1989

M.A.R. Colledge, *The Parthians*, London 1967

J. Cribb and G. Herrmann (eds), *After Alexander, Central Asia before Islam, Proceedings of the British Academy* 133, 2007

N.C. Debevoise, *A Political History of Parthia*, Chicago 1938

G. Erdosy, 'Early historic Cities of Northern India', *South Asian Studies* 3, 1987, 1–24

R.M. Errington, *The Dawn of Empire, Rome's Rise to World Power*, London 1971

R.M. Errington, *A History of Macedonia*, California 1990

R.N. Frye, *The Heritage of Central Asia*, Princeton NJ, 1996

A. Fuks, 'The *Bellum Achaicum* in its Social Aspect', *Journal of Hellenic Studies* 90, 1970, 78–89

J.-C. Gardin and P. Gentelle, 'Irrigation et peuplement dans la plaine d'Ai Khanoum de l'epoque achemenide a la époque musulmane', *Bulletin de l'Ecole Francais d'Extreme-Orient* 61, 1976, 59–99

D. Gera, 'Tryphon's Sling Bullet from Dor', *Israel Exploration Journal* 35, 1985, 153–163

J.D. Grainger, *Wars of the Maccabees*, Barnsley 2012

J.D. Grainger, *The Cities of Pamphylia*, Oxford 2009

N.G.L. Hammond *et al*, *A History of Macedonia*, 3 vols, Oxford 1972–1988

N.G.L. Hammond, 'The Western Part of the Via Egnatia', *JRS* 64, 1974, 185–194.

J. Hansman, 'The Problem of Qumis', *Journal of the Royal Asiatic Society* 1968, 111–139

J. Hansman, 'The Measure of Hekatompylos', *Journal of the Royal Asiatic Society* 1981, 3–9

J. Hansman, 'Charax and the Karkheh', *Iranica Antiqua* 7, 1967, 21–35

J. Harmatta, 'Parthia and Elymais in the second century B.C.', *Acta Antiqua Academiae Scientiarum Hungaricae* 29, 1981, 189–217

J. Harmatta, 'The Second Elamaean Inscription from Bard-e-Neshandeh', *Acta Antiqua Academiae Scientiarum Hungaricae* 32, 1989, 161–167

J.M. Helliesen, 'Andriscus and the Revolt of the Macedonians 149–148 BC', *Ancient Macedonia* IV, Thessaloniki 1986

G. Holbl, *A History of the Ptolemaic Empire*, London 2001

F.L. Holt, *Thundering Zeus*, California 1999

F.M. Holt, *Lost World of the Golden King, in Search of Ancient Afghanistan*, California 2012

A. Houghton, 'The Revolt of Tryphon and the Accession of Antiochos VI at Apamea', *Schweizer Numismatische Rundschau* 71, 1992, 119–141

A. Houghton *et al.*, *Seleukid Coins: a Comprehensive Catalogue*, Lancaster PA, 2002–2006

R. Kallet-Marx, *Hegemony to Empire*, California 1984

K. Kartunen, *India and the Hellenistic World*, Helsinki 1997

W. Kunkel, *An Introduction to Roman Legal and Constitutional History*, trans. J. M. Kelly, 2nd ed., Oxford 1973

J.A.O. Larsen, *Greek Federal States*, Oxford 1968

P. Leriche, 'Baktria, land of a Thousand Cities', in Cribb and Herrmann (eds), *After Alexander*, 121–154

G. Le Rider, *Suse sous les Seleukides et les Parthes*, Paris 1965

K. Liampi, 'Der Makedonische schild als propagandisches mittel in der Hellenistischen Zeit', *Meletemata* 10, 1990, 157–171

E. Maroti, 'Diodotos Tryphon et la Piraterie', *Acta Antiqua* 10, 1962, 187–194

H. Mattingly, 'Scipio Aemilianus' Eastern Embassy', *Classical Quarterly* 36, 1986, 491–495

M. Mitchiner, *The Early Coinage of Central Asia*, London 1973

W. Moore, 'The Divine Couple of Demetrius II Nicator, and his coinage at Nisibis', *American Numismatic Society Museum Notes* 31, 1986

G. Morgan, '"Cornelius and the Pannonians", Appian, Illyrica 14.41 and Roman History, 143–138 B.C.', *Historia* 23, 1974, 183–216.

O. Morkholm, 'A Greek Coin Hoard from Susiana', *Acta Archaeologica* 36, 1965, 127–156

A.K. Narain, *The Indo-Greeks*, Oxford 1957 and 1980

A.K. Narain, 'The Greeks of Baktria and India', *Cambridge Ancient History*, VIII, 2nd ed, 1989

E.T. Newell, 'Late Seleukid mints in Ptolemais-Ake and Damascus', *Numismatic Notes and Monographs* 84, 1939

E.T. Newell, 'The First Seleukid Coinage of Tyre', *Numismatic Notes and Monographs* 10, 1921

S.A. Nodelman, 'A Preliminary History of Charakene', *Berytus* 13, 1931, 91–121

D. Ogden, *Polygamy, Prostitutes and Death*, London 1999

L. Pietila-Custren, 'Some Aspects of the Life of Lucius Mummius Achaicus', *Arctos* 12, 1978, 115–123

C. Rapin, 'Nomads and the shaping of Central Asia', in Cribb and Herrmann, *After Alexander*

H. Raychaudhuri, *Political History of Ancient India*, 8th ed., with a commentary by R.N. Mukherjee, Delhi 1996

J.S. Richardson, *Hispaniae, Spain and the Development of Roman Imperialism, 218–82 BC*, Cambridge 1986

L. Robert, *Gnomon* 35, 1963

A.J. Sachs and H. Hunger, *Astronomical Diaries and Related Texts from Babylon*, vol. 3, Vienna 2002

H.H. Scullard, *Roman Politics, 220–150 BC*, Oxford 1951

A.N. Sherwin-White, *Roman Foreign Policy in the East, 168 BC to AD 1*, Norman OK 1984

S.M. Sherwin-White and A. Kuhrt, *From Samarkhand to Sardis*, London 993

R. Thapar, *Asoka and the Decline of the Mauryas*, rev. ed., Delhi 1997

A.J. Toynbee, *Some Problems of Greek History*, Oxford 1969

C.B. Welles, *Royal Correspondence in the Hellenistic Period*, New Haven, 1934

Index